# ACKNOWLEDGMENTS

Some of the material in *Faithful & True: Sexual Integrity in a Fallen World* was originally published in *The Secret Sin: Healing the Wounds of Sexual Addiction* by Zondervan Publishing House. *The Secret Sin* has been rereleased and retitled *Faithful & True* and is available in Christian bookstores. We would like to thank Zondervan Publishing House for making this book available to LifeWay Press.

*Faithful & True: Sexual Integrity in a Fallen World*
Copyright © 1996 • Mark Laaser
Third printing 2002
*All rights reserved*

ISBN: 0-8054-9819-2

Dewey Decimal Classification: 306.7
Subject Heading: SEXUAL BEHAVIOR

Unless otherwise indicated, biblical quotations are from the Holy Bible, New International Version (NIV), copyright © 1973, 1978, 1984 by International Bible Society. (MLB) indicates Scripture from *The Modern Language Bible, The New Berkeley Version.* Copyright 1945, 1959 © 1969 Zondervan Publishing House. Used by permission. (RSV) indicates Scripture from the *Revised Standard Version of the Bible,* copyrighted 1946, 1952, © 1971, 1973 by the National Council of Churches of Christ in the U.S.A., and used by permission. (KJV) indicates the *King James Version.*

To order additional copies of this resource: WRITE LifeWay Church Resources Customer Service; One LifeWay Plaza; Nashville, TN 37234-0113; FAX order to (615) 251-5933; PHONE (800) 458-2772; EMAIL to Customerservice@lifeway.com; ORDER ONLINE at www.lifeway.com; or VISIT the LifeWay Christian Store serving you.

*Printed in the United States of America*

Adult Ministry Publishing
LifeWay Church Resources
One LifeWay Plaza
Nashville, TN 37234-0175

# TABLE OF CONTENTS

**Mark Laaser, Ph.D.**, lectures and conducts workshops nationally and internationally. He also consults with hospital programs which treat sexual addiction. Dr. Laaser has worked with hundreds of addicts and their families. He has consulted with a variety of church congregations in which the pastor committed sexual sin as well as working with many pastors themselves. Dr. Laaser and his wife Deb have been involved in helping couples heal from the pain of sexual sin and other problems. He serves on several national boards including the Interfaith Sexual Trauma Institute and the National Council on Sexual Addiction/Compulsivity.

Dr. Laaser was trained as a pastor at Princeton Theological Seminary and received his doctorate in religion and psychology at the University of Iowa. He currently lives in Chanhassen, Minnesota with his wife and three children. In his spare time he is trying to figure out how to coach youth sports in a healthy way and how to survive Minnesota winters.

**Eldridge (Eli) Machen** is a licensed clinical social worker in Florida, and a certified social worker in North Carolina. He leads intensive workshops, conferences, training seminars, and provides program consulting throughout the U.S.

Eli is a graduate of Southwestern Baptist Theological Seminary and earned his Master of Social Work degree at the University of Connecticut. Eli currently lives in Black Mountain, North Carolina with his wife and son.

# FOREWORD

Never before have husbands and wives had a greater need for a deep commitment to a healthy marriage and family. Mark Laaser has eloquently unraveled the mystery behind addictive behavior, and he has helped us to see that when our relationships are not alive and growing the temptation for various kinds of addictions is unleashed.

The author clearly and concisely defines what a healthy relationship is and what it isn't. He explains what to avoid in your marriage and family that would move you toward the unhealthy range of behavior and what to maximize so that you can move toward the healthier range.

One of the things that attracted me to this book is Mark Laaser's description of healthy and unhealthy families. Unit 9 alone, in which he traces the roots of sexual addiction in families, is worth the price of the book.

Rarely have I called the authors of books I have read. In fact, I've only called two authors in my life. Mark Laaser was one of them. This is a book everyone needs to read.

Gary Smalley

# Healthy Sexuality

Everyone struggles to some degree with the issue of sexuality. *Faithful & True* gives you an opportunity to understand yourself better as a sexual being. It will help you cope in a world of sexual immorality as a faithful marriage partner or as a young adult or single adult living as a sexually whole person.

In *Faithful & True* you will encounter individuals who live out their sexuality in both appropriate and inappropriate ways. You will identify easily with some of the thoughts, attitudes, and behaviors. Others may not be your experience. All of us live somewhere between perfectly healthy and unhealthy sexuality. Through this study you will have opportunity to evaluate yourself and to discover meaningful ways to move in the direction of greater sexual health and more Christ-honoring behaviors.

Through *Faithful & True* you will learn to expand your thinking about sexuality. Sexual intimacy is a gift from God to be enjoyed between husband and wife. Sexuality is much more, however, than a physical act. Sexual intimacy with another person involves the physical, emotional, and spiritual dimensions of our lives. Paul compared the relationship between a man and woman to the relationship between Christ and the church (Ephesians 5:22-33). Many of us make the mistake of thinking that this spiritual union magically happens when we get married. We make the false assumption that the knowledge and ability to have sexual health will come to us instinctively. While we never would assume that we could play baseball, tennis, or golf without proper instruction, we assume that we will be able to deal with our sexuality on our own.

Experience in your home and culture has probably given you some incorrect messages about sexual health. You may have been the victim of sexual abuse, or exposed at an early age to pornography. Perhaps your family of origin was devoid of values. In some families any discussion of sexuality and intimacy is strictly taboo. Consequently, family members develop a limited understanding and develop anxiety about sexuality. Inappropriate behaviors often result. Even if you have not experienced any of these situations, all of us have the basic problem of sin—our alienation from God which leads to alienation from each other. This book will help you examine those influences and their effect on you.

## Plan of Action
You may choose one of two basic ways to use this material. The first approach is to study the first 6 units–Part 1–of this workbook. I call this section the sexual health model. This approach is for those
• who seek to grow in sexual health and to remain faithful to marriage vows, or
• who are single and wish to live as sexually whole and healthy persons.
Whatever your situation, you will develop a sexual health plan that you can use for the rest of your life.

The second approach to this workbook is for those who struggle in a more serious way with issues of sexuality. Those struggles may involve compulsive and addictive behaviors. Your first task will be to find sobriety—to stop the specific actions—and to gain peace from the slavery of powerful sexual thoughts and behaviors. Your group will start with unit 1 and then move directly to Part 2 which will explain the nature of sexual addiction, how the addiction began and grew, and how to use the sexual health plan to become sober and faithful again. You need to accomplish this task before you return to Part 1. Your group may need to work through Part 2 several times before you find lasting sobriety. You will be directed to other sources of support, therapy, and accountability to help you find sobriety and freedom from sexual lust and acting out. Research indicates that you will benefit most if you achieve 6-12 months of total freedom from sexual acting-out behavior before attempting more in-depth work.

Because of the unique 2-part approach of *Faithful & True*, you will encounter some material that may not apply to your life and experience. If you have difficulty relating personally to a particular section or activity, study that area to understand the experience of others.

## What's in it for you?

*Faithful & True* is not merely designed for you to understand concepts. The purpose of this material is life change. *Faithful & True* is part of the LIFE® Support Series. This series is an educational system of resources for study groups and support groups to provide Christian ministry and emotional support to individuals in the areas of social, emotional, and physical need. These resources deal with such life issues as chemical dependency, codependency, recovery from sexual abuse, eating disorders, divorce recovery, and how to grieve the losses of life. LIFE® Support Series courses are a form of focused discipleship. The Christ-centered recovery process helps people resolve painful issues so they can effectively minister to others.

*Faithful & True* is an integrated course of study—it combines personal study, interactive learning activities, and group interaction. To achieve the full benefit of this study, you will need to prepare your individual assignments and participate in the group sessions. This is not a course which you will study and forget. It represents an opportunity to understand yourself as a sexual being, as an individual in a world of sexual immorality, and as a marriage partner. Some of these issues will be difficult and you will need to be courageous in looking at your feelings. You may experience grief for past hurts and behaviors. You will find help and encouragement as you accept responsibility for your healing, emotions, and behavior.

Participating in a *Faithful & True* group will be the beginning of a journey. There will be times of pain and times of joy. Whether you are single or married, *Faithful & True* will lead to a new way of relating to yourself, to the world, and to others. When you complete *Faithful & True* we will suggest some possibilities for you to continue your growth.

### Study Tips

We all struggle at various levels with sexual issues. We are all sexual beings created in the image of God. How you react to this material will vary according to your own life experience. We do not impose any rigid schedule for your study of the book, particularly for those of you who discover that you are a survivor of sexual or other forms of abuse.

## Getting the most from this course

Some individuals are stabilized in their personal lives and highly motivated to deal with their sexual issues. If you are one of those individuals, you will find that *Faithful & True* is divided into 5 lessons per unit. The basic group plan is for you to cover one unit per week in preparation for your weekly group meeting. You may be able to study the material and complete the exercises in 30 to 60 minutes of study time each day. Even if you find that you can study the material in less time, spread the study out over five days. This will give you more time to apply the truths to your life.

On the other hand, you may experience extreme difficulty concentrating, or some of the material may be so challenging that you cannot complete a unit in a week, or even in many weeks. Do not shame or pressure yourself for needing to go slowly. Sexual health is a life-time process. Your group may decide to take a longer time to study each unit. Do not become discouraged if you cannot complete *Faithful & True* in 12 weeks. Remember that the purpose is life change, not speed reading. Some of us come from backgrounds, even in our Christian faith, that lead us to believe that we are not truly faithful or Christian if we do not find immediate answers to all of our problems.

 **In the margin read what Paul had to say about weakness in 2 Corinthians 12:7-10. Below write in your own words Paul's conclusion about weakness:**

_____

> To keep me from becoming conceited because of these surpassingly great revelations, there was given me a thorn in my flesh, a messenger of Satan, to torment me. Three times I pleaded with the Lord to take it away from me. But he said to me, "My grace is sufficient for you, for my power is made perfect in weakness." Therefore I will boast all the more gladly about my weaknesses, so that Christ's power may rest on me. That is why, for Christ's sake, I delight in weaknesses, in insults, in hardships, in persecutions, in difficulties. For when I am weak, then I am strong.
> –2 Corinthians 12:7-10

*Faithful & True* is like having your own tutor. Study it as if I were sitting with you helping you learn. When I give you an assignment, you will benefit most by writing your response (as you have just done). Each assignment is indented and appears in boldface type. When you are to respond in writing, a pencil appears beside the assignment. Lines, such as the ones above, will appear for you to use in writing your answer, but you may also use your own paper. No one will ever ask you to turn in an assignment or ask to see it. You may voluntarily show your work to someone if you wish.

In most cases your "personal tutor" will give you some feedback about your response. For example, you may see a suggestion about what you might have written. In the example above you may have written that weakness is normal or that weakness can, when submitted to God, glorify Him. This process is designed to help you learn the material and apply the concepts more effectively. Do not deny yourself valuable learning by skipping the learning activities.

At times you will be asked to respond in non-written fashion—for example, by thinking about or praying about a matter. An arrow will appear beside the assignment. This type of assignment will look like this:

> **Pause now to pray and thank God for unconditionally accepting you.**

Set a definite time and select a quiet place where you can study with little interruption. Keep a Bible handy for times in which the material asks you to look up Scripture. Make notes of problems, questions, or concerns that arise as you study. You will discuss many of these during your group sessions.

## Group Session

You will benefit most from *Faithful & True* if once a week you attend a group session. Others in your group will share your journey with you. They will affirm, encourage, and love you as you grow. Many of us have experienced problems that leave us with difficulty talking, being honest, and trusting others. You will have to practice talking, being honest, and trusting. The intimacy of your group will increase from week to week as you develop these skills. Your group can become the supportive family you may never have experienced before.

If you are not involved in a *Faithful & True* group, I encourage you to seek out a Christ-centered group. You will find that growth happens more quickly when you participate in a group. You may also need to be part of a 12-step support group for sexual addiction. A list of nationwide organizations that can help you find a group appears on page 224.

*Faithful & True* includes guidance for the group leader or facilitator. These leader helps begin on page 225. Do not attempt to conduct a recovery-type group without studying the facilitator's guide.

# A key decision

*Faithful & True* is written with the assumption that you already have received Jesus Christ as your Savior and Lord and that you have Him guiding you in the healing process. If you have not yet made the important decision to receive Christ, visit with a Christian friend or pastor about doing so. On page 17 you will find more information about receiving Jesus Christ as your Savior and Lord. You will benefit far more from *Faithful & True* if you have Jesus working in your life and guiding you in the process.

## THE ISSUE OF PROFESSIONAL COUNSELING

If you are a survivor of sexual abuse, some of the exercises and questions in this workbook may cause you to recognize deep emotional and spiritual issues. This is good. Most of us won't heal until we face these issues and talk about them. At first, however, they frighten and cause depression, anxiety, or even thoughts of suicide. You may feel that no one else will understand or that you are the worst person in the world, not even worthy of Christ's death. This deep shame, particularly about our sexuality, usually is a result of the abuse. Your group leader can help you identify these problems. He or she also can help you find professional help.

You may need to seek professional counseling from a skilled and committed Christian counselor who can help you talk through these feelings. If you experience a deep depression, for example, more aggressive help may be needed. You may desire to get a professional evaluation before you begin the group process.

Once you start the group process you will want to share with the other group members any feelings that you have. You will be surprised to find that many of them have had the same feelings. This is the value of a healing community. We are all fellow strugglers along the path to find a stronger relationship with Christ and a greater sense of peace in our lives. Sharing your feelings will let others know that you have a commitment to honesty. You will take a risk with others and open the door to intimacy. You will find that developing intimacy with others will be a major step on the road to wholeness in your life.

## My Basis for Writing

You may wonder, *What right does he have to tell me about sexuality?* The question is legitimate. Allow me to tell a part of my story. I was a young pastor. I appeared to all who knew me as completely well-adjusted and successful. I served a church, taught at the local Christian college, served on the local school board, and counseled many. People looked up to me and respected my opinion. I was a frequent guest on local radio and television shows. With three children, my wife and I seemed to exemplify an ideal family.

Few knew the sexual fire that burned inside me. The problem began when, as a young boy, I found myself preoccupied with female bodies. At age 11, I discovered pornography and became addicted to it. At first I stole pornographic magazines. Later I bought them. When I became a Christian I tried many times to give up pornography, and did for varying periods of time, but always came back to it.

In college I began to masturbate to fantasies of women. During this time I was dating my future wife and maintaining a "moral" relationship, waiting for marriage to have sex. I assumed that getting married would allow me to stop using pornography and masturbating. I was surprised and in despair when it didn't.

In graduate school I began going to massage parlors and spending money on prostitutes. As a pastor I began to have sex with women I counseled. In doing so I hurt and violated the trust of many people.

By the grace of God someone intervened and I sought treatment for my sexual problems. Many people were angry with me. Some of the women with whom I had been involved sued. My denomination turned its back on me. My story appeared in the local paper. But many others encouraged and prayed for me. Although shocked and angry, my wife decided to stay with me. Through a long and painful process, I have found sexual sobriety and my wife and I are finding spiritual, emotional, and sexual health.

I write to encourage you. Wherever you are on the spectrum of sexual health you can grow. You can experience greater intimacy with God and with others. As you work through *Faithful & True*, I pray that you will grow in health and godliness.

# A Foundation for Sexuality

## FOCAL PASSAGE

*Let us not give up meeting together, as some are in the habit of doing, but let us encourage one another—and all the more as you see the Day approaching.*

–Hebrews 10:25

## MEMORY VERSE

He who began a good work in you will carry it on to completion.
–Philippians 1:6

---

### A SECRET DESIRE

Fred was sick with anxiety. How could he have these terrible sexual thoughts? He had never been unfaithful to his wife, but for days he had driven past a newly opened nightclub that advertised nude dancing. More and more he felt the urge to go in. Fred had resisted the urge, but he was still angry at himself.

Fred wondered why the world was so filled with lust and perversion. How could his city allow this bar to be there in the first place? Fred was angry at the world.

Sometimes Fred was angry at his wife. *If my sex life with my wife were more exciting maybe I wouldn't have these temptations,* he thought. How could he talk to his wife about his feelings? Fred was angry at her for not being more available. But they didn't talk about sex--or much of anything that really troubled him. Fred didn't know how to share himself with another person. He often felt lonely.

Most of us have a difficult time talking about our feelings. In this unit you will learn how to build a support system for yourself so that you will have someone to talk to. You will also learn that, whatever your thoughts and feelings, you are not alone.

---

## GROWTH GOAL

In this unit you will identify reasons to have a system of accountability and support. You will begin to develop a support system and set goals for your growth.

| The Value of a Group | Building A Support System | Group Rules | Account-ability | Measuring Your Success |
|---|---|---|---|---|
| LESSON 1 | LESSON 2 | LESSON 3 | LESSON 4 | LESSON 5 |

# The Value of a Group

You met Fred in the unit story. He is struggling with his sexuality. Like many of us, Fred suffers from shame about his sexual feelings. Fred is also angry. Many of us are afraid of our anger, thinking that it is a totally destructive emotion. We've seen few good models of how to deal with and express anger. By keeping his emotions secret, Fred is allowing them to build quietly but powerfully. His thoughts are beginning to get out of hand. His temptations may soon cause him to fall into sexual sin.

Fred has other thoughts that are difficult to talk about. For example, he sometimes wonders if he made the right choice in a marriage partner. Fred looks at other women and thinks to himself, "If I had only found someone like her, I wouldn't have these sexual temptations." He wants his wife to be more sexually active, to initiate, to be more spontaneous and playful. He is frustrated with the "dullness" of their sex life.

Fred desperately needs to talk to someone about his thoughts and feelings. However, he thinks that he is alone in having them. He also is afraid of what they mean spiritually. His definition of being a Christian man tells him that he should never have thoughts like this.

✎ **Review the previous three paragraphs. What one word describes what you think keeps Fred from dealing with his problem?**

_____

_____

✎ **Read 1 Corinthians 10:13, appearing in the margin. Below describe what the verse says to you about the common nature of even our worst thoughts and feelings.**

_____

_____

_____

No temptation has seized you except what is common to man. And God is faithful; he will not let you be tempted beyond what you can bear. But when you are tempted, he will also provide a way out so that you can stand up under it.
–1 Corinthians 10:13

You may have chosen one of many words to describe Fred's behavior. Words such as *silence, isolation, fear, shame,* or *secrets* all describe the key to Fred's problem. Fred is not talking about his thoughts and feelings. Most of us feel that if others knew our private thoughts and feelings they would reject us. Paul often reminds us that we are all sinners; we all fall short of God's glory. We may think that others are better than we are, that they never do the things we do, think the thoughts we think, or feel the feelings we feel. This fear keeps us silent, trying to put on a "false front," proving to others that we are worthy of respect.

## Support and Sharing

We live in a war over sexual values. As Christians we must be aware of the decay of values and the sexual preoccupation that our culture currently experiences. Ask yourself the question, How many sexual stimuli have I been bombarded with today? Think of the advertising, songs on the radio, television shows, movies, and magazines you have encountered that convey sexual messages. Sexual stimulation even fills the magazines in the check-out lanes at your local grocery store.

Many of us have become so desensitized to the presence of these stimuli that we don't consciously focus on our reactions to them. Even if we did try to make healthy choices in the midst of such pressure, most of us have not had instruction at home or church about how to do so. Our situation today resembles what Paul described in Ephesians 4:17-19.

No longer live as the Gentiles do, in the futility of their thinking. They are darkened in their understanding and separated from the life of God because of the ignorance that is in them due to the hardening of their hearts. Having lost all sensitivity, they have given themselves over to sensuality so as to indulge in every kind of impurity, with a continual lust for more.
—Ephesians 4:17-19

As a society we have lost sensitivity and given ourselves over to sensuality. As a result, we continually desire more sensual stimulation.

Sexual struggles, dealing with temptations, and falling into sexual sin have been a problem for people of faith since biblical times. God's strongest man, Samson; God's greatest king, David; and God's wisest man, Solomon all succumbed to sexual lust.

The Bible is very open about the reality and destructive nature of sexual sin. Yet the church often pretends by its silence that sexual temptation doesn't exist. A Christian doctor friend of mine says that for many of us the church is like a new car showroom. We get ourselves all polished up to sell ourselves to other members of the church. He says that the church should really be like the auto body shop, a place where we go when bumped and cracked, damaged and bruised. It should be a place of restoration. This is a book for a group of Christians committed to support each other in the quest to be faithful and true. Developing a support system isn't just for people with problems. Every person needs a network of people with whom he or she can be honest.

✎ **Read Hebrews 10:25 that appears in the margin. Check the response below that describes what the verse says to you about the importance of a group.**

> ❏ I need to be strong and deal with life on my own.
> ❏ Only wimps need supportive relationships.
> ❏ All Christians need each other to stay on track.

The author of the Book of Hebrews wrote to a group of discouraged Christians. He told them how to stay together and find support. He said we are tempted to go our own way and take care of ourselves. This temptation tells us no one will understand us. No one will like us. No one will be like us in our thoughts and actions. Hebrews assures us that if we stay together and encourage one another, we will find strength and fellowship together.

Howard Hendricks strongly calls us to honesty and accountability. In *Seven Promises of a Promise Keeper,* he says every man needs three kinds of relationships. Every man needs:
- a Paul—an older, wiser, or more experienced man who can be a mentor.
- a Timothy—a younger man for whom he can be a mentor.
- a Barnabus—an equal who will hold him accountable.[1]

In this unit I hope to lead you to identify your need for supportive and accountable relationships. In our society most people—especially men—have never experienced a group in which they can be totally honest and be held accountable with love. This study may begin in what seems a peculiar place by urging you to build a support network, but supportive and responsible relationships are essential to growth in sexual health.

## You will begin to develop a support system and set goals for your growth.

✎ **This unit's growth goal appears in the margin. Below circle the feelings you experience when you think about people in a group offering you support, love, acceptance, and encouragement to help you be faithful and true.**

| | | |
|---|---|---|
| excited | numb | afraid |
| angry | detached | hopeful |

other_____

In this unit I will encourage you to take several specific actions toward building a support network. Remember that having a support system does not mean you are weak or weird. Building a support system is healthy and normal. To hide from or deny our fear, pride, and isolation is dangerous. You have heard many cultural messages saying things like: "real men don't show their emotions." Those messages are destructive lies.

Note: You may already be a part of an ongoing group. It may be a group in your church who regularly met together for prayer, study, and encouragement. You may have formed a group just for this study. If you are not part of a group, you will not get as much out of this study as those who regularly meet together to talk openly about their issues and pray for and encourage each other. If you are in a group, some of the following information about groups you will already be familiar with. Read it to refresh your commitment to the ground rules that make a group function best. If you are not in a group, be open to the possibilities as you read.

✎ What do you think can be gained from attending a group?

_____

_____

## I HAVE DIFFICULTY TALKING ABOUT—

_____

_____

_____

Can you list in the margin a thought or feeling that you are afraid to talk about?

The experience of talking about yourself for the first time may be a time of great anxiety. It may also be a time of great relief. You will experience that when you share, no one will run screaming out of the room. You will lose the burden of secrets you have been carrying. People will listen and understand. As you talk, others will be encouraged to talk also. Your group will be a process of learning to share, encourage, and accept each other. In the process of talking and sharing, you will experience support and fellowship.

Through relationships with others you will understand more about a relationship with Jesus. You may be confused about what such a relationship means. You may feel angry with God for allowing you to experience the thoughts, feelings, and events that you have. Even being angry with God is an emotion that is acceptable to Him. Share your doubts and questions with your group and your facilitator. Be who you are, where you are.

## Assignment for the Lesson

✎ Write your own paraphrase of Philippians 1:6, this unit's Scripture memory verse.

He who began a good work in you will carry it on to completion.
–Philippians 1:6

_____

_____

➤ Say aloud this affirmation five times.

I can find support and acceptance.

➤ As you reread the concerns and fears you listed on the previous pages, remember the words of 1 Peter 5:7, "Cast all your anxiety on him (God) because he cares for you." Pray and ask God to be with you as you begin your group process.

# Building a Support System

Fred, whom you met in the unit story on page 10, is not a bad man. He is a good man who desires to be a good husband and father. Some of the things going on in Fred's life, however, may destroy both him and his family.

➤ **Do you know anyone who is, or has, gone through the struggle that Fred is experiencing? Do you know anyone who suddenly began to have affairs, or to practice other forms of sexual immorality? Pause to pray for that person right now.**

Could it be that people who "suddenly" fall into self-destructive sexual sin are people who first struggled with thoughts and feelings that they do not know how to control? Are we all vulnerable to these same pitfalls? In this lesson we will consider why and how to break the silence.

James Dobson says that any man who does not have a support and accountability group is an accident waiting for a place to happen. Everyone needs a support network. Getting help may not come easy to you. You may have to practice the skills and exercise the courage necessary to get support. Your group will be a good place to start that practice.

Your *Faithful & True* group may be the first part of an entire system of support that you need to maintain healthy sexuality in your life. Other individuals--such as a spouse, family members, and friends--can be a part of that system.

 **On the first scale below place a mark to indicate your level of ease or difficulty in talking about your emotions. On the second scale indicate your level of difficulty talking about sexual issues.**

Easy                                                          Extremely Difficult

No one person can give you all the help you need to stay healthy. Many of us have made the mistake of thinking we could find support in just one person. Perhaps we place this all-or-nothing desire on a spouse, a close friend, or someone we plan to marry. Often we get mad at that person for not meeting all our needs. No one person can ever meet all of our needs, even if we ask. Some of us are too good at asking or demanding, and we drain one person of his or her time and energy. We must find a system of support, a group of people that we can turn to at the right time and place to get what we need.

## Self-Evaluation

Note that *Faithful & True* addresses a number of life situations, from the person who struggles with the universal challenge of sexual temptation to the person who is sexually acting out addictive or compulsive behavior. Part of your task as you study this material is to do honest self-evaluation. You may determine that your level of sexual struggle is relatively minor. In that case, a system of support/accountability will help you grow. If, however, you determine that you are struggling with a more serious level of sexual temptation/behavior, you need to build a stronger support network.

The process of restoration and discipleship involves more than the isolated individual. You may discover that your struggle involves relationships with your spouse and other

**KEY POINT**
Support means people who will allow me to talk about my struggles, people who will encourage me, people who will help me be faithful and true.

family or friends. You cannot control them or "make" them change. You may need to pursue growth work together.

## The Shame Barrier

When we think of getting help for healthy sexuality, most of us confront a part of ourselves that prevents us from getting support—the feeling of shame. Genesis 2:25 appears in the margin. In their original, innocent relationship to God and each other, Adam and Eve could be naked and not be ashamed. They must have experienced their bodies and their relationship to each other as gifts of creation from God. After the fall, shame about their bodies and sexuality entered their lives (Genesis 3:7).

**The man and his wife were both naked, and they felt no shame.**
–Genesis 2:25

**Then the eyes of both of them were opened, and they realized they were naked; so they sewed fig leaves together and made coverings for themselves.**
–Genesis 3:7

### A WORD ABOUT SHAME

The word shame often is misunderstood. It can have many meanings. Some shame is healthy. Healthy shame reminds us that we need God; we can't take care of ourselves without Him. We acknowledge our weakness and submit to God's strength. Healthy shame also tells us that we need others in our lives and asking for help is OK. Healthy shame is the opposite of the pride that led to the first sin. This pride says that we do not need God, that we can take care of ourselves.

Unhealthy shame makes us feel we can never be acceptable in the sight of God. This kind of shame tells us we are bad, worthless people, hated by God and everyone else. Unhealthy shame convinces us that we are unworthy of love or support.

In the final analysis, healthy and unhealthy shame are radically different. Unhealthy shame convinces us that we are a mistake and everything we do is wrong. Healthy shame reminds us that we make mistakes and we need to confess them, repent, make restitution, and find forgiveness in the grace of God. Unhealthy shame is a major enemy in our effort to grow. Healthy shame constantly reminds us that we need God and others.

**KEY POINT**
We must overcome unhealthy shame to experience sexual health.

If talking about sexuality with others automatically triggers our sense of unhealthy shame, we must overcome this shame to experience sexual health.

✎ The idea of healthy shame may be a new concept for you. In the explanation above, circle the words that describe the benefits of healthy shame.

Did you circle "reminds us that we need God"? Did you note that healthy shame leads us to submit to God's strength? Healthy shame leads us to the greatest relationship in life. It causes us to turn to God through Jesus Christ.

**For no one can lay any foundation other than the one already laid, which is Jesus Christ.**
–1 Corinthians 3:11

➤ What does 1 Corinthians 3:11 (margin) say to you about the importance of a relationship to Jesus Christ?

Have you come to a time and place in your life when you recognized your separation from God? Have you accepted the fact that Jesus died on the cross to pay for your sins? And have you made the choice to receive that already-paid-for gift of forgiveness and peace with God? In this lesson you are studying building a support system. The most vital part of a support system is a love relationship with God.

If you have not yet taken this key step of faith, I have great news. Now is the time. You can receive Jesus Christ right now by inviting Him into your life. If you desire to trust Christ and accept His payment for your sins, tell Him so in prayer. You may use this simple prayer to express your faith.

> *Lord Jesus, I need You. I want You to be my Savior and my Lord. I accept Your death on the cross as payment for my sins, and I now entrust my life to Your care. Please help me grow in my understanding of Your love and power so that my life will bring glory and honor to You. I hereby commit myself to love You, to honor You, and to serve You so long as I live. Thank You for forgiving me and for giving me a new life. Amen.*

_____ (signature) _____ (date)

If you have made this key decision, or if you have questions, call your group leader, pastor, or a Christian friend whom you trust. Share your decision with him or her. By telling others about your decision you will confirm your faith and enlarge your support network.

➤ **Do you have a friend, family member, or member of your *Faithful & True* group who you can ask to support you and hold you accountable?**

If you confess with your mouth, "Jesus is Lord," and believe in your heart that God raised him from the dead, you will be saved. For it is with your heart that you believe and are justified, and it is with your mouth that you confess and are saved. As the Scripture says, "Anyone who trusts in him will never be put to shame."
–Romans 10:9-11

### Assignment for the Lesson

✎ Write on a card Philippians 1:6, the Scripture memory verse for this unit. Carry the card with you. As you work through *Faithful & True,* regularly review your memory verses.

➤ Say aloud the following affirmation three times.

I am worthy of support and have the courage to get it.

➤ Remember 1 Peter 5:7 from the previous lesson? Ask God to help you overcome your anxiety and to share your story with the person or people He has helped (or will help) you choose.

LESSON
3

# Group Rules

Building intimacy and trust in a *Faithful & True* group depends on well-defined group rules. We sometimes call these group rules *boundaries*. Boundaries are rules that create safety. A boundary is a way of defining conduct. It is an invisible barrier keeping out dangerous, negative, and destructive behaviors and letting in healthy, positive, and constructive ones.

Most of us have had life experiences in which we didn't feel safe to express our thoughts and emotions. We may have been criticized, judged, or teased. Some of us have participated in groups in which confidences have been violated or where people were angry, judgmental, and blaming.

➤ **Think about a time when you were with people where you didn't feel safe to be honest. How did that experience feel?**

Whatever our experience, many of us fear participating in a group. We wonder what other people will think. We believe that we need to please them or somehow prove ourselves. I would like for your *Faithful & True* group to be a much safer place for you. I hope you will learn to practice being honest and open. The following group rules will help you build the kind of trust your group needs.

GROUP RULES
1. This group is safe; we can be honest.
2. This group is safe; we can be angry (even at God).
3. This group is safe; we can have conflict.
4. This group is safe; we can be sad, lonely, or frightened.
5. We will not put ourselves or others down.
6. We will make no self-righteous statements.
7. We will not blame others; we will take responsibility for our own actions.
8. We will strive to affirm ourselves and others.
9. We will practice confidentiality.
10. We will only give feedback when asked.
11. Group time will be divided among those who ask for time to share.
12. We will pray for God's presence and guidance in all of our discussions.

➤ Read the rules at the beginning of each *Faithful & True* group meeting.

Your group facilitator will help monitor these rules. As the group becomes more comfortable with each other, members will be able to monitor themselves and each other.

The first four rules declare that to express feelings is safe. These rules encourage us to be honest. They are group affirmations. They remind us that emotions are subjective. Our feelings are real to us. Someone else's perception of truth or reality should not prevent us from expressing ourselves. We must feel safe to tell who we are and what we feel without worrying about what someone else thinks.

The safety rules also remind us that we may disagree with each other. We may not always like what other group members say or do. Being angry with others—including God—is not destructive. Anger is a sign of how much we care for others and how much we have felt hurt. How we express anger can be positive or negative. Conflict is OK when we seek to express honestly how we feel in non-blaming and non-judgmental ways. Rules 5, 6, 7, and 8 help us have constructive conflict.

The last four rules aid the process of the group. Confidentiality is the cornerstone. We must agree that we will not share what we hear in group with anyone outside the group. As group members begin to trust each other, a sense of safety will grow.

To give feedback is to be a mirror for another group member. Giving feedback means telling another group member only what we see. Advice or instruction is not feedback. Getting feedback from other group members will often be vital to us. So often our own perceptions and thinking can be distorted by our faulty beliefs about ourselves and others. Feedback allows us to get a more objective perspective. Group safety, however, demands that we give feedback only when asked. However vital, astute, and magnificent we think our thoughts and opinions might be, we must be asked for them. Every member of the group deserves the freedom to speak without being lectured to or bombarded with unsolicited opinions.

You may not be comfortable asking for your needs to be met. Asking for time to share is something you must learn to do. You will find that sharing will come more easily as your *Faithful & True* group builds trust and support with each other. Rule 11 also asks that time be shared equally. If you tend to be too talkative, never really getting to the point or never really getting to your true feelings, you will need to learn to be honest and timely, respecting the needs of others.

➤ **Practice right now. Say out loud, "I need time to share my thoughts and feelings."**

Finally, the last rule simply reminds us that we seek God's presence in all that we do.

✎ **Read Romans 8:26, appearing in the margin. Below write what you think Paul is saying to you through the verse.**

_____

_____

> Likewise the Spirit helps us in our weakness; for we do not know how to pray as we ought, but the Spirit himself intercedes for us with sighs too deep for words.
> –Romans 8:26, RSV

The Scripture promises us the strength of the Holy Spirit. In our times of greatest fatigue we can be assured of the presence of the Holy Spirit. Your *Faithful & True* group may experience moments of emotional exhaustion. At those times, take a deep breath and remember the sigh that is too deep for words that is the assurance of God's presence in our life.

✎ **All of us have different experiences with groups going back to our earliest days of school. In the space below write any other rules that you would like to see your group observe.**

_____

_____

_____

Share these with your *Faithful & True* group. If everyone agrees, then other rules can be added to your group list.

## Assignment for the Lesson

➤ Make a list of the group rules that you can carry with you. Try practicing them in other relationships.

➤ Say the following affirmation five times.

I will be a great group member.

➤ Pray for each of the members of your group.

## Accountability

In groups we say: "you're as sick as your secrets," but in our culture we have treated sexuality as an exclusively secret issue. Developing and maintaining sexual health requires openness, honesty, and supportive relationships. We need to talk very specifically about one form of supportive relationship—namely accountability relationships.

Accountability means that you make an account—give a report—of your life to someone else. What you account for varies and may include your intentions and plans to stay faithful and true.

**ACCOUNTABILITY:**
willing to be held answerable for agreed on attitudes and behaviors.

✎ In the margin read John 5:6. Below describe what you think Jesus meant when He asked the paralytic man if he wanted to be healed.

_____

_____

**When Jesus saw him lying there and learned that he had been in this condition for a long time, he asked him, "Do you want to get well?"**
**–John 5:6**

The central question of this lesson is: *Do you want to grow?* The paralytic man at the pool of Bethesda gave Jesus excuses for why in 38 years he hadn't been able to get down to the pool.

**COMMON EXCUSES NOT TO CHANGE**
I'm too old.
I don't have the strength.
I don't have the wisdom or skill.
No one ever helps me.
Something always happens when I try.
My spouse doesn't support me.

✎ Below write excuses you've used to avoid making some needed change in your life, such as changing impure sexual thoughts or behaviors.

_____

_____

The real reason some of us don't want to change or be more healthy is because our old ways are familiar. They are comfortable. We know them. We know how to do them. To change would be to try something new and different, unfamiliar. Change feels uncomfortable, even painful. Many people live with old, even destructive, behaviors because they are familiar.

✎ Below write an area of your life in which you've tried to change and found yourself slipping back to old ways of doing things.

_____

Old, negative, and destructive patterns may even serve a purpose. Sometimes our behaviors gain attention for us or instantly gratify our needs and desires. Even our impure sexual thoughts and actions may have been ways we sought to get love and nurture.

Nothing is quite so instant as imagining (or fantasizing) about sex. This may sound strange but think about ways our culture has taught us to equate sex and love (songs, movies, television shows). Think also how culture (advertising) teaches us to get our needs met instantly.

✎ Write below one example of a cultural message that promotes the idea that sex and love are the same. For examples, look at the advertisements in a magazine or on television.

_____

**Now think of a message that encourages you to gratify your needs instantly.**

_____

Advertisements, television, movies, music are filled with such messages. If characters on television and in movies even think they love each other they are soon in bed together. We even say about sexual intercourse that we are "making love." Sex can be the expression of love between husband and wife, but the act of sex never "makes" love.

Negative, destructive, and impure thoughts or actions can deceive us by making us feel that they are "good friends." Despite their sinful nature they are things we did that felt good, helped us to relax, or soothed us at times of stress, anger, or crisis.

Whatever is true, whatever is noble, whatever is right, whatever is pure, whatever is lovely, whatever is admirable—if anything is excellent or praiseworthy—think about such things.
–Philippians 4:8

**SPECIAL ISSUE ALERT:**
Philippians 4:8 (margin) alerts us that we need to guard our thought life carefully. We need to think about wholesome and pure issues. As you work through Faithful & True, you will honestly need to examine the unhealthy and impure aspects of your thought life. The apostle Paul says "we take captive every thought to make it obedient to Christ" (2 Corinthians 10:5). As you respond to learning activities like the one below or as you share in group meetings, begin to train your mind to acknowledge the fact of wrong behaviors without dwelling on the details of the behavior. Remember that fantasizing is a behavior.

One of your tasks in Faithful &True is to evaluate your own level of sexual struggle. Some of this material describes an extreme level of sexual behavior or sexual addiction. If you do not identify with these issues, study to understand what others are experiencing. If you do identify with some or most of the material, study to experience life change.

✎ Check the types of impure sexual thoughts that you have had that you know bring you instant gratification.

❑ Fantasizing about imaginary sexual encounters
❑ Fantasizing about past sexual encounters
❑ Watching movies for the sexual content
❑ Reading books or magazines with stimulating sexual content
❑ Fantasizing about specific individuals.

❑ Other _____

To grow we must be willing to let go of these "old friends." Sometimes we must say good-bye to lifetime patterns of behavior. Change includes a grieving process. An accountability group can encourage you as you go through this grief process. We need to find people who themselves are strong enough and well enough to challenge us to change and confront us when our life is not reflecting a change.

**Both types of groups are supportive**

**All groups involve accountability**

**Support groups involve greater accountability**

**As you move toward the center of the circles, the level of accountability increases.**

If one falls down, his friend can help him up. But pity the man who falls and has no one to help him up! Though one may be overpowered, two can defend themselves. A cord of three strands is not quickly broken.
–Ecclesiastes 4:10,12

## Accountability and Support Groups

May I attempt to clarify some confusing terminology concerning groups? This workbook is designed for use in several situations. I am using the terminology that a *support* group is a gathering of people who wish to change something in their lives—such as a group of addicted persons committed together to overcome a specific behavior or a group of people who have suffered a loss gathered to work through their grief. Thus not everyone needs a *support* group, but everybody needs to be accountable. An *accountability* group is a collection of people who desire to develop specific character traits. They commit together to help each other grow. Thus while not every person needs a support group, everybody needs accountability groups in their lives. Using my terminology, every support group is an accountability group but not every accountability group is a support group. Part 1 of *Faithful & True* is for an accountability group. Part 2 is for a support group, though the support group will also use Part 1. The drawing in the margin pictures the relationship between accountability and support groups.

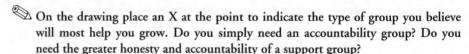 On the drawing place an X at the point to indicate the type of group you believe will most help you grow. Do you simply need an accountability group? Do you need the greater honesty and accountability of a support group?

Healthy and effective people know that they need systems of accountability. Accountability requires a specific network of people you ask to help you maintain or achieve healthy behaviors. They also will be people who help you avoid unhealthy and sinful behaviors. Your accountability group or accountability partners are not responsible for your behavior. They don't have the power to control or change you. Only God and you together can do that. They will be there, however, so that you can make an "accounting." They will listen, support, and encourage you. They also will give you feedback or even confront you if they think you're slipping into wrong behaviors.

In lesson 3 we discovered that everyone needs a support network (accountability). Depending on your level of struggle with sexual temptations and sexual behaviors, you may need more than a support group. If you have tried and failed repeatedly to overcome compulsive thoughts and behaviors, you need to enlist an accountability "team" specifically to help you. In the drawing, picture a smaller circle inside the first two. An accountability team is one of the strongest accountability systems. If you need to build such a team, start by choosing two individuals to be on your accountability team. The process for asking them is much the same as asking for support. The following are qualifications to look for in enlisting people to be your accountability partners:

## Guidelines for Selecting An accountability team:

1. Pray for wisdom as you select supportive people.
2. Look for people who are:
    a. able to be confidential, won't gossip about you
    b. mature Christians
    c. able to be honest and lovingly confront you when needed
    d. have learned how to make changes in their own lives
    e. further ahead in the process of developing healthy sexuality than you. They may be people who have already completed a LIFE Support Group. You will know these people by the peace and maturity you sense in them.
3. Surrender any resentment toward those who have not supported you in the past. They may not have known how to help.
4. Determine how much of your story you want to tell initially. Write it down on paper as a way of practicing.
5. Pray for the persons you choose.

You may be wise not to choose close friends for your accountability team. You may think close friends know you well, but you may not have been honest with them about your secret thoughts, desires, and actions. Close friends may be unable to be honest and confrontive with you for fear of hurting your feelings.

### If You Struggle Seriously with Sexual Sin

While you are participating in a *Faithful & True* group, you will learn to be accountable for your sexual temptations and sins. You also will need to be accountable for your safety. Work in this book can involve such deep pain that you may be tempted to do something destructive to yourself or to others. If you choose to study Part 2, I will be more specific about an action plan for your sexual feelings and actions. As you begin your *Faithful & True* group, you will need an action plan for times of emotional crisis and danger.

If you struggle with guilt, depression, or addictive sexual thoughts and behaviors, take time to seriously complete the following personal crisis plan.

---

## PERSONAL CRISIS PLAN

*I agree that when I experience painful and dangerous thoughts, I will call:*

_____

*If he is not home I will call people on the following list until I can find one that is:*

_____

_____

_____

_____

_____

*I further agree that I will not harm myself.*

*Signed*_____

---

## Assignment for the Lesson

➤ Say aloud this affirmation five times

I desire to be sexually whole. I can and want to change old patterns of thought and behavior.

✎ Below write Philippians 1:6 from memory. Check your work on page 10.

_____

_____

# Measuring Your Progress

John had always been faithful to his wife. He was a busy executive with a growing company. The demands of his job often required long hours and entertaining prospective clients. John's wife Sarah coped as best she could with the house and the kids. She developed her own set of friends and was active in church. John and Sarah resembled ships passing in the night. Often John felt that sex at the end of the day would be nice but Sarah seemed tired and disinterested. John was hurt and angry and told her so, but it only served to increase the distance between them.

John became interested in one of his female coworkers. She was attractive and nice to him. He found himself fantasizing about sex with her.

What John is experiencing is a common temptation. John's schedule is also rather common as is the lifestyle that he and his wife Sarah experience. John's sexual temptation is a symptom resulting from his natural desires, the stress of his work, and the distance that has developed between him and his wife.

As you work through this book you will encounter many normal life scenarios and problems that you also experience. Sexual temptation may be one of them. Feeling depressed, anxious, lonely, and tired may be others.

✎ **What are some of the symptoms that you experience in your life that suggest you have a need to grow?**

❑ sexual temptations ❑ relationship problems
❑ job stress ❑ financial tension
❑ other _____

John wants to control his sexual temptations and be sexually whole. He wants to be faithful to his wife. To do that he will have to look at the "big picture" of his life. John will have to work on the tensions, problems, and stresses in his life in order to deal with the problems in his marriage, particularly the sexual problems. You will know you are making progress not just by the reduction of sexual temptations and sins but also by your improved stress management and proper use of emotions.

✎ **Read over the following checklist. Put an ✳ by those items that apply to you; put a ✔ by those that you need to work on, and leave the others blank.**

_____ I often feel angry. _____ I often feel afraid.
_____ I often feel alone. _____ I often feel tired.
_____ I avoid relationships. _____ I work too hard.
_____ I don't like my work. _____ I often feel stressed or "burned out."
_____ I have an increased awareness of my value and worth.
_____ I am overcoming feelings of shame and false guilt.
_____ I am willing to face my problems.
_____ I experience financial hardship.
_____ My sexual thoughts, feelings, and actions are out of control.

When John recognized that his problem was larger than just his sexual thoughts, he felt overwhelmed. Gradually, however, he came to see that solving the nonsexual problems would enable him to achieve healthy sexuality. By identifying and finding solutions to these smaller problems, he began to make progress.

In the same way, you will enhance your sexual health by identifying the nonsexual problems that affect your sexuality. In the next units we will discuss strategies for growth in major areas of your life. You will establish action steps and monitor your progress very specifically in each of them.

## A Look Ahead

Congratulations on completing unit 1 of *Faithful & True*. You now have the opportunity for a decision. If you and your group are working to overcome sexually addictive and compulsive behavior, you will want to proceed to unit 7 on page 112. You will first work through the material on recovering from sexual sin. Then your group will work through units 2-6, the sexual wholeness model.

If you and your group are concerned for spiritual growth but are not seeking to change sexually sinful behaviors, you will want to proceed to the next unit. Units 2-6 contain a model to create a plan for sexual wholeness. You may choose to end your study when you complete Part 1, or you may choose to study Part 2 for ministry purposes. Understanding Part 2 will improve your abilities to understand and minister to others.

## Assignment for the Lesson

➤ Review the concepts in the checklist on page 23 and ask God for courage to face the issues on which you need to work. Recognize that change is a process over time and remember that God answers prayer.

➤ Discuss the challenges you face with your group.

➤ Say aloud the following affirmation.

I can grow in relating to God, others, and myself.

➤ Repeat Philippians 1:6 three times from memory.

## Discussion Group Questions

- Like Fred in the unit story, do you ever feel angry about sexual issues?
- What does 1 Corinthians 10:13 say to you about even your worst thoughts and feelings?
- What do you hope to gain from participation in this group?
- How would you respond to Jesus' question in John 5:6: *Do you want to get well?*
- Read Philippians 4:8. Why does the apostle Paul give this instruction? How doe Jesus' words in Matthew 15:18-19 apply to guarding your thought life?
- Can you name a thought, feeling, or topic (sexual or otherwise) you have difficulty talking about?
- How has your life been impacted by a sense of unhealthy shame?
- Read and discuss the group rules on page 18.
- Share examples of cultural messages that sex and love are the same.

---

Notes
[1] Howard Hendricks, *Seven Promises of a Promise Keeper,* (Colorado Springs, CO: Focus on the Family Publishing, 1994), 53.

# PART ONE

# A MODEL FOR SEXUAL WHOLENESS

In the next 5 units you will create a personal plan for sexual wholeness. Your work will be based on the Sexual Wholeness Model created by Ginger Manley, a sexual therapist from Nashville, Tennessee. Through Ginger's professional experience with sexual dysfunction and addiction she found that recovery involved more than behavior modification and biological knowledge. True recovery includes a sense of well-being and peace based on your relationship with God, yourself, and others. Recovery involves understanding five dimensions of yourself and striving for health in all of them. Diagrammed, it looks like this:

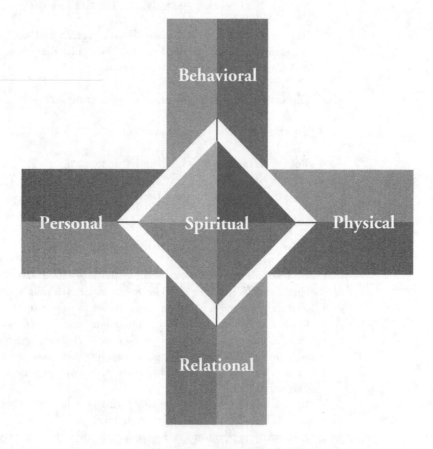

As we will see, each of the five dimensions is related to the others; each one influences all the others, and spirituality is at the center. As you do the work of this unit you will begin to see how the dimensions influence each other.

# The Physical Dimension

## FOCAL PASSAGE

*Do you not know that your body is a temple of the Holy Spirit, who is in you, whom you have received from God?*

—1 Corinthians 6:19

### MEMORY VERSE

So God created man in his own image, in the image of God created he him; male and female created
he them. God saw all
that he had made, and it was very good.
–Genesis 1:27, 31

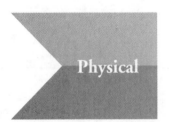

Physical

### TED'S STORY

Everyone thought Ted was a very attractive person—everyone except Ted. He never liked the way he looked. At times he bought expensive clothes to impress women. At other times he totally ignored his appearance and looked like a "bum." Most of the time he neglected his body and didn't eat properly, exercise, or get enough sleep.

Being self-conscious about his appearance, Ted was very shy around women. He "just knew" they would not find him attractive. Friends tried to set him up on dates, but these usually were one time events. Several women in the church liked Ted, but he could never believe they were interested in him.

While in the army, Ted's buddies talked him into going to a prostitute. As his frustration about not being married or even having a girlfriend grew, Ted's interest in prostitutes grew also. For the right price these women would treat him nicely and he found temporary "relief." Sex was not the main issue for Ted. He just wanted to be with women who didn't reject him. Ted knew he needed to stop this behavior. He quit for various lengths of time but always came back. As he thought about his inability to stop, he felt the most out of control when he was lonely, tired, and hungry.

### GROWTH GOAL

You will plan how to like, care for, and nurture your body even with its inadequacies and dysfunctions. You will learn that this is honoring God's temple.

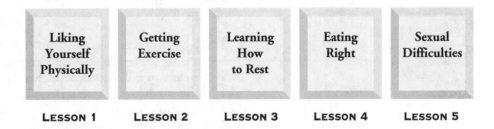

| Liking Yourself Physically | Getting Exercise | Learning How to Rest | Eating Right | Sexual Difficulties |
|:---:|:---:|:---:|:---:|:---:|
| **LESSON 1** | **LESSON 2** | **LESSON 3** | **LESSON 4** | **LESSON 5** |

# Liking Yourself Physically

You met Ted in the unit story. Ted needs to do many things to find sexual wholeness. He is like many people who, because of physical shame, are uncomfortable with themselves. These people tend to be emotionally and spiritually distant in relationships.

To wonder how we look in comparison to others is normal. One of the consequences of the sin in the Garden of Eden was that Adam and Eve were ashamed of their nakedness. One aspect of being in relationship with God is to remember that He created us in His image and declared us "very good."

So God created man in his own image, in the image of God created he him; male and female created he them. God saw all that he had made, and it was very good.
–Genesis 1:27, 31

In the margin read this week's memory verse. Which of the following most nearly represents your reaction to the idea that God considers you a "very good" creation?

❏ He could never look at me and say, "very good."
❏ I am filled with awe that God created me.
❏ Sexuality is a good part of God's creation.
❏ I believe God is disappointed in me and in my appearance.

Many people have experiences in life that turn their natural sense of shame into unhealthy shame. Some develop unhealthy shame at an early age when they are criticized for their outward appearance. Even friends, particularly as adolescents, can be very cruel to each other. Many people try to convince themselves how attractive they are by putting others down. You may have great difficulty believing your body is God's good creation.

Below describe a time when you felt put down or criticized for some aspect of your appearance.

_____

_____

A lack of affirmation can cause shame about our bodies. We need parents and others to teach us we are created in God's image and that we each are attractive in our own way. Unfortunately, not all families convey these positive messages. Many people come from families in which no one thinks he or she is attractive, affirmations are non-existent, and no one practices personal hygiene. In this kind of family, members feel a general sense of disgust for the human body. No one talks about physical things except in negative ways.

Check the attitudes concerning sexuality and the human body that your family displayed.

❏ Nobody would ever talk about sex in my family.
❏ Talk about the body usually involved complaints, shame, and put downs.
❏ Compliments and encouragement were common in my family.
❏ My parents displayed affection for each other.
❏ My parents talked openly with us about our bodies and about sexual issues.
❏ My parents got very nervous when sex was mentioned.
❏ Other _____

When a family frankly discusses sexuality and the body, children develop healthy attitudes about themselves. When sexuality is treated as dirty or a source of shame, the children develop unhealthy shame about their bodies.

Another way that bodily shame can develop is related to the first two. Some parents never teach children basic personal hygiene such as how to comb their hair or brush their teeth. The parents do nothing to make the children feel good about themselves physically.

Finally, and most destructively, we develop shame about our bodies when we are victims of sexual abuse. We will work more on this in Part 2 of this book. Until they find healing, most survivors of sexual abuse take some responsibility for what happened to them. Since sexual abuse is both a shame-filled experience and a physical experience, bodily shame often results. Some of you may be in recovery from sexual abuse. The LIFE Support Group Series resource *Shelter from the Storm* deals specifically with sexual abuse. You may need to work on sexual abuse issues either before continuing your work in *Faithful & True* or after you complete this group study.

✎ **Have you had experiences in your family that brought feelings of shame about your body? Below briefly describe the experience(s).**

_____

_____

➤ **Think back to school days. Most of us had the experience of having to take a shower or get dressed for the first time in the presence of our peers. Can you remember the first time this happened for you? What were your feelings as you compared yourself to others? Discuss with your group how this experience made you feel.**

Getting in touch with your shame about your body may be isolated to one particular part of your body (hair, nose, feet, hands, teeth, genital size, breasts, etc.) or one aspect of yourself (too short, tall, fat, skinny, slow, etc.).

✎ **What part of yourself do you most dislike? Can you share your feelings in a group?**

_____

_____

**KEY POINT**
Often our sexual temptations result from our need for physical affirmation.

✎ **Consider the Key Point statement appearing in the margin. Have you ever considered the possibility that sexual temptations might result from our need for physical affirmation?**

❏ No, but I can identify with wanting others to affirm my appearance.
❏ No, and I don't see any connection between desiring affirmation and temptation.
❏ Yes, I know my desire for physical affirmation is a powerful force.
❏ Yes, I can see how the principle operates, but I don't think it affects me.

✎ **Think about the ways our culture associates physical attractiveness with sexual attractiveness. Below write three examples of advertisements that suggest that if you use their product you will be more attractive and sexually successful.**

_____

_____

_____

Advertisements are only one way culture sends us the message that we must be more attractive. We learn to associate being attractive with being sexual. For some of us the only time we get touched or held is in a sexual act. For example, many men go to prostitutes simply because they want to be touched, held, or be told they are attractive.

When we equate touch and physical affirmation with sexual intimacy, we put a tremendous amount of pressure on the sexual dimension of our lives. In marriage this pressure often results in pressure to have sexual intercourse. If the spouse says no, for whatever reason, this pressure can create a great deal of anger. Think of all the jokes about the pressure in marriage for greater frequency of sex. Behind this humor lies a great deal of anger, fueled by a sense of personal rejection.

➤ For those of you who are married, or who have been, remember a time when your spouse said "no" to sexual intercourse. What was that like? What did you feel? Discuss this with your group.

## Strange Ways We Seek Affirmation

Our sexual fantasies and pursuits of new sexual experience can be ways of trying to create a perfect sexual partner who gives us lots of affirmation. Some sexual practices, such as oral sex, symbolize physical acceptance to some of us. Even exhibitionists, for example, may be people who were starved since childhood for physical touch and affirmation. They learned that even the frightened reaction they got to their nakedness is better than no reaction at all.

Exhibitionism is a relative thing. You don't have to wear a rain coat and go out at 2 o'clock in the morning. It may be a matter of the provocative nature of your dress or the way you flaunt your body. Remember the key point. Your sexual fantasies and pursuits may be ways in which you seek physical affirmation, love, and nurture. In Part 2 we will explore this further. This unit will help you learn to appreciate and, therefore, take better care of your body.

### Assignment for the Lesson

Do you not know that your body is a temple of the Holy Spirit, who is in you, whom you have received from God.
—1 Corinthians 6:19

✎ Write your own paraphrase of the focal passage of this unit, 1 Corinthians 6:19. What does it mean to you to be a "temple of the Holy Spirit"?

_____

_____

_____

So God created man in his own image, in the image of God created he him; male and female created he them. God saw all that he had made, and it was very good.
–Genesis 1:27, 31

✎ The Scripture memory verses for this unit appear in the margin. Begin to memorize the passage. Write the verses on a card and carry the card with you. Whenever you get a drink of water, review the passage.

➤ Say aloud this affirmation five times.

I am created in the image of God.

➤ Pray for yourself and each member of your *Faithful & True* group.

# Getting Exercise

Battling against sexual temptation requires lots of energy—spiritual, emotional, and physical. We need physical exercise to develop energy. When we feel chronically tired, we may not need more sleep. We may need more exercise.

Appreciating our bodies requires us to be in good physical shape. This does not mean the kind of shape our culture presents to us in advertising, television, movies, or pornography. We can set our own goals for how we realistically can look. We must also be careful because in the past we may have used physical attractiveness to gain sexual attention. We may have used physical conditioning at a health club or other exercise facility to make sexual connections.

**KEY POINT**
We all need exercise that will give us physical energy and help us feel good about our bodies. We must seek balance and not try to be something we are not.

✎ **In the margin read the Key Point for today's lesson. How do you feel about the issue of exercise?**

❑ Guilty—I know I need to change my patterns concerning exercise.
❑ Fearful—Using exercise in inappropriate ways has been a problem for me. I am afraid of falling back into that trap.
❑ Encouraged—I'm relieved by the statement that exercise is important.
❑ Angry—I don't want to deal with the issue of exercise.
❑ Numb—I don't feel anything.
❑ Affirmed—I am doing something right.

✎ **In your own words, describe your image of the physically fit person.**

_____

_____

➤ Ask yourself if this a realistic image. Get feedback from your group.

One person I know said, "The only exercise I get is sitting in the bathtub, pulling the plug, and fighting against the current." What has been your history with exercise? Have there been times when you regularly exercised? Maybe you are doing so now. Have there been times when you felt like you were in good shape? Have there been other times when you have been frustrated with your attempts to exercise? Some of your experience may have been associated with athletic endeavors.

```
┌─────────────────────────────────────────────────┐
│              MY EXERCISE HISTORY                 │
│  Successes:                                      │
│                                                  │
│  _____    │
│                                                  │
│  _____    │
│                                                  │
│  Failures:                                       │
│                                                  │
│  _____    │
│                                                  │
│  _____    │
└─────────────────────────────────────────────────┘
```

You may have convinced yourself that you don't like exercise. Your attitude may be shaped by experiences when exercise was used as punishment—like running laps or doing push-ups. Your problem may be that you simply need to try new forms of exercise that you like. You just haven't discovered the forms of exercise you can enjoy. Many people have misconceptions about what exercise really is. It can be fun.

*A Few Alternative Forms of Exercise*
- Walking in an enjoyable setting
- Singles tennis as opposed to doubles
- Walking a golf course instead of riding in a cart
- In-line skating
- Cross-country skiing

These are just a few ideas to get you started thinking on your own. Now you need to create a plan for yourself.

✎ **Below describe how you'd like to look and feel.**

_____

_____

✎ **Write down the forms of exercise that you think would help you achieve those goals. (You may need to get some consultation from an exercise expert.)**

_____

_____

Many of us have difficulty getting started on an exercise plan unless we have support and encouragement. We may need to find someone to exercise with, go with to a health club, or hold us accountable to our plan. (This is one of the places where an accountability group can help you.)

✎ **Who will you ask to participate with you in your exercise plan?**

_____

You may have age or health concerns that require you to consult a physician before you try any strenuous activity.

✎ **If you need to consult a physician before starting your exercise plan, write your appointment time here.**

_____

## Assignment for the Lesson

➤ Share your total plan for exercise with the members of your *Faithful & True* group. Get their feedback about it. Then START!

➤ Say this affirmation five times.

I am the temple of God's Holy Spirit. I can look and feel better.

✎ Below write your own paraphrase of Genesis 1:27, 31. Continue to memorize the passage.

_____

_____

➤ Pray for patience and courage to change years of old behaviors and to overcome lethargy.

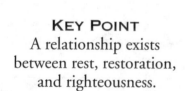

# Learning How to Rest

_The Lord is my shepherd, I shall not be in want. He makes me lie down in green pastures, he leads me beside quiet waters, he restores my soul. He guides me in paths of righteousness for his name's sake._

—Psalms 23:1-3

✎ On the lines below, describe what this familiar passage of Scripture says to you.

_____

_____

Sheep are peculiar animals. Shepherds know that sheep will graze all day long without taking a rest or drinking unless they are forced to. In Psalm 23, David is describing our relationship to God as being like that of sheep to a shepherd. In that relationship, notice that the first thing David mentions is rest in green pastures and beside still waters. Immediately after talking about rest, David says God restores our soul and leads us in paths of righteousness.

**KEY POINT**
A relationship exists between rest, restoration, and righteousness.

The Key Point in the margin is not surprising. Being tired all the time makes us vulnerable to a variety of temptations. Like sheep, however, many of us are not accustomed to resting. We are like little children whose parents have to make them go to bed.

Tony has problems sleeping. His job is stressful. His children are having trouble in school. He smokes and drinks alcohol and coffee. Tony believes that sexual intercourse with his wife at night will help him sleep. He often uses this as an excuse to persuade her to have sex with him. When she says no, he becomes angry. His anger makes it more difficult for him to go to sleep. Fantasizing about sex helps him to relax. Many nights he lies in bed and finds himself lost in a world of imagined sexual activity.

You may have difficulty sleeping. Not all sleep difficulties stem from sexual difficulties. For some, sleep disorders may require medical intervention.

✎ The following list contains some obvious reasons why sleep may be difficult. Place a check by those factors that may contribute to your difficulty sleeping.

❑ caffeine          ❑ eating before bedtime       ❑ alcohol
❑ nicotine          ❑ exercising before bedtime   ❑ lack of exercise
❑ sugar             ❑ chronic pain
❑ stress (anxiety, worry, unresolved conflicts and problems)

Other parts of this book will deal with some of these problems. If some of the examples apply to you, you need to establish a plan to get help.

✎ **If you are having difficulty sleeping what changes do you need to make?**

_____

_____

Getting rest is more than getting sleep. Rest also means being still, relaxing, and recreation. According to God's plan for creation, one seventh of our time (the Sabbath) should be for resting. Be careful not to believe that work only involves making money. Some of us spend our rest time working on the house, working as chauffeurs for our children, or working at golf (some of us really don't enjoy it).

> He makes me lie down in green pastures, he leads me beside quiet waters.
> –Psalm 23:2

Psalm 23 describes green pastures. Perhaps you have experienced times and places in your life that you would say were restful. Where were these green pastures in your past?

✎ **Describe at least two of the restful times and places you have known.**

_____

_____

You may feel guilty when you are not working. You may think that God only loves the righteous worker or that you will only get approval from others if you work continuously. Maybe your parents "put the fear of God in you" about work. If they always worked and never enjoyed themselves, they modeled an unhealthy attitude to you. You may think your entire worth is tied to your performance. You may be a workaholic.

> After Jesus had sent the crowd away, he got into the boat and went to the vicinity of Magadan.
> –Matthew 15:39

Note that in Matthew 15:39, and on several other occasions recorded in Scripture, Jesus was surrounded by needy crowds, but He sent the crowds away and retreated with His disciples to rest.

✎ **How do you feel about Jesus' action of leaving the crowd to take care of Himself?**

_____

_____

✎ **On the scale below place an X to indicate with what difficulty or ease you can say "no" to needs or demands on your time and say "yes" to taking care of yourself.**

Easy                                              Extremely Difficult

Many of the people around Jesus that day needed healing and preaching, yet He got in a boat and went to the other side of the sea. I imagine many a personnel committee or church council would be mad at Him for missing this opportunity. Jesus needed to get away, to rest. We need to ask ourselves if we are stronger than He was.

✎ **What are your fears about not working hard enough or about playing too much?**

_____

_____

✎ Where are your "boats"—your ways to get away from work and stress? Where is the "other side" for you?

_____

Many of us fear becoming lazy or being considered lazy. We may have forgotten how to take time off or how to play at something we enjoy. Some of us may never have known how to play.

➤ Make an appointment with a child (your own, your grandchild, or the child of a friend who trusts you) to learn to play. Possibly you can join in a game with a group of children. Or go to a toy store and pick up a game you might enjoy playing with others. It might be a puzzle—you could have a puzzle party.

The word recreation literally means to re-create. Remember our key Scripture passage. We are created in the image of God. Rest, vacation, or play allows God to re-create us and restore our souls.

### Assignment for the Lesson

➤ Discuss with your accountability group your plan for better sleep, rest, play, vacation, or trips to green pastures and still waters. Discuss how they will hold you accountable to do some of these things.

✎ In the margin attempt to write Genesis 1:27, 31 from memory. Check your work on page 27.

➤ Say aloud this affirmation five times

I am created in the image of God

➤ Pray for rest for yourself and for members of your group.

LESSON
4

# Eating Right

Jay often felt lonely, though he did not lack for friends. He was a very social person. Everyone at church liked him. He had a good job. No one, however, really knew him. Once, when he was young, Jay had an affair. He ended this quickly, confessed to his pastor, and has been faithful to his wife ever since. He never told his wife. He felt that it would hurt her too much. He also felt that if she knew she might leave him.

Both Jay and his wife are successful, busy people. Their children make many demands on their time. Always pleasant to each other, Jay and his wife never really talk. Their sex life has dwindled to being very infrequent. Late at night, after his wife has gone to bed, Jay often finds himself in the kitchen—eating. He is now 50 pounds overweight.

Taking care of and appreciating ourselves physically is also a matter of eating properly. The Book of Deuteronomy is full of injunctions about eating and diet. Gluttony has always been considered one of the seven "deadly" sins.

✐ **Ask yourself this question, If I wanted to treat my body like the city dump, what would I put into it? Below list those things you already "dump" into your body.**

Maybe you wrote things like too much sugar, fat, cholesterol, or salt. Maybe you wrote too much food, caffeine, nicotine, or alcohol. You probably already know a lot about what is bad and good for you. What prevents you from making the changes you need to make?

Perhaps you are like Jay. He ate when he was lonely. Food is a great comforter. As babies, much of the time we were held was for the purpose of eating. This association stays with us. Eating can be associated with being held. We also eat at family gatherings, special occasions, and times of fellowship at church. Eating can be associated with family, friends, and fellowship. When we are lonely, food can be our friend.

At other times you may eat because you are anxious, afraid, or angry. Putting food into your stomach causes blood to be transferred from the brain to the stomach for the purpose of digestion. The process has a relaxing effect on the brain. Food can be a tranquilizer.

Sometimes we eat when we are bored. Eating provides something to do. We see or smell food and we eat it for lack of something better to do.

On the other hand, some people do not eat enough. They don't eat because they don't have time. They may never feel hungry, or they're afraid of being fat and unattractive.

✐ **Which style(s) of eating just described seems to fit you?**

- ❏ eating to feed my emotions
- ❏ eating to hide (or hide from) my emotions
- ❏ eating out of boredom
- ❏ not eating because "I don't have time"
- ❏ not eating for fear of getting fat
- ❏ none of the above

When we are lonely, anxious, afraid, or angry, food can be a substitute: for—
- intimacy
- being with family and friends
- talking
- a relationship with God.

Not eating can be a way of controlling how we look and, therefore, how other people respond to us. Eating or not eating can be a way we control our emotions and seek nurture. When we use food in these ways, we miss the intimacy that will make us healthier people.

You may have one or more medical conditions (hypertension, diabetes, heart disease, etc.) which require that you watch what you eat. If you have difficulty maintaining your diet, you may be denying—pretending the consequences of unhealthy eating do not exist or do not apply to you. Disease and death frighten us all. Unhealthy eating does not always have immediate consequences, so we ignore what is happening inside our bodies.

➤ **If you have a medical condition that requires a specific diet, tell a friend or member of your group what the consequences will be to you if you don't follow your diet. Be honest about how frightened you are about these consequences.**

We may not eat properly for a variety of other reasons. Sometimes we don't understand proper nutrition. Eating right may simply be a matter of getting more information about what is or is not healthy. Seeing a doctor or dietitian may be important. For more information about healthy eating and for a group resource to help you with healthy lifestyle change, read about *First Place: A Christ-Centered Health Program* on page 221.

Some of you have been conditioned by your history of eating. You know you like certain things and that they taste good. Giving them up would be to give up something that is very pleasurable. Doing so might make you angry. Changing life long patterns may be a matter of grieving the things you can no longer do.

✎ **Do you enjoy a food you need to give up but that would make you angry to do so? ❑ Yes ❑ No If so, in the margin write the food with which you have difficulty.**

➤ **Tell a friend or member of your group how difficult it will be to give up the food you named.**

Finally, in considering a plan for balanced eating, you need to consider your ideal and your realistic weight. Beware of what the media displays as "ideally" attractive. Take into consideration your genetic makeup. Some people are naturally thin, while others are heavier. You may need a doctor, dietitian, or friend to give you a more objective opinion.

✎ Write your ideal weight _____

✎ Now write one pattern of eating that you would like to change in the next several weeks.

_____

➤ **Tell your accountability group about these goals and include them in your regular check-ins with them.**

If you find that the work of this lesson has just been too difficult, if you don't understand it, or if you're just too resistant, you may be suffering from an eating disorder. You may need to get professional help. To learn more about eating disorders, see *Conquering Eating Disorders: A Christ-Centered 12 Step Process* (see page 221).

### Assignment for the Lesson

✎ Other than during regular meal times, the next time you feel like eating ask yourself if you are really hungry. If the answer is *no* and you are able to refrain from eating, then ask yourself what you are feeling. Write your answer in the space below.

_____

_____

➤ Be prepared to tell your group about your answer.

➤ Say aloud this affirmation five times.

I can eat right and feel better.

**KEY POINT**
Healthy eating is balanced eating. We need good foods when we genuinely are hungry.

➤ Pray for yourself and for members of your group in times of loneliness.

➤ Practice repeating this unit's memory verses. Review your Scripture memory verse from Unit 1.

# Sexual Difficulties

LESSON
5

David felt ashamed but knew he couldn't talk to anyone. He thought, *Men just don't talk about these things.* Several months ago while having sexual intercourse with his wife he was unable to maintain an erection. Both he and his wife were frustrated but didn't talk about it. He had been tired and stressed by a situation at work. After that, whenever they tried to have sex David would become preoccupied with whether or not this problem would reoccur. More often than not, it did. Gradually he began to lose hope, thinking he may never be "normal" again.

David's wife tried to be understanding, but she too was frightened about what this meant. Did David no longer find her attractive? She also felt ashamed. This situation was something that she had never heard any of her friends talk about.

Not being able to talk about their problem, David and his wife found that it was easier to just avoid the whole issue of sex. Then one day David saw some sexual images in a movie. The experience excited David to the point of having an erection. He was embarrassed by this, but also thrilled that it could still happen. That night, David and his wife were able to be sexual again, but only while he secretly fantasized about what he had seen.

David is really no different than most men who have experienced times of impotence. Impotence is one of many forms of sexual dysfunction. The problem is not that the stress of his life caused this condition, but that he was not able to talk about it. His shame kept him silent. His family, his friends, and his church had given him no experience of talking about these kinds of problems. The movie provided him with a sinful experience of sexual excitement and this drove him into a world of sexual fantasy.

Some of the most common sexual dysfunctions, in addition to impotence, include:
- premature ejaculation
- inability to sustain erection
- inability to reach orgasm
- inability to communicate about sexual likes and dislikes
- conflict over frequency.

**KEY POINT**
Sexual dysfunctions are disturbances of normal sexual functioning. They are very common and can, in most cases, be treated. They can't be treated, however, if the person will not talk about them.

These examples are not a complete list. As the key point in the margin suggests, any time a married couple experiences frustration, pain (emotional or physical), or silence about their sexual life, they are dealing with sexual dysfunction.

Many possible reasons for sexual dysfunction exist. Some dysfunctions are biological in origin. A variety of factors can cause impotence including: medical conditions, such as diabetes; medications, such as hypertension drugs; and other factors such as stress and anxiety. If you experience this problem, you may need to consult a physician about the underlying cause.

If medical reasons are ruled out, as they would be in David's case, the reasons can be psychological. David experiences a great deal of stress and tension. After the first time his impotence occurred, the resulting fear of it happening again served to compound the problem. In David's case simply hearing how normal his problem is may serve to relieve the anxiety enough to solve the problem. If not, counseling will help him.

Some sexual dysfunctions are caused simply by lack of knowledge. Education may be enough to deal with these kinds of problems. Books and seminars in the Christian community can help with education. For example note *Restoring the Pleasure* or *The Gift of* Sex by Clifford and Joyce Penner, or *Intended for Pleasure: New Approaches to Sexual Intimacy in Christian Marriages* by Ed and Gay Wheat.

Some couples are too embarrassed or ashamed to communicate about their sexual likes and dislikes. They don't know how to talk to each other about sexual matters. Many couples have had buried feelings about sex for as long as they have been married. Not talking about their feelings creates anger and resentment. These unexpressed emotions may cause sexual dysfunction. Support to start talking may be all these couples need. Education may help, or counseling may help them learn to communicate.

Abuse, particularly sexual abuse, in a person's childhood can have a profound effect on a couple's sexual health. Mary loved her husband deeply. She had never been able to tell him, however, about her sexual abuse as a young girl. She didn't fully remember it. She was ashamed of it, felt responsible, and didn't want him to think that she was somehow "damaged." While she desperately wanted to be available to him sexually, she often found his sexual advances frightening. When she felt this way, she would shut down and either say *no* or comply in a cold and unresponsive way. This hurt and frustrated her husband. He tried to understand but at times found himself getting angry. He pleaded, argued, and even got angry with Mary. His anger, of course, just reminded her of her trauma and made things worse. This pattern continued for years and their mutual frustration eventually led to a life of total sexual abstinence.

Mary and her husband are experiencing sexual dysfunction. With help they can overcome the problems. Mary must learn to share her secret in order to heal as a survivor of sexual abuse. Her husband needs to be supportive and patient, allowing her time to heal. Together they must learn to participate in sex in ways that will help Mary feel safe, loved, and nurtured.

✎ **Have you experienced sexual dysfunction?** ❏ Yes ❏ No **If so, check those you have experienced.**

    ❏ premature ejaculation
    ❏ inability to reach orgasm
    ❏ inability to communicate about sexual likes and dislikes
    ❏ inability to sustain erection
    ❏ conflict over frequency
    ❏ other _____

✎ **Describe your feelings when you experienced sexual dysfunction.**

_____

_____

_____

➤ **Share your feelings with your group.**

## Assignment for the Lesson

✎ If you have experienced sexual dysfunction, check which of the following you would be willing to explore, seek, or work to develop.

- ❏ medical evaluation
- ❏ more education about how the body works
- ❏ a greater ability to share and communicate about sex with my spouse
- ❏ psychological help for me
- ❏ counseling for us as a couple

✎ Write the name of the person(s) from whom you will first seek help.

_____

➤ Be prepared to share this plan with your accountability group.

✎ Write from memory your Scripture memory verses for this unit.

_____

_____

_____

➤ Say the following affirmation five times

I can enjoy God's gift of healthy sexuality with my spouse.

➤ Pray for yourself and your spouse (if you have one).

## Discussion Group Questions

- When you were an adolescent, how did you feel about your physical appearance? How do you feel about it now?
- How do you react to the statement in the Scripture memory verses (Genesis 1:27, 31) that God considers you a "very good creation?
- Describe a time when you felt put down or criticized about some aspect of your appearance.
- When you were growing up, what attitudes did your family display toward sexuality and the human body?
- What does it mean to be a "temple of the Holy Spirit" (1 Corinthians 6:19)?
- If you are or have been married, how have you felt when your spouse says "no" to sexual intercourse?
- How would you describe your exercise plan?
- How do you feel about Jesus' action of leaving the needy crowds to take care of Himself (pray, eat, and rest)? (Matthew 15:39)
- Discuss your answers to the assignment at the bottom of page 37.
- Describe your feelings when you realize that in the real world we experience things like sexual disfunction. Have you sometimes felt pressure to perform sexually or felt inadequate sexually?

# The Behavioral Dimension

## FOCAL PASSAGE

*For everything there is an appointed season, and there is a proper time for every project under heaven...a time to weep and a time to laugh, a time to mourn and a time to dance....a time to embrace and a time to refrain from embracing....a time to be silent, and a time to speak.*

—Ecclesiastes. 3:1,4,5,7, MLB

## MEMORY VERSE

Cast all your anxiety on him because he cares for you.

–1 Peter 5:7

Behavioral

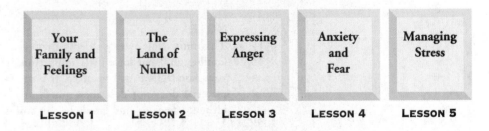

### BOB'S STORY

Bob and Helen are a young working couple in a deteriorating marriage. Bob grew up in a home where no one talked about feelings. Daily life was "calm." No one ever got angry. Bob medicated his feelings with work, games, television, and food. Bob's father got drunk a lot. No one ever confronted his alcoholism since he was a "quiet drunk." Bob became the "man" of the house, especially during times when his father was drinking. Bob's mother and father mainly co-existed and tried to keep things running smoothly.

Now Bob drinks too, but not like his dad. He also smokes but believes that one day he will give that up. Bob eats too much, especially when he watches television, but he is young and believes this behavior hasn't affected him. He is "up-and-coming" in his job, and this way of life seems normal for a young man in his profession.

Because of their lack of relationship, Helen avoids sexual intimacy. Bob doesn't know that the lack of relationship has anything to do with why Helen avoids sex. He thinks she just doesn't like it. The more she says "no," the more Bob demands. They never talk about this tension. Bob is angry, but never says so. He feels attracted to other women and wonders if they are more available to their husbands. Sometimes he fantasizes what it would be like to be with a woman who seemed to enjoy sex more.

## GROWTH GOAL

You will evaluate your relationship to your feelings. How comfortable are you expressing emotions? You will identify behaviors you have used to "hide" from your feelings as well as ways to begin expressing them. Learning to express and manage your feelings in healthy ways will enhance your ability to be intimate. Intimacy is a key to healthy sexuality.

| Your Family and Feelings | The Land of Numb | Expressing Anger | Anxiety and Fear | Managing Stress |
|---|---|---|---|---|
| LESSON 1 | LESSON 2 | LESSON 3 | LESSON 4 | LESSON 5 |

# 1

**INTIMACY:**
the ability to be honest
about thoughts,
actions, and feelings.

**A Key Family Assumption**
(Usually unspoken) If we express our
feelings, they will get worse!

# Your Family and Feelings

Like Bob in our introductory story, your family may not have expressed feelings well. Your goal in this lesson is to understand your background and identify what you can do to more effectively express feelings. Healthy sexuality is the expression of spiritual and emotional intimacy. Your ability to be intimate depends on your ability to be honest and open with your feelings.

 Has your spouse or a friend ever said to you, "You need to be more open with me, tell me what you're really feeling"? Or have you ever wondered to yourself, Why can't I identify and talk about my emotions? ❏ Yes ❏ No Explain.

_____

_____

If you have had this kind of experience, you are not alone. Most families don't model healthy and adequate ways of dealing with emotions. You may have deeper reasons why talking about your feelings is difficult. We will deal with those in Part 2.

The assumption in the margin affects us in a variety of ways. For example, someone might think, _If I get angry, I will kill someone; If I admit that I feel sad, I'll be depressed for the rest of my life;_ or _If I become anxious, I will have a nervous breakdown._

 Remember a time in your family when something really sad happened. Remember the event that caused the sadness, who was present, and what did they say or not say about it? Describe what you felt at that time.

_____

_____

You are beginning to understand your family's pattern of dealing with emotions. Many families use tried and true methods to keep family members from feeling certain things. Here are a few common examples:

"Big boys (or girls) don't cry."
"That's a stupid thing to feel."
"Only crazy people feel that way."
"God doesn't like it when you feel like that."
"Grow up and stop feeling sorry for yourself."
"Calm down, get a hold of yourself."

NOTE:
**This unit deals with subjects that powerfully affect some people and families and that have little impact on others. If this material applies to your family, you will want to give special attention to this unit. If this material does not describe your family, you still can learn more about intimacy, feelings, and family by this study.**

In some homes, parents quote Scripture to squash feelings. One of my family's personal favorites was, "In all things God works for the good" (Romans 8:28). The implication was that you don't need to feel the way you do because God is going to work it out. While the theology may be sound, it serves to suppress emotions.

✎ **Write any sayings, excuses, put-downs, and/or Bible verses that you remember being used to avoid feelings in your family.**

_____

_____

_____

_____

These messages are words imprinted in our brains and are difficult to erase. Sometimes even if the psychology or theology of a statement is correct, the timing is inappropriate. For example, at funerals we often think we should not feel sad, because we will see the loved one again in heaven. We might even consider it a lack of faith to feel sad. But even though we will see the loved one again, it might not be for years. To be sad is appropriate.

Another way families deal with feelings is by avoiding or changing them. Some of your family members may have the ability to act as if they don't even have feelings. These people seem distant or quiet, certainly even-tempered. In many families, such behavior receives affirmation. Family members say: "Look at Sam, he is so strong, nothing ever bothers him."

Other families use substances or behaviors to deal with feelings. In Bob's story, his father was an alcoholic. Drinking is a way to depress and avoid feelings. Alcohol chemically alters the brain. It temporarily erases feelings of fear, anxiety, stress, and loneliness. We know, of course, that this is a terribly destructive solution, but alcohol and many other substances will work to change the way we feel.

Likewise, behaviors can distract us from our feelings. Some of these behaviors may also work to change chemicals in our brain and help us avoid feelings. For example, compulsive working can distract us from everything else around us. If the work is challenging and exciting, with demands, pressures, and deadlines, it causes our bodies to produce adrenaline to deal with the challenges. Adrenaline can have a mood-elevating effect.

When Mary was a little girl, her mother was very busy and didn't like to be disturbed from important house cleaning, church work, and the care of Mary's brothers and sisters. When Mary was bored, sad, or frightened, her mother would say, "Can I fix you something to eat?" Sometimes it was just a matter of a cookie or something else full of sugar. At other times mom would fix something to eat, get out a TV tray, and turn on Mary's favorite programs.

Today, Mary is 50 pounds overweight. Her husband complains, but she can't seem to stop her eating. She spends her days in front of the TV with her favorite soap operas.

Certain substances or behaviors can raise or lower our moods. For example, caffeine raises our mood. Nicotine can lower mood. Work raises our mood, eating can lower it. The diagram at the top of the next page illustrates this concept.

|  | Substances | Behaviors |
|---|---|---|
| Elevate Mood | caffeine<br>amphetamine<br>sugar<br>cocaine | work<br>shopping<br>cleaning<br>danger<br>sex |
| Depress Mood | alcohol<br>heroin<br>narcotics<br>nicotine | eating<br>watching TV<br>sex |

 From the sample behaviors listed in the chart, underline any that your family used to deal with feelings. Add other examples as you think of them.

You will notice that sex is listed as a behavior that can either raise or lower mood. Fantasizing about sex, the excitement of a new experience, and the pursuit or even the danger associated with it can raise adrenaline levels and thereby elevate mood.

People also use sexual fantasy, sexual humor, and the release of tension associated with orgasm to relax or calm anxieties. We can use sex as either a stimulant or a depressant, and either way it can create chemical reactions in our bodies and our brains.

All of the substances and behaviors on the chart share a common characteristic. Any of these can be used in excessive ways and can become addictions.

## Addictions

An addiction is an unhealthy attachment to or relationship with some substance or behavior. In any addiction the person loses control. Life, at least in that one area, becomes unmanageable. The person intends to stop but can't do it. An alcoholic, for example, can't control drinking. If the alcoholic chooses to drink, the addiction takes over—sometimes gradually, sometimes rapidly. An addiction progressively gets worse and leads to destructive consequences.

 Researchers suggest that many or even most families are affected by some form of addiction. In the space below, or on separate paper, write the names or initials of people in your family who you fear suffer or have suffered from addictions.

*Addicts in my family*                    *Their addictions:*

_____          _____

_____          _____

Be gentle with yourself and with your family. Recognizing the presence of addiction does not imply that a family is bad or evil. It simply recognizes a fact of life—all families are imperfect. Many studies have shown that most addicts can trace addictions in their families back for many generations.

Addictive behavior generates many feelings. When families don't know how to deal with these feelings, they find ways of covering-up, making excuses, and even lying to protect the image of being a "normal" family. We call this kind of behavior *enabling*. Enablers pretend the addictions don't exist. They excuse, cover-up, lie, minimize the seriousness, or blame others for the problems. For example, an alcoholic comes home drunk and can't go to work the next morning; the enabling spouse calls the boss and makes excuses. Family members who enable may also be referred to as "co-addicts."

✎ **In the space below, identify persons in your family who fit this description.**

*Enablers in my family (co-addicts):*        *They enabled (which addict/addiction)*

_____        _____

_____        _____

You may be getting a clearer idea of the suppressed feelings that existed in your family and how people coped with them. The experience of addiction and co-addiction may be models that you learned. As you search for creating intimacy in your life you will need to examine these powerful influences.

### Assignment for the Lesson

✎ **In light of today's lesson, write your own interpretation of this unit's focal passage that appears in the margin.**

_____

_____

➤ Say aloud the following affirmation five times.

I am safe. I can feel my feelings.

➤ Pray for your family.

For everything there is an appointed season, and there is a proper time for every project under heaven...a time to weep and a time to laugh, a time to mourn and a time to dance....a time to embrace and a time to refrain from embracing....a time to be silent, and a time to speak.
—Ecclesiastes. 3:1, 4, 5, 7, MLB

**LESSON 2**

# The Land of Numb

Now that you have looked at how your family deals with feelings, you can examine your own patterns. Healthy sexuality, remaining faithful and true, requires the ability to be intimate. To be intimate you must be able to express yourself emotionally and spiritually.

### Escape from Emotions

When we seek to escape rather than deal with our feelings, we create an imaginary world I call the "Land of Numb." It is a place where we avoid unwanted emotions. No anger, sadness, fear, or loneliness exists there. These feelings are forbidden. We run away from these scary realities into our dream world. The Land of Numb is a place of imagination and fantasy. Imaginary friends and lovers can be there. They always are willing to listen and respond to our desires. They always seem to like us. Perfect scenes, perfect people, perfect experiences—all live there. No one ever judges you in the Land of Numb.

Some people use chemicals to take them to the Land of Numb. Others find behaviors that will do the trick. Some are so good at getting there that they just throw a switch in their minds and go. The Land of Numb, by its very nature, is a land of imagination. It really doesn't exist. It is my way of describing what some of us do to escape or "exit" our feelings. You may be a frequent traveler to the Land of Numb if—

• You often feel lonely.
• You have few, if any, real friends.
• Your marital relationship is distant.
• You very often think about certain behaviors, like sex, or substances like alcohol.
• You never seem to have enough time for important activities.
• You often daydream.
• You avoid times to talk with family and friends.

## Barry's Story

Barry and his wife grew apart. They never talk about what they feel. They love each other, but the excitement is gone. Other activities consume their time. They are outstanding members of their community and church, with many acquaintances but no real friends. They never go out socially together except with other couples.

Barry rarely initiates sex with his wife. He simply finds it easier to watch television, eat, or smoke. Usually he combines all three, particularly late at night. The sexually provocative movies on cable television feed his active imagination. The sex depicted there is exciting and passionate. Even at work these images "pop up" in his mind, and he loses himself in them. His work is beginning to suffer because he can't concentrate.

We accomplish nothing by blaming either Barry or his wife. Neither of them had the skills they needed coming into their marriage. They both need the ability to identify and express their feelings. Barry is caught up in sexual temptation. As his story suggests, however, this is not only a problem of sexual lust but also of loneliness. Barry is lonely because of the distance in his marriage and because he has no real friends.

Barry distances or "exits" his feelings by isolating. His isolating behavior protects him from immediate pain, but it keeps him from facing and solving the problems in his life. The total result is greater pain. Barry has a variety of strategies for accomplishing his exits. None of his exit strategies are very dramatic so the damage they are doing is not readily apparent. This same pattern may be true for you.

Look back at the diagram of mood altering strategies on page 44. Have you developed one or more of those patterns?  ❑ Yes ❑ No
Below complete a copy of the diagram for yourself.

|  | Substances | Behaviors |
|---|---|---|
| Elevate Mood | | |
| Depress Mood | | |

You may find that you have numerous ways you raise or lower your mood. You are beginning to understand how you exit your feelings and how much time you spend in the Land of Numb. Sometimes these behaviors are not all bad. If they are not sinful or destructive in themselves, it may be appropriate to use them at certain times. For example, a cup of coffee in the morning is probably not that destructive and will get you going. Watching television may help you relax. However, overuse of any of these substances or behaviors becomes destructive.

You will have an opportunity to share your list in your group this week. When you share your list with your group and listen to theirs, their examples may remind you of more substances or behaviors that you need to add to your list.

✎ **Below list all the behaviors or substances you use to raise or lower your mood in a typical day—from the time you wake up to the time you go to sleep. (Use separate paper if necessary.)**

| Time | Substance or Behavior | Used to raise/lower what mood? (e.g. anger, sadness, fear, loneliness) |
|---|---|---|
| ____ | _____ | _____ |
| ____ | _____ | _____ |
| ____ | _____ | _____ |
| ____ | _____ | _____ |

You may notice in doing this activity that you are a major pharmacist and that your only patient is yourself. How skilled you must be to keep yourself in balance!

✎ **Do you use any of these substances or behaviors to avoid talking honestly or being with someone? If so, in the space below write their names or initials and the issues you try to avoid.**

_____

_____

You may recognize some of these substances or behaviors as addictive for you. You might be in recovery from them, or you may need to take a courageous look to see if they have become unmanageable and destructive. You may recognize that sexual fantasy or activity is an addictive activity. If so, Part 2 of this workbook will help you deal with those behaviors.

✎ **Go back and reread the definition of addiction on page 44. Below check any substances or behaviors that seem to be addictive for you.**

❑ alcohol or other drugs
❑ work
❑ sexual behaviors (from fantasy to overt behavior)
❑ gambling
❑ gaining approval from others
❑ shopping
❑ other _____

➤ Tell your accountability group about any patterns of behavior or addictions you need to confront. Have them hold you accountable to get the help you need to make these changes.

If you have an addiction you will need very specific help to find sobriety. On page 224 you will find a list of resources for dealing with some types of addictions. A variety of groups, meetings, and counselors can help. Your pastor may be able to direct you to help.

✎ The Scripture memory verse for this unit appears in the margin. Begin to memorize the passage. Write the verse on a card, and carry the card with you. Whenever you get a drink of water, review the verse.

➤ Say the following affirmation five times.

I can stop negative and addictive behaviors. I can be in touch with my feelings.

➤ Pray for yourself and for members of your group as you deal with these new issues.

**Cast all your anxiety on him because he cares for you.**
**–1 Peter 5:7**

LESSON
3

# Expressing Anger

Anger is one of the most basic emotions and the one many of us have the most difficulty expressing. We all *experience* anger, but not all of us *feel* our anger. Even fewer of us acknowledge and appropriately deal with our anger. If we are going to experience intimacy, we must be able to constructively to deal with and communicate about anger.

## Gary's Story

Gary's family didn't discuss anger. When family members were angry, they never said so. His family had indirect ways of expressing anger. They used sarcastic put-downs. They never affirmed each other, just joked about each other's faults and peculiarities. When tension would reach a critical level, someone would tell a joke or make a funny comment. Occasionally, Gary's dad would blow up at something, usually when he was drinking. Gary's father never hit anyone, but he did break things and occasionally kicked the cat.

Gary fears anger. He doesn't know how to express it. Lately Gary has become increasingly angry at his wife. She doesn't discipline the children to suit him. He wishes she would keep the house cleaner. He doesn't like her friends. Although she is always available for sex, she never seems to enjoy it and this makes Gary really angry. Gary has become just like his dad, blowing up frequently. He yells at the kids for insignificant things. He is stressed at work and angry because he isn't moving up in the company. Gary often finds himself withdrawing into his own world. His state of depression is growing deeper. When his wife asks him if he is OK, he makes a sarcastic reply. Gary is a walking time bomb. His is a case of growing, unexpressed anger.

Like Gary, many people grow up in homes where anger is ignored or where violence is common. They do not experience any healthy model for dealing with anger. Like Gary, they often fear anger. Their inability to deal with anger damages their ability to experience intimacy, just as Gary's anger at his wife has affected his sexual feelings about her.

✎ **Have you ever been angry at your spouse about sex?**  ❑ Yes ❑ No

Repressed anger—anger that is bottled up—is the source of a variety of physical and emotional conditions. Anger is a feeling that cries out for physical action. God created us with the ability to become angry as a form of protection. When we don't express anger, we don't use the energy anger generates inside us. Over time this unexpressed energy damages our bodies. When we create energy that never is used, we literally get burned-out. Anger can cause physical conditions from headaches to heart disease. Energy that burns us out also makes us emotionally tired. This kind of burnout can cause depression. Anger also can come out "sideways." We become angry about insignificant things or at people we're not really angry with.

✎ **In the space below describe the last time you became angry at something or somebody that didn't really deserve it.**

_____

Maybe you've had someone say to you, "Why did you get so upset about such a little thing? That was really trivial." Perhaps you became angry at your spouse or kids for something that really isn't significant.

Anger is about being hurt. A part of us is afraid and wounded. We interpret that someone else caused that pain and is responsible for it. Our perception may or may not be true. We must talk about it to discern the truth. Sometimes when we feel anger toward someone in the past we put that anger on someone in the present. For example, if we are angry with our parents, we may displace the anger on spouse or children.

Unless we learn to identify and appropriately deal with our anger, we will continue to use unhealthy strategies. Typically we use one of the following six dysfunctional methods:

1. **Stuff it.** Through our childhood conditioning, we learn to not recognize we feel anger. If we do recognize it, we feel afraid of it and need to control it so we deny that we feel it. We stuff the anger down inside and deny that it exists.
2. **Delay it.** Since we're afraid of being angry, we think that putting it off until later will be safer.
3. **Displace it.** We take the anger that we feel and put it onto some place, thing, event, or person—including ourselves—that we think is safer.
4. **Minimize it.** We rationalize our anger, telling ourselves that it really isn't that bad. We sometimes try to "understand" the other person, "He really didn't mean it." As Christians, we often tell ourselves that it is not proper to feel as angry as we do.
5. **Numb it.** We use a chemical or substance to numb our anger and try to avoid it completely.
6. **Avoid it.** We get involved in excessive work, play, hobbies, or other activities in order to distract us from our anger.

✎ **Which of these approaches do you use? On the lines below write the ones that you do and give an example of each.**

_____

_____

_____

_____

**Anger is like a cancer. If it is not dealt with early, it will grow and kill.**

The key to expressing anger is not whether or not we do it, but how we do it. Physical violence, yelling, screaming, or revenge are inappropriate ways to cope with anger. Internalizing or "stuffing" anger is also destructive. Discovering ways to constructively express our anger is helpful. Physical activity of a non-destructive nature (hitting a tennis ball, chopping wood, or running) can be ways of releasing the physical energy that comes with anger. Sometimes talking about our anger to a trusted friend or writing down what we're angry about can be helpful.

**IMPORTANT NOTE:**

**For some of you, your anger may sometimes get out of control. You get angry at the slightest thing. Perhaps you yell and scream, use sarcasm, or put people down. You may even use physical violence when you get angry. Some refer to this as "rage-aholism." If this is true for you, you can change. A large part of you wants to stop this behavior. Seek professional help so that you can stop. Consult with your pastor or a Christian counselor if you don't know who to turn to.**

**You sold your people for a pittance, gaining nothing from their sale. All this happened to us, though we had not forgotten you or been false to your covenant.**
**–Psalm 44:12, 17**

You may be angry with God. Anger toward God is a difficult emotion for any Christian to express. We fear that God will be mad at us, or that our anger shows a lack of faith. Yet, the Bible contains many examples of anger directed toward God. Many of the writers of Scripture expressed anger to God. In the Book of Psalms, for example, the writers freely and often express their anger at God for allowing them to suffer. (See Psalm 44:9-21, or Psalm 88.) Jeremiah the prophet raged at God (Jeremiah 20:7-18).

Perhaps the psalmist's anger indicates why we become angry at God. He isn't answering our prayers as we like. Because of this selfishness on our part, we have a difficult time understanding God's will for our lives and the timing of His plan. Our anger is sometimes a product of our immaturity or of our limited understanding, but we need to express the anger in healthy and Christ-honoring ways. When we repress our anger we damage both ourselves and our relationships.

✎ Have you ever been angry with God? ❏ Yes ❏ No If so, below describe what you were angry about.

_____

Notice that God did not strike you with lightning because you admitted your anger. You have chosen to have a more intimate relationship with God by telling Him how you feel. In revealing to God exactly how you felt, you may have experienced a feeling of relief. Or you may have felt guilty for expressing your anger. No matter what you feel about expressing anger toward God, you demonstrate to God how much you care for Him as you share your anger.

## Assignment for the Lesson

✎ Think of someone with whom you have become angry in the recent past. Describe in the space below what you were angry about.

_____

➤ Practice expressing your anger in constructive ways. Enlist someone to help you practice. Ask them to listen and to play the part of the person toward whom you feel anger. Express your feelings. Start with a statement like this,

"I care about you (or love you) as a person (friend, spouse, etc.). What I have to say is not about judgment or blame, but I need to tell you how angry I am. When you_____, I felt_____. I wanted you to know so that we can talk about it and continue our relationship.

✎ Below list the ways you usually express, deal with, or avoid anger. Include in your list any behavior such as stuffing or displacing anger.

_____

_____

In the margin list some more appropriate or effective ways of dealing with anger. Be prepared to discuss them with your group.

➤ Say the following affirmation five times.

I can express my anger safely.

➤ Pray for those with whom you are angry.

**BETTER WAYS TO DEAL WITH MY ANGER:**

_____

_____

_____

_____

# Anxiety and Fear

*Do not worry about tomorrow, for tomorrow will worry about itself. Each day has enough trouble of its own.*

—Matthew 6:34

Have you struggled with the passage above? The Bible tells us we need not be anxious or afraid, yet we can't ignore our feelings. You may desperately want to control your anxieties and fears. Just as we disguise anger, we find ways to avoid or suppress our fears. We sometimes use the substances or behaviors as an alternative to facing our fears and anxieties. We can even use prescription medication to deal with anxiety.

Anxiety and fear can be crippling. You may have feelings of panic and dread in certain situations. Others may have "phobias," or a fear of specific things like bugs, heights, flying, or public speaking. Maybe you're afraid of relationships, that people won't like you if they really get to know you. Because of this, you may avoid relationships altogether. Sex can cause great anxiety and fear in many of us. As we learned in unit 2, this kind of fear can cause men to be impotent or to just turn away from sex. If you are to be sexually healthy and find intimacy with God and others, you need to understand and be able to express your anxieties and fears.

## The Nature of Anxiety

**Anxiety** is an overwhelming sense of panic about something large, ultimate, awesome, and difficult to explain. Anxieties differ from fears in that fears are more specific, such as fear of snakes. Anxieties are more general. They do not have an identifiable, describable

**KEY POINT**
Anxiety is an overwhelming sense of panic about something large, ultimate, awesome, and difficult to explain.

object. A number of theologians have identified the four most common anxieties. The "big four" anxieties are: death, condemnation, meaninglessness, and isolation.

## The "Big Four" Anxieties

**Death**—How do you talk about death? The thought of it can cause panic. To some, even thinking about death is difficult. Death anxiety is not the same as fear of the process of dying. We fear sickness, pain, and hospitals. Attempts to control our fate reflect our anxiety about death. We try to control our lives and circumstances in the hope that we can avoid death.

**Condemnation** is related to death anxiety. What will happen when we die? As Christians, we believe in heaven. Will we make it there? Feelings of guilt often attach themselves to this anxiety. We wonder if we have been good enough to avoid condemnation.

**Meaninglessness** follows closely on the heals of death and condemnation. What if my life really counts for nothing? Fear that life is futile creeps in like a spider. Does God really give meaning to life?

**Isolation** is the massive anxiety about being alone. Does anybody like me? Will anyone stay with me? Do I have any friends? If I don't, how will I live and protect myself? These thoughts lead me right back to the anxiety of death. Loneliness is the feeling I get on the edge of the anxiety of isolation.

✎ As you read the previous paragraphs, what thoughts did you have?

❑ I identify one or more of these anxieties in my life.
❑ I understand anxieties, but seldom experience them.
❑ I wonder what anxiety has to do with sexuality.
❑ I often feel anxious for no reason that I can explain.
❑ other _____

**KEY POINT**
Fear is the specific translation of anxiety.

Maybe you had a difficult time with the exercise above. Thinking about these anxieties is challenging. This is where fear comes in. Fear is more specific than are anxieties. We can identify the things we fear. We fear things we can see, hear, taste, or touch. Since anxiety is so ultimate and difficult to define, many of us translate it down to something specific that we can try to control.

## My Story

Every fall I used to get a vague sense of anxiety. I didn't quite know why. Perhaps it was the anticipation of winter, the cold, the snow, the harshness of the elements around me. It was something I couldn't control. As a boy, I was once trapped in a car during a blizzard. My parents and I waited for hours for the tow truck to come. After that experience, the idea of winter made me anxious.

Every fall I busied myself with preparations. The yard had to be raked just so, the driveway resealed, the gutters cleaned, and every thing tied down and covered. I tuned up the snow blower, put extra supplies in the basement, and carefully placed emergency kits in the trunks of the cars. I was proud of how the yard looked. I was an honest, hard working, God-fearing man. The neighbors must know that I was a prepared and decent Christian man. Still whenever the first snow came, I worried.

The experience in the blizzard was my first experience of fearing death. I was just a boy. Consciously, I hardly remember it, but the memory is buried in my mind. Later it caused great anxiety. Not being aware of the memory or knowing how to talk about it, I busied myself with more specific fears that I could think about and attempt to control. The difference between anxiety and fear is that fear is specific while anxiety is generalized. When I don't talk about or deal with my fears, my mind may turn fears into anxieties.

✎ **What are your fears? Below list all the fears you even occasionally experience.**

_____

_____

_____

✎ **How do you relate to my experience? What specific fears do you have that are related to larger anxieties? Write your thoughts below.**

_____

_____

_____

Did you think of examples for each of the anxieties? My attempt at winter preparations was an example of death anxiety expressing itself in an irrational way. For another example, I tend to believe that if my desk is neat and tidy, everything is right with the world. People who clean obsessively seek to control a deeper sense of anxiety by controlling a part of their environment. When anxiety-driven behaviors get out of hand psychologists call the result obsessive-compulsive disorder.

✎ **Think of your fears related to being good. Have you ever felt guilt even for things over which you had little or no control? ❑ Yes ❑ No Below describe the areas in which you feel you must excel and the areas in which you fear failure.**

I must excel in _____

I fear failure at _____

For years I thought that I had to be the smartest person in the room. If I wasn't, I wasn't a good person. Beneath that fear was my anxiety of condemnation. Some people fear having inadequate answers to life's most important questions. They may become rigidly invested in black and white answers they will defend to the death. They believe that if they can rigidly control one area of life then they will be OK.

What fears do you have about relationships or friends? Do you fear losing your spouse? Would you do anything, no matter how manipulative, to keep him or her around? To what lengths of self-sacrifice will you go to impress your friends? To what lengths do you go to avoid being abandoned?

A fear may express more than one anxiety. For example, think of people who go to great lengths to look younger so as to have more or younger friends. They may fear that age means death, or they may fear that age means loneliness. In either case, they may fear the loss of youth because it represents–and triggers–deep anxieties.

Then Jesus went with his disciples to a place called Gethsemane, and he said to them, "Sit here while I go over there and pray." He took Peter and the two sons of Zebedee along with him, and he began to be sorrowful and troubled. Then he said to them, "My soul is overwhelmed with sorrow to the point of death. Stay here and keep watch with me."

Going a little farther, he fell with his face to the ground and prayed, "My Father, if it is possible, may this cup be taken from me. Yet not as I will, but as you will."

Then he returned to his disciples and found them sleeping. "Could you men not keep watch with me for one hour?" he asked Peter. "Watch and pray so that you will not fall into temptation. The spirit is willing, but the body is weak."

He went away a second time and prayed, "My Father, if it is not possible for this cup to be taken away unless I drink it, may your will be done."

When he came back, he again found them sleeping, because their eyes were heavy. So he left them and went away once more and prayed the third time, saying the same thing.

Then he returned to the disciples and said to them, "Are you still sleeping and resting? Look, the hour is near, and the Son of Man is betrayed into the hands of sinners."
–Matthew 26:36-45

But we see Jesus, who was made a little lower than the angels, now crowned with glory and honor because he suffered death, so that by the grace of God he might taste death for everyone.
–Hebrews 2:9

 Review your list of fears. Below write your fears and try to relate your fears to one of the four larger anxieties: death, condemnation, meaninglessness, or isolation.

| Fear | Anxiety |
|------|---------|
| _____ | _____ |
| _____ | _____ |
| _____ | _____ |
| _____ | _____ |

You may have noticed that in my story about winter that my current fears had their origin in a childhood event. Early-life traumas, buried deep in our memories, commonly cause present anxieties. We will examine in Part 2 what these early traumas may be for you.

➤ As you work through this book, you may want to keep a separate journal of early memories that come to you. However trivial they may seem, write them down. You will want to refer to them later.

Many people experience anxiety related to intimacy and sexuality—including individuals who have never been abused or molested and individuals with no sexual compulsions or addictions. Early life sexual experiences greatly influence current anxieties and fears about sex. Many individuals have experienced a lack of attachment and bonding throughout childhood and into adulthood. Some have experienced repeated rejections by significant others, including parents, friends, and persons of the opposite sex. Some have been told that sex is dirty or naughty, genitalia are dirty and should not be touched, or that sex is only for procreation, not pleasure or intimacy. These experiences and messages lead to inappropriate ways to handle sexual anxieties. Sexual trauma, for example, sometimes causes people to seek to control sexual activity by either:
1. always being aggressive about and initiating sex or
2. by withdrawing from sex completely and never enjoying it.

Has one of these approaches been your pattern? Think of the complications involved when a #1 marries a #2. Both patterns, in the extreme, are about anxiety and fear of sex. We will deal more extensively with these anxieties and fears in Part 2.

➤ Read Matthew 26:36-45, appearing in the margin. As you read, try to feel the sense of anxiety that Jesus must have felt as He faced the cross.

In this passage, we see that Jesus experienced the stress, fear, and anxieties that we face. He experienced the anxiety of death and dread about what was going to happen. Surely, He felt abandoned when the disciples couldn't stay awake. On the cross, He felt abandoned by His Father. Jesus cried, "My God, my God, why have you forsaken me?" (Matthew 27:46). Hebrews 2:9 says that Jesus suffered so that He could "taste death for everyone." He fully entered into the pain, alienation, and condemnation of death, hell, and separation from God. By conquering death, Jesus made complete provision for our anxieties. We cannot defeat them ourselves. We must rely on God's grace.

Jesus surrounded Himself with friends to support Him in His darkest hour. We too need the support of the community of faith—the fellowship of believers. Like Jesus' friends, ours may sometimes fail us or be unable to solve our problems, but community gives us a sense of security, attachment, and belonging. We share our common problems, help each other, and support each other. We find a sense of peace in belonging.

## Assignment for the Lesson

➤ Choose a member of your support group to discuss one of the anxieties or fears that you wrote about in this lesson.

➤ Review and practice your Scripture memory verses for this and the previous units.

➤ Say the following affirmation five times.

I can find peace in my relationship with Christ.

➤ Pray for the courage to face your anxieties and fears.

# Managing Stress

How do you manage stress? You can deal with stress so that it becomes a growing, strengthening experience, or it can be damaging to you. Some stress in our life is healthy and we need to be able to distinguish between the healthy and unhealthy responses to stress. Healthy stress pushes us to grow. Unhealthy stress results from unresolved problems, anxieties, or circumstances that lead us to feel life is unmanageable. Using abusive, addictive substances or behaviors to deal with stress is only a temporary solution.

Stress is a frequently misunderstood word. Stress is the physical reaction of the body to anxiety and fear. The body responds to the perception that it must deal with something dangerous. We call stress the "fight or flight" response because, in preparing to deal with danger, the body creates the physical resources to fight or run away. The body prepares for action by dumping various chemicals, like adrenaline, into the bloodstream. The heart starts racing, breathing becomes more rapid, the stomach seeks to empty itself, and the muscles tense. The body also makes various physical changes to protect itself. For example, the time it takes blood to clot decreases.

These physical reactions are natural and protective. Problems with stress arise when our minds feel anxious or afraid and no real physical danger exists. The body prepares itself for a non-existent battle. The body must use the excess energy in some way so it can return to its normal state. The process of using this excess energy is called relaxation. Unused energy will eventually lead parts of the body to "burn out." Since we need to be awake to run or fight, the stress response keeps us in a state of general alertness. Those who have trouble sleeping know how anxiety and fear keep them awake although they may be really tired. Think of expressions that use physical metaphors to express the feeling of fear. You might say, "That took my breath away," or "I have butterflies in my stomach," or "I was really uptight."

## Perpetual Stress Management

Living in a family that does not permit healthy expression of emotions is like growing up in a class on inappropriate ways to deal with stress. Whatever the feeling, including anxiety and fear, someone demonstrates a destructive way to raise or lower your mood.

In lesson 2 we learned how you may already be an expert at ineffective ways to manage stress, medicating your feelings on a daily basis. Sometimes these strategies may be appropriate to help you relax. If used all the time, however, they will lead to problems with chronic emotional and physical conditions. If you are one of these people, you need to find better ways of managing stress.

Two kinds of stress-management strategies exist. Both have value.
• One offers symptomatic relief; it only deals with the outward signs of the problem.
• The other strategy offers more therapeutic relief; it deals with the basic, underlying problem to promote long term healing or a cure.

What you do to relieve the symptoms of stress once you have them is symptomatic relief. Whatever you do to prevent the anxiety and fear that cause stress is more therapeutic.

✎ Look at the list of stress-management techniques below. The activities listed under symptomatic are designed to relieve the symptoms of stress. The methods listed under therapeutic deal with the underlying causes of unhealthy stress. Circle those methods you use to manage stress.

### Stress Management

| Symptomatic | Therapeutic |
| --- | --- |
| Medication (such as Valium) | Finding meaning in life |
| Meditation | Trust in God's providence |
| Listening to Music | Living in community |
| Laughter | Laughter |
| Physical exercise | Physical exercise |
| Working less | Working less |
| Prayer | Prayer |
| Bible Study | Bible Study |
| Sexual thoughts or actions | Healthy sexual relationship |

A cheerful heart is good medicine, but a crushed spirit dries up the bones.
–Proverbs 17:22

Some stress-management strategies can be both symptomatic and therapeutic. In the margin read Proverbs 17:22. Laughter improves heart rate and respiration and relaxes muscles. Laughter improves digestion. In this way, laughter is a symptomatic form of relief. Laughter also causes us to look at life less seriously and to change our perspective. When we laugh, we feel less anxiety and fear. This is therapeutic relief. Notice that prayer and Bible study are also in both categories. These two can be symptomatically relaxing, but they also are about ultimate connection with God and finding meaning in one's life.

The symptomatic examples could contain any activity that helps you calm down and relax. Exercise of any kind that uses up the energy of stress can allow the body to relax. As we discovered in unit 2, one of the keys to exercise is that it be fun and not work. Bringing our competitive instincts to exercise can cause it to be more stressful.

✎ What forms of symptomatic relief for stress have you found successful? List them below. In the margin list any unhealthy substances and behaviors you have used to relieve stress in the past.

## UNHEALTHY FORMS OF STRESS RELIEF I HAVE USED—

_____

_____

_____

_____

_____

_____

You are probably more of a stress management expert than you think. Part of your task now is to eliminate the unhealthy strategies and practice the healthy ones. Over 50 years ago Alcoholics Anonymous began using part of a prayer by the famous theologian Reinhold Niehbur.

God,
Grant me the serenity
to accept the things
I cannot change,
the courage to change
the things I can,
and the wisdom
to know the difference.

➤ Read Reinhold Niehbur's prayer that appears in the margin.

This prayer reminds us that we have limited control. It also suggests that those things we can change, we need to change. This prayer has come to be called the "Serenity Prayer." If practiced daily, it is an effective form of stress management.

Positive stress-management strategies are essential to healthy sexuality because they are essential to effective living. We will never find total relief from stress. The therapeutic strategies mentioned in the chart are goals that can be part of our daily walk with God. In many ways stress is a product of original sin, trying to take control back from God. We will learn more about creating a plan for therapeutic relief of stress in unit 4, the spiritual dimension.

## Assignment for the Lesson

✎ What new symptomatic strategies would you like to try?

_____

_____

➤ Share your list with your group. Ask them to help you practice these strategies. Be specific about how you will do so.

➤ Repeat the "Serenity Prayer" two times.

## Group Discussion Questions

• When you were growing up, how did your family deal with powerful emotions?
• What substances or behaviors do you use to elevate your mood? to depress your mood?
• Describe your relationship with "the land of numb."
• What do passages like Psalm 44:9-21, Psalm 88, and Jeremiah 20:7-18 say about being angry with God?
• Describe a time when you have been angry with God. If you cannot remember a time when you were angry at God, why? Is it OK for you to be angry with God?
• Which of the "big four" anxieties (death, condemnation, meaninglessness, isolation) is the greatest issue for you and why?
• Describe the areas in which you feel you must excel and the areas in which you fear failure.
• What unhealthy forms of stress relief have you used?
• What new strategies for managing stress would you like to try?

UNIT 4

# The Relational Dimension

## FOCAL PASSAGE

*The man said, "This is now bone of my bones and flesh of my flesh; she shall be called 'woman,' for she was taken out of man." For this reason a man will leave his father and mother and be united to his wife, and they will become one flesh. The man and his wife were both naked, and they felt no shame.*

—Genesis 2:23-25

## MEMORY VERSE

The Lord God said, "It is not good for the man to be alone." –Genesis 2:18

Relational

### JONATHAN'S STORY

Jonathan was lonely. He had been lonely most of his life. When he was young his parents rewarded him when he acted like an adult, but they didn't really listen to him. Neither his mom nor dad talked to him about emotional or spiritual issues. They didn't encourage Jonathan to play or make friends. Since his dad worked long hours, Jonathan's mom enjoyed having Jonathan around and treated him like the "man of the house." When his dad was home he didn't have much time for Jonathan. Mom was busy with all of her activities.

Jonathan married his high school sweetheart, Mary. They had known each other for years. Jonathan and Mary had three children. Gradually both of them got busy with work, church, and the children's activities. They didn't have much time to talk or go out together.

One night as Jonathan was flipping through the TV channels after Mary had gone to bed, an attractive and seductive looking woman appeared on the screen. "Do you need a friend tonight? Are you lonely? Call me," she said. He quickly changed the channel. Over the next several days, however, her image kept reoccurring in his mind. He had never called one of those numbers, and he wondered what it would be like. Jonathan knew he shouldn't, but something powerful, lonely, and deep inside of him yearned just to hear the sound of her voice. The appeal of the woman on TV was not so much about lust as a deep longing for companionship. Jonathan needs to know how to be emotionally and spiritually intimate.

## GROWTH GOAL

In this unit you will explore the importance of intimate relationships. You will understand the connection between sexual temptation and loneliness. You will learn how to be more intimate with others. Finally, you will explore how shame may be preventing you from being more open and vulnerable with others.

| Shame and Relationship | Developing Healthy Intimacy | Healthy Dependency | Contracts for Relationships | Restoring Trust |
|---|---|---|---|---|
| **LESSON 1** | **LESSON 2** | **LESSON 3** | **LESSON 4** | **LESSON 5** |

# Shame and Relationship

We talked about shame in unit 3. Below notice the difference between healthy shame and unhealthy shame.

### HEALTHY SHAME

- Makes me aware of my need for God. Reminds me that I am powerless without God in control.
- Points me to surrender to Christ as the way I can find salvation.

### UNHEALTHY SHAME

- Makes me feel worthless and unloved even by God.
- Leads me to try to control my life and save myself by being perfect.

**The Lord within her is righteous; he does no wrong. Morning by morning he dispenses his justice, and every new day he does not fail, yet the unrighteous know no shame.**
**–Zephaniah 3:5**

Unhealthy shame damages our ability to be intimate with others. It contributes to a negative self-concept—the feeling that no one would want to be intimate with me because no one likes me. Distinguish, however, between unhealthy and healthy shame. Shame in itself is not bad. The Bible warns that feeling no shame is very dangerous. Note the words of Zephaniah the prophet: "The unrighteous know no shame."

Unhealthy shame may arise for many reasons. In our opening story, Jonathan did not feel accepted by his parents. In more extreme cases, shame may result from various degrees of abuse. We will explore how past experiences lead to shame in Part 2. We all experience some degree of unhealthy shame. For now, begin to evaluate your level of unhealthy shame.

 **Do you remember a time in your life when you thought that no one liked you? Below describe what you remember about that time or incident.**

Every person can benefit from this study. Be aware that this unit describes beliefs and feelings that are a major problem for some individuals. If some of the material does not describe your situation, study for understanding. If the material does describe your thoughts, feelings, and behaviors, study for life change.

_____

_____

At some time in their lives, particularly during adolescence, most people feel that no one likes them. Some people move through these feelings and form healthy relationships. The people who overcome these feelings usually have experienced unconditional love and nurture from their home environment. They have resources to draw on during times of self-doubt. You may never have worked through childhood and adolescent feelings of non-acceptance. If you did not experience affirmation, love, and nurture, you may still wonder whether others, including your spouse or those closest to you, will really like you. Your life may have been filled with attempts to find love and nurture. Or, you may not know what you are looking for.

In his book, *Out of the Shadows,* Pat Carnes describes four core beliefs held by those who have problems with sexual addiction and compulsiveness. Everyone can learn by examining these core beliefs. In this lesson you will look at each of these individually.

## CORE BELIEFS ABOUT SHAME

1. I am a bad and worthless person.
2. No one will love me as I am.
3. No one will take care of my needs but me.
4. Sex is equal to love, and sex is my most important need.[1]

## 1. I am a bad and worthless person.

We previously discussed the feeling of worthlessness. We may desperately want to believe that Christ died for us but have real trouble accepting His care and forgiveness. We believe we are so bad that not even God could love us. Sometimes our actions can compound this feeling. We do things that confirm to us that we are bad and worthless.

✎ **What do you think is the worst thing about yourself?**

_____

**What is the worst thing you have ever done? Write your response. You may need to use initials or write in code.**

_____

_____

You may have difficulty admitting these things even to yourself. Do these things make you really unlovable in the sight of God? If someone else confessed these things to you would you tell them that Christ didn't die for that particular kind of sin?

Perhaps you're afraid that if you really accept God's forgiveness you wouldn't be able to commit that sin again. Remember that you must want to give up sinful behaviors to benefit fully from God's forgiveness. Forgiveness implies that you don't want to commit a particular sin again. You may have to begin by honestly telling God that you do not want to give up the behavior. Ask Him to help you become willing.

## 2. No one will love me as I am.

Feelings of shame often stem from abuse and put-downs experienced in the past. Everyone experiences some rejection. How much rejection you have experienced is not nearly as important as honestly examining the effects those experiences have had on your life.

Your parents or important others in your life may not have expressed love appropriately to you. Wherever feelings of shame begin, this belief says: "Hide. If they really know you, they won't like you." You may hold back parts of yourself and your history because you fear rejection. The fear of rejection strongly motivates this belief, making intimate relationships more difficult. Intimacy with another person requires the ability to be honest about who you really are. If you are hiding something, the thought resides in the back of your mind that if they knew _____ about me, they'd hate me.

➤ **What do you think of the definition of intimacy that appears in the margin?**

✎ **Has fear of rejection caused you to withhold information about yourself? If so, below list the names of people you have deceived. About what did you deceive them?**

| _Person I deceived_ | _My deception_ |
| --- | --- |
| _____ | _____ |
| _____ | _____ |

Be gentle with yourself about these deceptions. You were deceptive because you feared rejection. You want to be loved and cared for and you are lonely. This is not devious dishonesty. This is like a frightened little child.

**INTIMACY:**
the state of honesty and mutual acceptance between two or more people. Being intimate requires the ability to be honest about yourself, what you think and what you've done.

Have you ever been in trouble in a relationship because you did not tell the truth? Others probably thought you deceived them because you did not care. The reality may be that you lied to them because you were afraid of losing them. Revealing yourself to a relative stranger is much easier than being honest with those close to you. Rejection from a stranger is less painful. Spouses, in fact, may be jealous of the honesty that you have developed in your *Faithful & True* group. They may ask, "How can you be so honest with relative strangers when you have lied to me for years? You must not really love me!"

 **Below write the name of the person whose presence and acceptance you most fear losing.**

_____

### 3. No one will take care of my needs but me.

This third core belief is a matter of trust. If you don't trust anyone else to take care of your needs, you have to meet those needs yourself. This may be based on a history of abandonment. If you didn't get what you needed when you were small, you won't trust anyone to give you what you need now. Unmet needs at an early age lead to distrust at a later age. We will take a closer look at abandonment issues in Part 2.

You may also have discovered that you can take care of your needs in ways that are more immediate and pleasurable than what someone else could do for you. This is called *instant gratification.* We live in a culture that teaches us to gratify ourselves instantly.

 **When you were a child, did you experience a lack of love, care, or support from one or more important people in your life? Write their name(s).**

_____

A lack of safety, love, and provision for our needs when we are children teaches us that we must grab for what we need before someone snatches it away. We fail to learn to wait for what we need. This explains why many of us develop the need for instant gratification.

Some forms of instant gratification can lead to addiction. You can become so psychologically or physically dependent on the high, the relief, the medicating quality of a substance or behavior that it becomes an addiction. Remember that we worked on some of these behaviors in unit 3. Do you now see that some of these behaviors may be a search for the love and nurture that you feel you cannot get from anyone else?

 **Review your work in unit 3 on page 46. Which of the substances or behaviors you learned about involve a search for nurture (love, acceptance, and belonging)?**

_____

_____

> **Could we say that many of us have a "relationship" with alcohol, sex, work, sports, or some other object or event?**

### 4. Sex is equal to love, and Sex is my most important need.

Genuine relationships are my greatest need. The fourth false core belief says that sex is my most important need. Thus sex takes the place of relationships. When I don't challenge this belief, I equate sex with love. I begin to believe that if someone really loves me she

*If we hope for what we do not yet have, we wait for it patiently.*
–Romans 8:25

will be willing to be sexual with me. Sex is a great symbol of acceptance and nurture. Sometimes we associate specific body parts or various sexual acts with love and nurture. For some people, sex is equal to love.

✎ As an example of what you have just read, have you ever thought: If sex is frequent enough or good enough, our relationship must be fine?" ❑ Yes ❑ No

Sex can be a wonderful part of a relationship, but genuine intimacy comes from communication and self-disclosure. When people substitute sex for genuine relationship, they defeat themselves. They keep their own need from being met. For many people, a small group is one of the first places in their lives where they experience real intimacy—the ability to be honest about their worst qualities, thoughts, and behaviors.

## Assignment for the Lesson

➤ One of the ways to practice and develop intimacy is simply to tell your group how difficult honesty is for you. Tell your group if you are afraid they won't like you. Discuss how honesty is difficult at church because of the fear that people will think that you are not a "good" Christian.

➤ What was it like to be honest with the group? Describe to them any fears, any sense of relief, and any feeling of acceptance that you experienced.

✎ Begin to memorize your Scripture memory verse for this unit. Write the verse on a card and carry it with you. Whenever you get a drink of water, review the passage.

➤ Say the following affirmation aloud five times.

Nothing can separate me from the love of Christ Jesus.

➤ Pray for courage to be honest and to trust others.

The Lord God said, "It is not good for the man to be alone."
–Genesis 2:18

LESSON

2

# Developing Healthy Intimacy

Larry goes to church because he desperately wants to fit in. He hates being alone and fears that no one likes him. He enjoys being a member of one of the fastest growing churches in town. He is quick to point out to many what a "great" church it is and brags about it especially to people from other churches.

Yet, Larry is not a reliable member. He could attend many groups at the church, but he doesn't. He prefers to attend only Sunday morning worship. He constantly resists invitations to Bible study, prayer groups, men's fellowships, and support groups. Many times the choir director has invited Larry to join the choir, but Larry says he has no time. The pastor, likewise, has offered Larry various types of church-service projects, but Larry prefers to give money. "After all, that's what we pay the church staff to do," Larry's says. Larry rejected service on any of the church committees. He hates the arguments, conflicts, and decision making processes. At coffee hour, however, he is quick to blame members of those committees for work that is not getting done.

Larry's wife Betty has been trying for years to get him more involved in family activities. Larry prefers to spend his time with work, golf, and the TV. Betty is desperately lonely. So is Larry, but he is afraid to talk about his loneliness for fear of finding out how desperate the situation really is. Larry suffers from intimacy disorder. He is afraid to tell anyone who he really is and afraid to get involved. He doesn't trust anyone, not even his wife. He is afraid that she will leave him if she knows his feelings.

In *Couples in Recovery*, Pat Carnes, my wife Deb, and I have written about healthy intimacy as opposed to intimacy dysfunction. The following list compares healthy intimacy and intimacy dysfunction in categories with a brief description of the characteristics of each.[2]

 **Carefully study the following characteristics of healthy intimacy and intimacy dysfunction. Then after each description, evaluate yourself in each of the categories by using the graph to rate your ability or inability to be intimate. Place an *X* on each of the graphs in the spot you feel is most appropriate for yourself. For example, in the category of *Initiative*, if you sometimes struggle with some of the issues mentioned, but for the most part feel the description under "Able to take initiative" describes you, then place an X toward the left end of the scale.**

| HEALTHY INTIMACY | INTIMACY DYSFUNCTION |
|---|---|

**Initiative**

One of the characteristics of healthy intimacy is the ability to begin a relationship or reach out to others. This involves taking the risk to express how much you care for the person, how you want his or her time and attention, and how much you are attracted to the person (emotionally, spiritually, or physically). Initiative also includes the ability to invite a person to share in activities and a willingness to share your own problems and issues.

The inability to reach out and begin a relationship characterizes intimacy dysfunction. Instead, you stay passive and detached. At times you may assume a victim posture and blame others for bad things happening to you. You may also have the feeling that you have been abandoned and you are helpless to do anything about it.

 **Rate your ability or inability to be intimate. Place an *X* on the graph in the spot you feel best describes your ability to take initiative in relationships.**

Able to Take Initiative             Unable to Take Initiative

**Presence**

The ability to meet others, to listen, and to attend to another's thoughts and feelings-marks healthy intimacy. You can share your own reactions. You can reveal feelings honestly. The person you are with knows you genuinely are present in the relationship.

With intimacy dysfunction, you do not make your feelings available. You isolate yourself. You do not accept attention and may divert attention away from yourself. Addictions and other dysfunctional behaviors keep you numb to feelings and turn others away.

Present in Relationships             Isolate Myself

### Finish

Healthy intimacy involves the ability to finalize arrangements, complete transactions, end fights, and solve problems. You can respond to requests, desires, and attractions without getting lost in the other's identity. This includes the ability to accept help and to say "Thank you."

Without healthy intimacy skills, you tend to exaggerate problems instead of solving them, use excuses, and blame others for your problems. You may use chronic busyness and work overload as an excuse not to complete work. You hold issues open and avoid closure.

Able to Complete Projects — Difficult to Complete Projects

### Vulnerability

Vulnerability is the ability to share what you are thinking or feeling. You can talk about yourself with others, including problems that you are facing. You can ask for help in problem solving.

In unhealthy intimacy you keep your thought process private, do not ask for help, and may have private conversations with yourself and debate back and forth about what to do.

Able to Be Vulnerable — Difficult to Make Myself Vulnerable

### Nurture

With healthy intimacy you can care for others with no expectation of something in return. You have empathy for and can support others. You make suggestions and do not feel rejected if they are not taken. You show physical affection (holding hands, giving hugs) without it having sexual meaning. You can express feedback in affirming and supportive ways.

Relationships built on unhealthy intimacy lack nurture. You take care of others in order to control them or get something in return. You build your self-esteem on your ability to give care. You cannot accept another person's feelings and make efforts to discount the other's feelings. Physical touch may have ulterior motives, like sex.

Nurture Others — Attempt to Control Others

### Honesty

Healthy intimacy involves the ability to be clear about what you believe and feel, express anger in positive ways, express either negative or positive feelings, and openly share disagreements or resentments.

Unhealthy intimacy is dishonest. You claim to not have deep feelings, disguise your anger to avoid making waves or conflict, use anger as a way of controlling another person, do not share your beliefs, attitudes, or values, may tell lies to gain approval, and avoid direct communication by using others to relay messages.

Honest with Feelings — Dishonest with Feelings

### Play

People who have healthy intimacy skills see the humor in life and laugh easily. They put effort into non-work activities and search for opportunities to play. They feel free to take risks and try new

With unhealthy intimacy you may be compulsively busy and miss significant events. You take a grim, "Life is a problem," stance; refuse to try new things, take a risk, or go on an adventure;

ventures, and they enjoy children. They exhibit the ability to smell the roses, enjoy a sunset, and engage in celebrations of God's creation. They are willing to play in non-competitive ways and do not feel guilty just because they take time to play.

rarely laugh; express the belief that children should be seen and not heard; have few or no hobbies, unless in compulsive, competitive, or income producing ways; have no idea how to enjoy life with another person.

| Able to Play | Enjoyment Impaired |
|---|---|

Look back at all the graphs. Overall, do your marks tend to be toward the healthy or the unhealthy side? Ultimately, your ability to be intimate is about trust. Do you trust other people not to take advantage of your openness and vulnerability? Have you healed enough from your sense of shame to think that you deserve to be in a healthy relationship?

➤ Ask yourself, "Am I intimate with God? Am I able to be honest and open with Him? Do I allow myself to be vulnerable and surrender control to God, or do I think gloom and doom? Do I play the victim, blaming God for my problems? Do I enjoy His creation? Do I play and laugh and enjoy God's children?

➤ Share this exercise with your spouse or a close friend and ask him or her to rate you. How do the two compare? Have a conversation with him or her about what you have learned about yourself in this exercise.

Many of us must learn how to be intimate. We develop intimacy skills through practice. Most of us will not obtain intimacy overnight. Practicing requires taking some risks, experimenting with how others react to our new openness. Some of our experiences may not be as successful or rewarding as others, Some may even seem to take us a step back.

## Assignment for the Lesson

➤ Start your practice. Pick one of the problems you currently face, however major or minor. Reach out to one other person (spouse, friend, or someone in your group) and ask for help. You might start this way,
"I've really got a problem. I value your friendship and opinion and need your help. Let me describe my situation to you and tell you what feelings it creates in me. I'd really like to get it resolved."

➤ Begin thinking of how you might get involved in some service project that has absolutely no known reward for you.

➤ Tell one other person that you really care about him. Tell him if he ever has a problem you're available to listen and be of whatever help you can.

➤ Invite one other person to play with you in some way that is totally enjoyable and non-competitive. If you need help, consult with a child about what is really fun.

➤ Give your spouse or a friend an affirmation for something nice he or she has done this week.

✎ In the margin write your Scripture memory verse for this unit. You may check your work on page 58.

➤ Say aloud the following affirmation five times.
I am worthy of relationship and can trust.

# Healthy Dependency

Samson was chosen by God, set apart even before his birth. God blessed him with great strength. He defeated the enemies of Israel. Even with his fame and fortune, Samson had a deep loneliness that he sought to overcome on his own. He went to prostitutes, even at risk to himself. Eventually Samson fell in love with a Philistine woman named Delilah. The Philistine officials paid Delilah to discover the source of Samson's strength so that they could destroy him. Below read the rest of the amazing story of Samson and Delilah.

> *So Delilah said to Samson, "Tell me the secret of your great strength and how you can be tied up and subdued."*
>
> *Samson answered her, "If anyone ties me with seven fresh thongs that have not been dried, I'll become as weak as any other man."*
>
> *Then the rulers of the Philistines brought her seven fresh thongs that had not been dried, and she tied him with them. With men hidden in the room, she called to him, "Samson, the Philistines are upon you!" But he snapped the thongs as easily as a piece of string snaps when it comes close to a flame. So the secret of his strength was not discovered.*
>
> —Judges 16:6-9

You would think any sane person would have said: "This woman is no good for me" and would have run the other way. But twice more Delilah asked Samson for the secret of his strength, and twice more he lied to her. Each time Delilah betrayed Samson to his enemies. Below read the next act in their story.

> *Then she said to him, "How can you say, 'I love you,' when you won't confide in me? This is the third time you have made a fool of me and haven't told me the secret of your great strength." With such nagging she prodded him day after day until he was tired to death.*
>
> *So he told her everything. "No razor has ever been used on my head," he said, "because I have been a Nazirite set apart to God since birth. If my head were shaved, my strength would leave me, and I would become as weak as any other man."*
>
> *When Delilah saw that he had told her everything, she sent word to the rulers of the Philistines, "Come back once more; he has told me everything." So the rulers of the Philistines returned with the silver in their hands. Having put him to sleep on her lap, she called a man to shave off the seven braids of his hair, and so began to subdue him. And his strength left him.*
>
> *Then she called, "Samson, the Philistines are upon you!"*
>
> *He awoke from his sleep and thought, "I'll go out as before and shake myself free." But he did not know that the Lord had left him.*
>
> —Judges 16:15-20

✎ **Samson's story certainly raises questions in my mind. Below check one or more questions you would like answered about the story, or write your own question.**

❑ How could Samson be so stupid? He had to know she would betray him.

❑ How could someone so powerful in one area of his life be so weak in another area?

❑ Why would a man of Samson's abilities—obviously the most powerful man in his country—go to prostitutes?

❑ How could a man with such special connection to God make such destructive choices?

❑ other: _____

We certainly wonder: "Why would a man of such strength and devotion to God succumb to the temptations that Samson did? How could he let himself succumb to the obvious manipulations of Delilah?" This story is a comfort to some of us who have sexually sinned and wondered why we weren't stronger, smarter, or more faithful.

One answer could be that with all of his strength, Samson was lonely. He was a hero, but most heroes are lonely. Who do they talk to? Who can they be weak with? Who will let them be an ordinary person? Samson somehow became dependent on the sexual and emotional seductions of Delilah. This is a form of unhealthy dependency.

Unhealthy dependency usually happens out of loneliness. Some people, like Samson, are lonely because their role in life has been to be independent and strong. They will not take the risk of being vulnerable for fear of falling off their pedestal. Others may be lonely due to their own shame, feeling they are unworthy of anyone's attention.

Shame and loneliness lead us to search for approval, love, and nurture. When we find a person who seems to like us, we may be so afraid of losing the approval that we would do anything to keep it. We've talked about these things in lesson 1 of this unit. In many ways we can become addicted to that person or their approval. This is unhealthy dependency.

✎ **Following are some of the symptoms common to those who struggle with unhealthy dependency. Check the ones that seem to apply to you:**

- ❑ I feel shame and inadequacy; I hate this feeling, but I'm unable to talk about it.
- ❑ I experience a strong need for another's approval and I become anxious about not having his or her approval.
- ❑ I worry that others disapprove of and will reject me.
- ❑ I use money, status, power, or appearance to gain approval.
- ❑ I use anger, weakness, protectiveness, or self-sacrifice to manipulate approval.
- ❑ I ignore advice and distrust other's motives. I have difficulty accepting help.
- ❑ I am unpredictable and break promises.
- ❑ I look for a way to escape feelings especially when conflict occurs.
- ❑ I blame others to avoid taking responsibility.
- ❑ I lie about negative and sinful behaviors.
- ❑ I experience sudden and unpredictable moods.
- ❑ I am easily influenced by another's approval.
- ❑ I ignore my own needs in order to please others.
- ❑ I try to manipulate changes in others.
- ❑ I feel frightened about being abandoned.
- ❑ I relinquish my own beliefs, attitudes, and values to please or pacify others.
- ❑ I use sex as a barometer of the health of a relationship.
- ❑ I am afraid God will reject me.

If you checked a number of these symptoms, you have a problem with being dependent on others. You may often have been angry with yourself for not being stronger and following your own will. You may have been hurt by someone else and afraid to talk about it. You are angry at yourself because you can't express anger. You may feel like a coward for giving in or being so afraid.

Be gentle with yourself. When we were infants, we feared being left alone. When we felt alone, we cried. This is a natural reaction. Some of us have been nurtured and protected in healthy ways so that we learned to feel relatively safe. Others of us go through life trying to create safety for ourselves by attaching ourselves to others. Dependency is not a negative word. We are human beings. We need others. We certainly need God. To depend on God and on others is healthy.

The following is a list of characteristics of healthy dependency. Put a ✓ by those you are good at now. Put an *X* by those that you would like to work on.

❑ I can seek help and ask for advice.
❑ I can identify trustworthy people and people who are not trustworthy.
❑ I trust others who are trustworthy.
❑ I can talk about my feelings including anger, sadness, anxiety, fear, loneliness, and inadequacy.
❑ I do not seek to please or manipulate others for selfish purposes.
❑ I can make commitments and follow through with them.
❑ I am dependable.
❑ I admit mistakes and take responsibility for my own behavior.
❑ I can set healthy limits for myself.
❑ In times of conflict I can identify my contribution to the problem.
❑ I can be alone and not feel lonely.
❑ I can operate independently.
❑ I can hold opinions, beliefs, and values which may conflict with other's.
❑ I state my own needs and ask in healthy ways that they be met.
❑ I affirm myself and others.
❑ I let others solve their own problems. I will offer help and advice when asked.
❑ I can share leadership and cooperate with others to solve problems.
❑ I find strength in my relationship with God.

Healthy dependency will allow us to develop healthy community. Our homes, schools, cities, and churches will benefit from our efforts. How do we develop this kind of trust if we have lived a lifetime of experience with unhealthy dependency? We must practice this kind of surrender one person at a time and one day at a time.

**KEY POINT**
Trust and courage are the keys. If we trust God and surrender to Him, we must also trust others and surrender our fears of rejection and efforts to control approval.

## Assignment for the Lesson

First, you must make a decision about the most important people in your life. These are the people to improve relationships with. In the margin write the names of your top three important people. Your list might include your spouse, other family members, or friends. Be careful to choose those that you think will have the ability to respond in reasonably healthy ways.

Make an appointment to have a conversation with each of these people. In the margin record the date and time of your appointments.

On a separate sheet of paper make two lists. On the first list, write the characteristics of unhealthy dependency that you checked in the exercise on page 67. Beside each characteristic in your list, write specific examples of how you think you have been dependent in an unhealthy way.

On the second list write the characteristics of healthy dependency that you checked. Write any characteristics that you want to work on and suggest ways that you might do so. (Don't worry if you don't get this exactly right. Do your best. We will be doing more practicing in the next two lessons.)

In the margin write your Scripture memory verse for the unit.

➤ Say the following affirmation five times.

I am strong. I am worth relating to. I depend on God and others for my strength.

# Contracts for Relationships

Bob and Ruth had been married for 23 years. Their children were growing. They both worked and participated in church and community. Everyone thought they were an ideal couple. Yet they were strangers to each other. When they dated they were anxious to please each other. Their romance was exciting—filled with bells ringing and music playing. They talked about almost everything, but each of them had secrets about their past, nothing serious really, but facts they were afraid to reveal. The past didn't seem to matter. They were "made" for each other.

Their relationship deteriorated slowly. The deterioration started with sexual frequency. They did not talk much about sex. For Bob sex was not often enough. Ruth felt Bob was too sexually demanding. She wanted to be a faithful partner, but she felt used and angry. They also did not talk about money. They never really argued or fought, but both worried about money. Occasionally, Bob would become angry at Ruth for things she bought. Bob felt inadequate about his salary but was afraid to admit his feelings to Ruth.

They involved themselves in work, family, and school. They rarely went out by themselves, and never went on vacation. Although they were both very active at church they didn't even sit together because Ruth sang in the choir. They prayed before meals, but that was all. Bob and Ruth did go to a Sunday School class together, but they never did their homework or lessons together. Ruth felt ashamed when she started noticing that one of the other men in the class was really intelligent, knew his Scripture, seemed like a wonderful godly man, and was so funny. How lucky his wife must be! Bob was really frustrated by how attractive and understanding many of the women in the class were. How lucky their husbands must be!

Bob and Ruth are headed for trouble. They are good people who had an exciting romance but now suffer from intimacy disorder. They depend on each other in unhealthy ways. Their marriage can become healthy, but they must make some major changes. Bob and Ruth need help to achieve and manage change. Contracts for change can help couples grow in their relationships. In this lesson you will consider six of these contracts. As you will see, some of them can be applied not just to marriage, but to other relationships as well. The contracts we will consider appear in the margin.

This lesson is a key for your entire study. You will require extra time for this lesson. You cannot complete all of these contracts quickly. You will need to work on this section for an extended time and refer to this lesson again and again.

## SIX CONTRACTS FOR CHANGE

Sexuality
Fighting
Communication
Roles
Play
Spirituality

## Sexuality

When we marry, most of us assume our sexual relationship automatically will be healthy. At first, it may be; romance and newness sometimes override other issues. Sooner or later, our past traumas, ignorances, shame, and fears take over. Frequency, initiation, and the mechanics of our sexual relationship can become problems. Very few things create as much anger in relationship as sexual problems.

For those of you who are married you may want to share your work from lesson 5 of unit 2 with your spouse and invite him or her to work with you on it. Remember that some of this conversation may be very difficult for you. You may need to enlist the aid of a professional counselor, particularly if you are experiencing sexual dysfunction. You may need to deal with the following issues related to your sexuality contract:

**Education.** Participate in some form of Christian sexual education. (Be advised: many secular approaches to sex education teach immoral values. They use what is, in effect, pornography in a misguided attempt to solve sexual problems.) Many Christian marriage books provide excellent tips on how each partner can bring pleasure to the other. Tell each other what you like or don't like, and what you would enjoy adding to your sexual experience.

**Frequency.** Negotiate expectations about how often sex will occur in a week or a month. Beware of the trap of thinking that good sex is always "spontaneous" and that sex must always be connected to dramatic romantic moments. Planning for sex may insure that it doesn't get neglected in our busyness and fatigue.

**Initiation.** Most relationships have a primary initiator, the one who always raises the issue. Discuss your relationship up to this point and negotiate for a shared balance. If you or your partner has a problem with initiating, consider whether unresolved issues from the past such as sexual shame, trauma, or abuse might cause the reluctance. Any of these problems may be reasons for professional counseling.

**Abstinence.** Some couples use periods of abstinence to remove the pressures of sex from their relationship. During this time of abstinence the lack of sexual tension will allow more intense work on other areas of the relationship. Sexual abstinence is like a fast. It can enhance the emotional and spiritual nature of a relationship. Periods of abstinence must be mutually negotiated for a specific period of time.

> Those of you who have experienced sexual trauma and addiction will need to work through these issues first before you even try negotiating a healthy sexuality contract. Part 2 of this workbook will deal more directly with overcoming sexual addiction. Shelter from the Storm can help those who suffer from the trauma of sexual abuse.

Sexuality contracts can also help in other relationships. In Bob and Ruth's story you noticed the sexual tension in their Sunday School class. Sexual tension exists in many of our relationships at church, at work, and in our other friendships. If we never talk about it, the power of those temptations stays secret, festers, and may explode.

Since we are always sexual beings, we exist with a level of sexual temptation whenever we're in a mixed gender setting. Knowing that I am male and that others in the room are female, sensing an attraction to some that is beyond my attraction to others, and enjoying the opportunity to be around those persons—these are normal, healthy sexual dynamics.

This healthy awareness of the sexual dynamics in male-female relationships is a far cry from falling prey to sexual temptation. Lust takes the sexual energy beyond its harmless and engaging quality and transforms it into the power to hurt and destroy. Lust is the selfish use of another human for my own sexual gratification. When thoughts of attraction turn to thoughts of sexual actions, I have stepped across the line of appropriate behavior. (Remember that thoughts are behaviors.) Monitoring my thought life will enable me to effectively manage sexual tensions in relationships.

You can combat sexual tension in relationships with the following two strategies:

**KEY POINT**
When we talk about sex it takes the power of the temptation away.

1. If you feel sexual temptation, talking about it with someone you trust (like your *Faithful & True* support group, another support group, or a 12-step group) will help to keep you accountable. This also serves to take the power of the temptation away. Talking about temptation removes the secrecy that adds the power and excitement of danger to the feeling.
2. In church groups, the workplace, or any other organization, sexual boundaries should be very specifically defined. We will not act on any sexual feelings or temptations. We will avoid situations that lead to such behaviors. We will actively guard our hearts.

❏ Contract negotiated.

✎ Check the box in the margin when you have discussed and developed a sexuality contract with your spouse or with your support community.

## Fighting

Everyone experiences hostile emotions. We need the skills to deal with these powerful emotions in healthy and positive ways. A fighting contract means we develop healthy ways to express anger and resentment.

✎ What kind of situations or behaviors make you feel unsafe? In the following list circle those circumstances that have made you feel unsafe in the past.

- using profanity
- hitting or other forms of physical violence
- throwing things
- yelling and screaming
- making blaming statement

- fighting in front of the kids
- threatening divorce or separation
- leaving or "exiting" during the fight
- fighting when both people are too tired to be rational
- other _____

These are just a few. Every relationship is different. Review your list. What do you or the other person do that causes you to feel unsafe?

✎ Now create some fighting rules. What do you need for a safe environment and what rules do you need to be more comfortable having an honest disagreement?

_____

_____

_____

_____

_____

> Some counselors say that men use sex to make up—to resolve issues and to feel close—while women want sex after the relationship feels close. This difference can cause him to feel rejected and her to feel he's not taking the relationship seriously.

You may find that certain locations feel safer. Deb and I discovered that a certain restaurant created safety for us. It also allowed us to be away from the children. Yelling and screaming were much more difficult. Other rules that you might follow include:

- Take personal responsibility for your own contribution to the problem.
- Express your anger or resentment in non-threatening ways. Don't threaten divorce or separation. Don't leave in the middle of the conversation.
- Don't rehearse every past instance that proves your point.
- Have a time limit, don't argue into the middle of the night when both people are too tired to be rational.
- Take time outs if you need to cool down.
- Reschedule a fight if you don't finish.
- Search for cooperative solutions. Negotiate.
- Seek to listen to your partner's anger. It is a gift he or she gives you. Your partner is taking a risk. Anger may be a powerful evidence that he or she cares about you.
- Pray before you start.
- Make "I" statements, not "you" statements.

Again, these are just a few suggestions. Review the list of safety rules. Have your spouse or friend do the same exercise and compare notes. Create a combined list of safety rules that you can use for a safe and fair "fight."

Because of past hurts some couples simply cannot abide by rules without help. If you need help, one of your rules in the early stages may be that you will only bring up or confront an issue in the presence of a counselor, pastor, other couple, or friend.

Some people in relationship don't fight. Both people are just too afraid to bring issues out into the open. In this case schedule a time together on a regular basis. During the week before you meet, make out a list entitled "Things that made me angry this past week." When you get together exchange lists and talk about them if you can.

✎ **Check the box in the margin when you have negotiated your fighting contract.**

❑ **Fighting contract completed.**

## Communication

Poor communication doesn't mean both people don't know how to talk. It means they don't know how to listen. Communication contracts include ways to practice talking and listening. You can employ many strategies to improve communication. Have you ever had a conversation in which your volume steadily increased? Maybe your spouse or partner did the same thing. Raised volume indicates that the speaker doesn't feel heard.

✎ **In the next two paragraphs look for and underline specific actions to improve communication. After you have underlined all the actions you can find, circle two specific actions you will seek to apply this week.**

One of the most basic communication rules is to take turns talking. For a prescribed period of time (for example, 5 minutes) only one person may talk. The other person must listen. Both people get equal time. Another strategy is to repeat back to the other person what you think he or she said. Allow your partner to say it again until you get it right.

Make "I" statements, not "you" statements. When you begin a statement with "you," it usually alerts the other person to be on the defensive because blame usually follows. Even starting, "I feel _____ when you _____," may change this dynamic. A communication contract may include a specific time to talk. This may be as basic as agreeing to talk for 30 minutes every Sunday night at eight. Like my wife and I, you may agree to go someplace away from home to have these conversations. Hold yourselves accountable to this commitment. Ask someone else to hold you accountable if you find it difficult to maintain this contract.

✎ **Negotiate with your spouse or friend which of the strategies you will try. Check the box in the margin when you complete your communication contract.**

❑ **Communication contract completed.**

## Roles

Many relationships flounder because of different expectations about who is going to fulfill certain roles. Some common roles that couples have problems with in marriage include:

| | | |
|---|---|---|
| • Earning money | • Housecleaning | • Disciplining children |
| • Laundry | • Managing money | • Cooking |
| • Yard work | • Attending school functions | |

These are just a few. Couples need to negotiate their expectations about each role. Some of those expectations may be based on old family modeling. For example, if you grew up in a family in which the father always managed the money, you may expect the man to deal with finances. Conflict can result if the woman wants to be involved.

> Talk with your spouse about any anger or resentment that either of you feel about roles. Explore who played those roles in your families of origin. Negotiate who is going to fill those roles now. You may have to make some changes. You may feel awkward or angry. Talk about your feelings as you monitor your progress.

❏ Role contract completed.

✎ Check the box in the margin when you have negotiated a role contract.

## Play

Many people in relationships don't know how to have fun or play together. Some of us have forgotten how. In the next unit we will explore how to get back in touch with your sense of play. In a marriage, don't assume that you can just go back to your dating period and remember how you had fun together. You may have been so busy trying to please the other person that you never stated what you enjoyed doing. You may have to remember back to your childhood to find what you are good at playing.

Some couples do not play because they have communication and fighting problems. They simply have trouble being together. Make sure your contract is in place before you try to play. Contract together to go out on a date. Find a regular baby-sitter if you need one. Experiment with what is fun. Be silly. Roll down a hill. Have a snowball fight. Swing in swings. Play in a sandbox.

People in other than marital relationships also need to experience play. Often we take ourselves too seriously. We sometimes are guilty of thinking that our work, our friendship, our church activities are too serious to play. Remember that play is a way of re-creating ourselves so we will be more productive at other times. Plan in this relationship for times of play.

❏ Play contract completed.

✎ In the margin check the box when you have contracted for play time together.

## Spirituality

Like Bob and Ruth in our opening story, you may find that you don't have a spiritual life in your relationship. Many of us are good at individual spirituality but don't do anything together. Our relationship with God is the most intimate and important relationship. If we experience shame which leads to intimacy problems, that shame will most profoundly affect the spiritual dimension of our relationship.

> Discuss whether you feel embarrassed to pray together and why.

All relationships should establish a spirituality contract. What will you do to bring spirituality into your relationship? Following are some sample ideas:

• Do a Bible study course together.
• Read a book of prayers aloud to each other.
• Attend a Sunday School class and do the assignments together.
• Take a trip to a place that has spiritual significance to you.
• Ask another couple to work with you as spiritual mentors.
• Go to church together and discuss the sermon.
• Read a devotion together.
• Go on a retreat together. Your church has information about possibilities (see page 222).

As with the other contracts, agree on regular times to complete the activities you choose.

❑ Spirituality contract completed.

✎ Check the box when you've negotiated a spirituality contract.

You now have a list of six contracts. This is a start. All contracts can be re-negotiated and changed as needed. Be creative. Be patient. Be gentle with yourself. Many of these skills take a lifetime to develop fully. The effort required is worthwhile as you experience greater intimacy and less loneliness.

## Assignment for the Lesson

➤ You have done a lot of work. Take a break. Do something nice for yourself.

➤ Say the following affirmation five times.

I can make changes. I can take risks. I can be in healthy relationships.

➤ Pray for your spouse or a friend.

LESSON

5

# Restoring Trust

You already know my story from the introduction. You do not know Deb's story, the story of a wife damaged by sexual sin. As a pastor's wife, Deb suddenly lost the congregation she was a part of because her husband, the pastor, had to leave. Deb read about her husband's adultery on the front page of the local newspaper. She had to decide what to tell her children. She heard the unspoken comments, "If she had been a better wife, maybe this fine man of God wouldn't have done the things he did." Deb's is the story of a woman whose heart and trust were broken.

I can't begin to describe the courage and strength Deb displayed. I can only thank God for this remarkable woman in my life. Deb's story has been one of hurt and anger, lots of support and therapy, and of dedication to restoring the marriage. She did not look for ways to blame her husband for his sins. Instead she worked to understand her contribution to the loneliness of a relationship. Deb and Mark's story is the account of a couple who have worked to restore trust and intimacy in their marriage.

This lesson is for everyone. For those who have experienced a breech of trust in your relationship, such as sexual sin, this lesson is about restoration of trust. For those who seek to build a trusting relationship, it is about the things you must practice to build trust.

We have been blessed to know many couples struggling to restore or rebuild trust. They have taught us much. We have tried to condense their wisdom into seven principles of trust building. Those seven principles appear below. Healthy trust must be:

- **Christ Centered**
- **Committed**
- **Continuing**
- **Communicating**
- **Consistent**
- **Considerate**
- **Control Surrendered**

> For this reason a man will leave his father and mother and be united to his wife, and they will become one flesh.
> —Genesis 2:24

## Christ Centered

Marriage is unique among human relationships because marriage pictures Jesus' love for the church. In his letter to the Ephesians, Paul describes marriage as a stage where we play out our relationship to Jesus in front of others. Through the marriage relationship a man and a woman become one flesh. They are a unity made up of two individuals. Have you heard children say, "my parents." Parents are a collective unity in the minds of the children. A spiritual union occurs between a man and a woman in marriage. It is God-ordained.

All relationships are sacred. We are brothers and sisters in Christ. All of our relationships must be Christ centered. Recognizing this sacredness will help us understand the seriousness of our trust-building work.

➤ For all relationships in which you seek to build trust, pray with your spouse, family member, or friend. Thank God for your union in Christ.

## Committed

Sometimes we agree to something before we feel like doing it. When we seek to build trust, we may not feel trust, but we can be committed to try. Recognizing the Christ-centered nature of relationships, we can want to trust. This is important. It signals to our spouse, family member, or friend that we will exert the emotional and spiritual effort required to build trust.

 Sign below if you are willing to be committed to build trust. Have your spouse, family member, or friend sign also.

*We are committed to trust each other.*

_____      _____

## Continuing

Many times when a sexual sinner repents of the sexual sin, he wants his partner to trust him immediately. He may even quote various Scriptures about forgiveness to win his argument. Is this request really fair and reasonable? I think not. Damaged emotions and wounded spirits take time to heal. With God's help and lots of support, they will. The healing, however, is a process. Those of us who have damaged trust must recognize that our partners will be grieving a loss, the loss of their trust. Grieving takes time.

When we first talked to our oldest son about his new driver's license and being able to drive the car by himself, we set some limits. He objected and said, "Don't you trust me?" The answer is that we are in a Christ-centered relationship with our son in which we seek to guide and protect him. We are committed to trusting him. He has never done anything to damage our trust. This is a new experience of driving, however, and building trust will be a process over time. He will earn our trust on an ongoing basis.

➤ If you have damaged trust, tell your spouse that you are willing to be patient and you understand that trust building is a process. If you have not damaged trust through sexual sin, talk with your spouse about how you can strengthen the trust in your relationship.

## Communicating

In the previous lesson we talked about communication contracts. Building trust demands communication. Few things damage trust as much as feeling the other person isn't being honest. Make sure that you schedule regular times to talk and that you have strategies in place for being honest about feelings.

Remember the shame core belief that says, "No one will like me as I am." This belief has caused some of us to withhold information or lie about some of our past and present behaviors. Our partners can interpret these behaviors to mean we really don't love them, otherwise we'd tell the truth. Developing trust can mean that we take the time to tell about our past—even the sinful behaviors. The thought of doing this can be really frightening. We are afraid of losing those close to us if they react negatively.

➤ **Ask yourself the question, "Do I really want to live the rest of my life wondering,** *"If my spouse finds out _____ about me, will he or she be repulsed and leave me?"*

Keep these things in mind concerning truth telling:

1. Never tell the truth to punish someone else. For example, "If you had been a better wife I wouldn't have had to go out and have that affair. Now I'm going to tell you about it." This does not mean that you should hide the truth to avoid hurting the other person. The key is your intention. If you are telling the truth for the purpose of developing intimacy and building trust, then the process can be healing.

2. Never tell the truth to manipulate forgiveness. For example, "I'm going to tell you the truth, the whole truth, and nothing but the truth. Now you need to forgive me and we need to move on." This "forgive and forget" strategy is selfish and doesn't take into account the other person's pain and the time it may take to heal.

3. Never use learning about someone else's past as an opportunity to punish the person for telling the truth. Do not assume that knowing about some past failure justifies your becoming hyper-vigilant to watch for symptoms of sinful behavior in the future.

You need to get feedback from your group about your motives for truth telling.

➤ **Write down the information about yourself you need to tell your spouse, family member, or friend in order to build trust.**

_____

_____

## Consistent

Consistent behavior over time builds trust. If you say you are going to change a behavior, you need to make that change. In the case of addictive behavior this is called *maintaining sobriety*. If you pledge to do something, such as remain faithful to a marriage vow, you must be consistent in your performance of your vows over time.

Some marriages have involved lies for years. Restoring trust may not take years, but it certainly will not take just a few days or weeks. Behavior that is consistently repentant, humble, and corrected will eventually heal the wounds.

I have often seen persons who have repented of sexual sins tell their spouse, "You can trust me now." Such expectations are rather naive. If lies, deceptions, and various inconsistent behaviors have been a part of the past, you must demonstrate now that you are different. You must be able to do so over time.

Consistency applies to all behaviors. If you say you're going to be home for dinner at six o'clock, be home at six o'clock. Keep your promises. Do what you say you're going to do. If something comes up that prevents you from doing so, offer explanations that are not self-serving or blaming.

## Considerate

If trust has been violated in your relationship by your sinful behaviors, you have damaged your partner. You must be considerate of this. This means several things:

1. Don't expect your partner's feelings to heal overnight.
2. Expect current events to occasionally trigger past pain.
3. Be willing to listen to your partner's pain no matter how old it is.

Rich had a number of affairs years ago. He confessed, repented, and has been faithful ever since. Kate has forgiven him, and the consistency of Rich's behavior has helped her to trust him again. One day, however, Kate saw Rich talking to an attractive woman at church. Although the encounter involved nothing sexual, Kate remembered her past pain. She felt hurt and angry, and she stormed out of church.

✎ **Rich has two response choices. Pick which one you think will build trust faster.**

❏ Rich can get angry with Kate. He can say, "Don't you trust me after all these years. You embarrassed me by storming out of church. What you saw was nothing."
❏ Rich could find Kate and say, "I can see that my talking with that woman must have looked bad. Can you tell me about your hurt? If you'd like, I'm willing to explain that nothing was going on with her."

Rich must be willing on an ongoing basis to accept that one of the consequences of his sin is the damage done to Kate. While he desperately wants her not to be hurt and he is honestly embarrassed by her reaction, expressing his anger is not a good choice.

Being considerate of the needs and emotions (however unique they may be) of your spouse, family members, or friends will build trust.

## Control Surrender

Our love and trust relationship with Jesus Christ demonstrates building trust. We surrender our lives to Christ and give up control. This surrender is moment-by-moment, not a one-time decision. We find joy, peace, and eternal life in return. We must be willing to give up our lives to get them back. Surrendering control over the actions of spouses, family members, or friends works the same way. We can't control their behavior, keep them liking or loving us, or prevent them from sin. They must be motivated on their own. We must be willing even to give up our relationship in order to get it back. We must surrender our partners to God's care. This applies to all relationships. Think of times when you had to let go:

• Your child learns to walk, you let go of his hands.
• Your child goes to school, you waved good-bye.
• Your child learns to drive, you gave her the keys.
• Your child gets married, you gave her away.

➤ **Recall the joy and peace of being saved by Christ. Reaffirm your surrender to God and surrender your relationships to Him as well.**

## Assignment for the Lesson

➤ Say the following affirmation five times.

I can trust. I surrender my trying to control others. I am trustworthy.

➤ Pray for those whose trust you have damaged.

## Discussion Group Questions

- Discuss the difference between healthy and unhealthy shame. Give an example of how you feel each type of shame.
- Respond to the four shame-core beliefs. To what degree do they tend to affect your life? Which has the greatest impact on you? Which has the least?
- Has fear of rejection caused you to withhold information about yourself? Describe.
- Discuss the key concept that "The person(s) you are most afraid of losing will be the one(s) to whom you are least likely to tell the truth."
- How does the core belief that "No one will take care of my needs but me" contribute to addictive behaviors?
- Of the characteristics of healthy and unhealthy intimacy on pages 63-65, describe one characteristic that is a strength and one that is a weakness in your life.
- Discuss the checklist of symptoms on page 67. Choose the one(s) with which you struggle most.

---

Notes
1. Adapted from Pat Carnes, *Out of the Shadows*, (Minneapolis: CompCare Pubs., 1983).
2. Mark Laaser, Deb Laaser, Pat Carnes, *Couples in Recovery*, (Minnetonka, MN: Positive Living Press, 1994).

# The Personal Dimension

## FOCAL PASSAGE

*The word of the Lord came to me, saying, "Before I formed you in the womb I knew you, before you were born I set you apart; I appointed you as a prophet to the nations." "Ah, Sovereign Lord," I said, "I do not know how to speak; I am only a child."*

—Jeremiah 1:4-6

## MEMORY VERSE

"A time is coming, and has come, when you will be scattered, each to his own home. You will leave me all alone. Yet I am not alone, for my Father is with me."
–John 16:32

### NEAL'S STORY

Neal struggles with many sexual temptations. His struggle began when he was four or five years old. He was the victim of sexual abuse by two of his older sisters. They undressed in front of him, teased him about his body and about being a boy, and touched him in places he did not want to be touched.

Today, Neal struggles to understand why he lusts after pornography, strippers, and prostitutes. He is married and has a family. His wife does not know about his preoccupations. She is sexually available to him but wonders why he doesn't ask more often. Neal feels bored with sex with his wife. He has no idea how to talk with her about his problem, much less to discuss his emotions. While it is not his wife's fault, Neal does not trust her to understand. Neal feels bored with life. He has gone from job to job, never really finding anything that he enjoys. He has no hobbies or forms of recreation. He feels angry with his wife but cannot talk about his anger.

Neal was wounded as a child. He doesn't know yet how much this has affected him. His abuse created fear about sex, confusion about himself as a man, sexual dysfunction with his wife, and anger that he doesn't understand. Neal is intelligent but bored with his life. What will he do? The allure of sex and other temptations call out to him.

## GROWTH GOAL

In this unit you will learn how your emotions, ability to trust, sense of identity and purpose affect you. You will discover how problems with trust, emotions, and identity lead to problems with anger, stress, and loneliness. This combination can help to create the fire of sexual temptation.

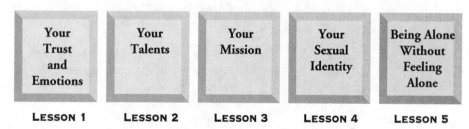

| Your Trust and Emotions | Your Talents | Your Mission | Your Sexual Identity | Being Alone Without Feeling Alone |
|---|---|---|---|---|
| LESSON 1 | LESSON 2 | LESSON 3 | LESSON 4 | LESSON 5 |

# Your Trust and Emotions

*Then little children were brought to Jesus for him to place his hands on them and pray for them. But the disciples rebuked those who brought them. Jesus said, "Let the little children come to me, and do not hinder them, for the kingdom of heaven belongs to such as these."*

—Matthew 19:13-14

✎ **What do you think Jesus meant about the kingdom of heaven and children? From the list below select the statement you believe best describes Jesus' purpose.**

❑ You must stop thinking like an adult and think like a child to go to heaven.
❑ In heaven, we will be carefree like little children.
❑ The kingdom of heaven involves a trust like that of little children.
❑ Only children will be able to get into heaven.

One of the points of this story is the importance of being a little child. Earlier, in Matthew 18:3, Jesus says that unless we become like a child we will not enter the kingdom of God. Like the disciples, we also have trouble with childlike qualities. What is it about us that needs to be more childlike? Certainly one characteristic, if not the main one, is the ability to be more trusting. Children have the innate ability to trust. Until they learn otherwise from parents, friends, life experiences, or culture, children trust others for their needs. I selected the third response in the learning activity above.

✎ **Can you think of a time in your childhood when your trust was betrayed, when someone you looked to for care somehow disappointed you, let you down, or hurt you? If so, write a brief description of the event. You might want to include who betrayed you, and what effect this incident had on your ability to trust others.**

_____

_____

_____

We must allow these wounds to be healed. A healthy relationship with God and with each other requires the ability to exercise childlike trust.

How do we develop the ability to trust? First, recognize that we all have the ability. We decide to exercise trust every day. When we turn the key, we trust our car will start. When we drive through a green light, we trust that someone else will stop at the red light. When we get in an airplane, we trust that the pilot knows what he is doing. When we see a doctor, we trust that she knows enough to help us. When we have surgery, we trust the surgeon to cut us open and somehow put us back together again.

We need courage to trust combined with the ability to identify trustworthy people. Trusting others is a choice we make. We choose to trust or distrust, based on our life experiences. Trusting God involves no risk. He will not violate our trust. Trusting others, however, involves some risk. Probably, everyone has violated a trust and been a victim of someone else's violation. We have to be willing to take the risk of a violation if we are to experience intimacy with others. We need the skill to identify trustworthy people and to trust them in appropriate ways.

✎ With whom would you like to be more trusting? List at least three people.

_____

_____

_____

Children express their emotions and trust. The tiniest baby expresses emotions so that those around know when he is unhappy or experiencing a problem. As we grow up, we begin to hide our emotions. Those around us may have no idea what we are feeling. If we cannot talk about our emotions, we cannot be intimate and have a relationship with Christ or anyone else. We doom ourselves, therefore, to loneliness. Loneliness is one of the feelings that Satan uses to tempt us in a variety of ways, including sexually.

In Part 2 we will talk more about how our families have affected our expression of emotions. Right now, let us assume that all families deal with emotions differently. Some families are very emotional, sometimes too much so. Other families are stoic; they don't talk about feelings. Most families are comfortable with some emotions and uncomfortable with others.

✎ Following is a list of emotions. As you read each emotion, try to remember how your family dealt with them. Recall a time when you felt that emotion. Ask yourself if you were able to express your emotion appropriately. Then for each emotion rate yourself from one to five, with five being excellent and one being poor, on how well you can express these emotions today.

| Emotion | Score |
|---|---|
| Fear | _____ |
| Anxiety | _____ |
| Anger | _____ |
| Sadness | _____ |
| Loneliness | _____ |
| Envy/Jealousy | _____ |
| Attraction (likes and dislikes) | _____ |
| Love | _____ |
| Hate | _____ |
| Boredom | _____ |
| Awe and Wonder | _____ |
| Curiosity | _____ |
| *Total* | _____ |

If you scored a 50-60, you are good at expressing emotions. If you scored between 12 and 24, you are a rather numb or stoic person. Do you see how it could be difficult for anyone to get to know you? Note that some people score high because they deny reality.

✎ Think again of the story of Jesus and the little children. Imagine yourself as a little child in the crowd that day. You wanted to see Jesus. Think of the disciples that try to keep you away. Hear the voice of Jesus telling you to come anyway. Can you picture being close to our Savior? Oh, how wonderful that would be! Below write what you would tell Jesus.

_____

_____

What a glorious day it will be when we have the opportunity to talk with Jesus face-to-face! Right now, however, we can talk to children of God, including our spouses. How wonderful to get to know each other better!

## Assignment for the Lesson

➤ Pick one person that you selected with whom you want to develop more trust. Tell that person how you feel today.

✎ Begin to memorize the Scripture memory verse for this unit. Write the verse on a card and carry it with you. Whenever you get a drink of water, review the passage.

➤ Say the following affirmation five times.

I am a trusting person. I can express my feelings.

➤ Pray for your spouse or closest friend.

LESSON
2

# Your Talents

Jesus said that the kingdom of heaven is like a man who went on a journey and gave his servants responsibility to care for his possessions while he was away. He gave one servant five talents (a talent was a measure of money, but the principles in the parable also apply to our gifts and abilities). He gave a second servant two talents, and to a third he gave only one talent. When the man returned, he demanded an accounting from the servants. The servant who received five talents gained five more. Likewise, the servant who received two talents doubled his money. The master commended both of these servants and rewarded them with greater responsibility.

> His master replied, "Well done, good and faithful servant! You have been faithful with a few things; I will put you in charge of many things. Come and share your master's happiness!"
> Then the man who had received the one talent came. "Master," he said, "I knew that you are a hard man, harvesting where you have not sown and gathering where you have not scattered seed. So I was afraid and went out and hid your talent in the ground. See, here is what belongs to you."
> His master replied, "You wicked, lazy servant! So you knew that I harvest where I have not sown and gather where I have not scattered seed? Well then, you should have put my money on deposit with the bankers, so that when I returned I would have received it back with interest.
> "Take the talent from him and give it to the one who has the ten talents. For everyone who has will be given more, and he will have an abundance. Whoever does not have, even what he has will be taken from him. And throw that worthless servant outside, into the darkness, where there will be weeping and gnashing of teeth."
>
> —Matthew 25:23-30

Does this story scare you just a little? It always has scared me. All of us spend time wondering if we are using our "talents" the way God wants and if they will bring a return?

This story contains two important elements. First, we must identify our talents. Second, we must risk using them.

## Conversations with Our Parents

Garrison Keillor, a famous humorist from my home state, has said he often has phone calls from his dad that always end, "Son, you never call me. Why don't you ever call me?" Garrison says, "Dad, I don't have to call you on the phone. I have conversations with you every hour of every day in my mind."

How many of us have those conversations with our parents? Do they approve of us? Do they think we are doing a good job? What do they think of our talents and abilities?

✎ **Describe a typical conversation with one or both of your parents in which you have a sense either of approval or disapproval from the parent.**

_____

_____

Perhaps you never have felt approval from your parents—that you can never do anything right. This kind of experience can lead you to believe that you have no talent. Or such experience can drive you to prove the parent wrong. Either way you continue to react to and be controlled by the parent.

✎ **Have you ever sought through money, status, or power to prove to yourself that you have talent or that others approve of you?** ❑ Yes ❑ No

Families use powerful methods to shape and control children. For example, some families assign names like "Uncle Bill the Doctor" to show what behaviors, vocations, and talents the family values. At other times the family may tell stories about the child's successes or failures to live up to the family expectations. These methods press the child into the mold of the family's choosing.

In a healthy family situation the children receive love, discipline, and affirmation. They discover for themselves God's purpose and what they want to do with their lives. Unfortunately, in many families the parents seek to live out their own unfulfilled hopes through the children. Thus the children do not have opportunity to discover their talents and dreams for themselves.

✎ **Can you recall a story that was repeated in your family, a story that told what you were or were not good at, or that told you what the family expected you to be or to do? Below describe one or more such stories.**

_____

_____

_____

Family choices sometimes conflict with what God chooses and with a realistic evaluation of our hopes, dreams, and talents. We often live in anger and frustration as a result of not exercising our God-given talents. We may be filled with rage and not understand the source of our frustration and anger.

- working
- playing
- laughing
- reading/Telling stories
- organizing
- cleaning
- public speaking
- thinking of others
- cutting the grass
- working on cars
- affirming others
- visiting the sick
- coaching
- teaching
- cooking

Below make a list of things that you have been good at. What have been your accomplishments? What have others told you you're good at? List them even if you don't believe it. Don't just think of the glamorous things in life. You may need to refer to the list of examples that appear in the margin.

_____    _____

_____    _____

_____    _____

_____    _____

Have you used your talents? ❑ Yes ❑ No If not, why not? In the list below check any of the excuses you have used and add any others you have used.

❑ I'm really not that good at it.
❑ People will think that I'm conceited if I do that.
❑ There's too much responsibility in doing it.
❑ I won't be able to do it again.
❑ Someone else is much better at it than me.
❑ I'll never do it perfectly.
❑ I'm too old to do that.
❑ People won't like me if I do that.
❑ It will take too much of my time.
❑ People don't really care about (or need) me to do that.
❑ I'll fail or mess up and be embarrassed.
❑ I could never make a living doing that.
❑ My parents (Mom and/or Dad) don't like me doing that.
❑ It's a silly and frivolous thing to do.
❑ (other)_____.

A meaningless life leads to the Land of Numb where we can feel important, at least in our own minds. In the next lesson we'll look at using our talents to create a mission for ourselves. Are you willing to take the risk that you may need to take to use your talents?

## Assignment for the Lesson

➤ Ask someone you trust to give you feedback on any talents you think you may have.

➤ In the margin write your Scripture memory verse for this unit. Check your work from your Scripture memory card.

➤ Repeat the following affirmation:

I have many God given talents and I can use them to God's glory.

➤ Consider the following Scripture and pray for God to show you your talents.

*There are different kinds of gifts, but the same Spirit. There are different kinds of service, but the same Lord. There are different kinds of working, but the same God works all of them in all men.*

—1 Corinthians 12:4-6

# Your Mission

Matt usually did what everybody told him to do. He was a man of many talents, good at almost everything he tried. His parents were the first to make suggestions as to what he should do. Then, his friends always seemed to know what was best for him. His wife frequently told him what he should do to fulfill his purpose in life. His pastor, also, had many suggestions about what God's will might be for his life. Everyone gave Matt affirmations when he did a good job at those things that they thought he should do.

Matt was an expert at accepting instructions from others, but he was not very good at accepting affirmations. While he knew what everyone else wanted, he didn't know what *Matt* wanted to do. He just knew he was frustrated and unhappy. He did not like going to work. He was angry at his boss. Matt felt he did not make enough money.

The only good thing at work, lately, was a new woman who had joined their office group. She was recently divorced and seemed very friendly. At least, Matt finally had something to look forward to when he went to work.

**VOCATION:**
From the Latin word for voice. It literally means to be called.

No one has ever encouraged Matt to find his true calling or mission in life. Everyone thought they knew what was best for him. Certainly his many talents lent themselves to many different interpretations. Matt's frustrations and anger will lead him into sin if he isn't careful. The excitement of sex might be more powerfully tempting in the face of an unfulfilled life.

In the last lesson you considered identifying your real talents. In this lesson consider how you might weave those talents into a tapestry that is your true calling and mission. To do so you may have to clear away some other voices. In lesson 2 you identified what others may consider are your talents. The same voices may be speaking to you about what your mission should be.

✎ **When I think about what I'm supposed to do with my life, the voice I most often hear is (check one):**

❑ My Father      ❑ My Uncle or Aunt
❑ My Brother      ❑ My Friend(s)
❑ My Mother      ❑ My Teacher
❑ My Sister      ❑ My Pastor
❑ My Spouse      ❑ Other _____

If you checked any of those boxes you have certain tapes in your head that you rewind and replay over and over again. Why do some of us do that? A variety of reasons exist.

✎ **If you have allowed others to make your life decisions for you, check the reason you've used the most:**

❑ The person I hear represents spiritual authority to me.
❑ The person I hear will be mad at me if I don't do what he says.
❑ The person I hear will leave me if I don't conform to her picture for my life.
❑ This person knows better than I do; I can't figure my life out.
❑ Whenever I decide things, I always mess up.

These are just a few of the thoughts we use to continue a pattern of allowing other people to take our responsibility from us. We need to assume responsibility for our own lives.

### How did God make you fast?

The movie *Chariots of Fire* told of two runners training for the 1924 Olympic Games. The first runner was Jewish and from England. He ran to gain the title *the world's fastest human*, the symbol of which would be winning the 100-meter dash in the Olympics. He was a driven perfectionist. In many ways he was striving to overcome a critical father and centuries of prejudice against Jewish people. When he won the gold medal, his victory was hollow and depressing. Winning did not bring him what he hoped.

The other runner, Eric Liddel, was a Christian from Scotland. He was studying to finish his theological degree so that he could return to work with his missionary parents in China. His sister, Jenny, was with him making sure that he stayed on task. Along the way he discovered that he was a good runner, so he began to train for the Olympics.

The training bothered Jenny. She thought that it was a waste of time. She chided her brother to finish the "real" work of his theological studies. Eric took her on a walk and gently told her, "Jenny, I know that the Lord made me for China. But, he also made me fast. When I run, I feel His pleasure. Not to run would be to disappoint God."

Eric Liddel's story illustrates two very important questions that you also need to ask yourself:
  1. How did the Lord make you fast?
  2. What are you doing when you feel His pleasure?

The first question asks about talents. What did the Lord create you with the talent to do? How did He make you "fast"? You explored your talents in lesson 2. You are "fast" when you are living out of the talents and gifts God gave you.

When you are using your talents, you should feel joy and God's pleasure. This is your mission. Don't be confused. This is not a matter, necessarily, of making money or of doing something productive in the eyes of the world. Nor is it a matter of feeling sensual pleasure. It is a matter of being in touch with God's will for your life and of experiencing the satisfaction of knowing you are serving Him.

✎ When you are working at cross purposes to God's will for your life, you will experience some of the following symptoms. Check any that you have felt:

❑ anger ❑ feeling stuck ❑ sense of meaninglessness
❑ resentment ❑ boredom ❑ lack of purpose
❑ frustration ❑ feeling like a failure

✎ Here, on the other hand, are a few symptoms that result when you are in touch with God's will for your life. Check any that you have felt. Then describe what you were doing when you felt that result:

| *Symptom* | *The last time I felt this I was:* |
| --- | --- |
| ❑ joy | _____ |
| ❑ peace | _____ |
| ❑ happiness | _____ |
| ❑ contentment | _____ |
| ❑ fulfillment | _____ |
| ❑ productive | _____ |

**KEY POINT**
Don't be confused by thinking that you have to feel good feelings all the time to be doing what God wants. Evil is at work in the world and will often tempt you with negative feelings to throw you off track.

This last exercise may give you some clues about your mission. Remember that whatever you wrote may not be a matter of making money or of being "productive." No book can lead you in enough directions to know exactly what your mission is. Continue to discover God's plan through prayer and following God's leading.

When you weave your talents into a tapestry of calling and mission you will experience the symptoms described above. You may also experience another symptom. You can work at your calling and often have more energy than you need. Read Isaiah 40:31 in the margin. If you are in touch with your calling and mission, you will know what this means. God's strength does not mean you will not struggle, but as you remain faithful He supplies strength for the struggle.

The symptoms I have discussed are internal signs of finding your mission. At least three outward signs of being on the right track also exist:

Those who hope in the Lord will renew their strength. They will soar on wings like eagles; they will run and not grow weary, they will walk and not be faint.
—Isaiah 40:31

## YOUR CALLING AND MISSION WILL BE

- Of service
- Meaningful to yourself and others
- An honor and glory to God

Once you think you know your calling and mission, the real challenge begins. You must have the courage to do it. This will be in spite of your doubts like:

- I'm not worthy.
- I can't do it.
- I won't be able to support myself.
- Others won't approve (like those voices in your head).
- It's really not that big of a deal.

The 12 steps of Alcoholics Anonymous tell us what we need to do with these doubts. Step 3 says that we: "Made a decision to turn our will and our lives over to the care of God as we understood him."

Pursuing your calling and mission is a matter of surrender to God followed by obedience.

### Assignment for the Lesson

➤ Pray about your mission. Write down a mission statement for yourself (if you can). Share your thoughts or your written statement with your *Faithful & True* group.

✎ Below write your Scripture memory verse for this unit. You may check your work on page 79.

_____

_____

➤ Say the following affirmation five times:

I surrender the will and control of my life to God. I trust Him to show me my mission.

➤ **Read Galatians 5:17-21. Pray that you will find God's pleasure.**

*The sinful nature desires what is contrary to the Spirit, and the Spirit what is contrary to the sinful nature. They are in conflict with each other, so that you do not do what you want. But if you are led by the Spirit, you are not under law.*

*The acts of the sinful nature are obvious: sexual immorality, impurity and debauchery; idolatry and witchcraft; hatred, discord, jealousy, fits of rage, selfish ambition, dissensions, factions and envy; drunkenness, orgies, and the like. I warn you, as I did before, that those who live like this will not inherit the kingdom of God.*

*But the fruit of the Spirit is love, joy, peace, patience, kindness, goodness, faithfulness, gentleness and self-control. Against such things there is no law. Those who belong to Christ Jesus have crucified the sinful nature with its passions and desires.*

—Galatians 5:17-23

LESSON
4

# Your Sexual Identity

In his early teenage years, James was typical of many other boys. His feelings of attraction to girls was emerging. This was confusing, frightening, and exciting all at the same time.

One of the ways we deal with confusing and difficult emotions is to joke about them. The group of boys that James spent time with was no different. They joked about sex. They teased each other about sexual conquest, made fun of women, and compared each other's genital anatomy.

James' friends also joked about masturbation; some bragged that they had done it lots of times. This group, like many adolescents, also teased each other about homosexuality.

One of the rituals of James' group was to steal pornography wherever they could find it, often from their fathers' hidden collections. This excited James, but it also made him feel guilty. However, to feel like one of the group James swallowed his guilt and acted like "one of the boys."

James' friends were also extremely competitive. They constantly compared themselves to each other athletically, socially, financially and intellectually. James believed that the more you won at anything, the more you became accepted.

Once, in his teenage years, James discovered his mother crying. She sobbed to him that his father was having an affair. What should she do? James didn't know. His father was always the "strong" one in the family, earning the money, being a leader at church and in the community. The tension in his home increased, but his father stayed and the subject was never discussed again.

James married a woman a lot like his mother. She idolized him, depended on him, and catered to his every need. On the one hand he loved this attention, but on the other hand he felt disturbing feelings of anger. He felt that she was controlling and smothering him. James tried to be like his dad; but he was frustrated with his job, and the pressure of earning enough income for his family was really getting to him. He envied his male friends who seemed to be "making it."

The wife of one of his friends had always been really nice to him. As difficult as it was to admit, James felt himself sexually attracted to her. Of course, he could never tell anyone about this.

## The Personal Dimension

James' friends as an adolescent and as an adult, his family, his church, his work, the TV he watches, the movies he sees, the magazines he reads are all part of the culture that teaches him what being a man is like. Feeling confused about his role leads James to search for culture's answers to being a "real" man. Culture's answers may lead him into sin. The personal dimension is about understanding yourself, your wounds, your emotions, your ability to trust, your true calling, and your mission. Knowing who you are as a man or woman is also a part of this dimension.

✎ We can identify lessons that James learned about life, love, sex, and relationships. Review the following list of lessons and check the ones to which you relate.

❑ Women are basically sex objects.
❑ Sex is not something to talk about seriously or in terms of relationship.
❑ Winning and being successful is everything.
❑ Money, status, and power are all indications of winning.
❑ The size of your genitals is important.
❑ Women (like his mother) are weak.
❑ Sex is a matter of conquest.
❑ Getting sex is a matter of winning.
❑ Certain women (like the ones in pornography) are willing to be sexual; they are, after all, always smiling.
❑ Sex and relationships are two different things.
❑ Men earn money. Women stay home.
❑ Men (like his father) have affairs and don't talk about it.
❑ Men who have any "feminine" qualities are homosexual.

✎ Do you identify other similar lessons that your family or experience taught you about these issues? ❑ Yes ❑ No If so, list them below.

_____

_____

So far, we have examined one man's life and the lessons he might have learned about being a man. Women also have cultural influences that teach stereotypical messages. For example, if men are learning that sex is a matter of conquest, women may learn to be self-protective and defensive. If men learn that sexual conquest is a sign of success, women may learn that being sexually attractive and desirable is their measure of success.

✎ Consider the question, *What is my learned definition of a successful man or woman?* For each of the cultural categories listed below list one example of what your experience with that group of people has taught you about your sexual identity.

| Cultural Category | Your Example |
| --- | --- |
| Your family | _____ |
| Your adolescent friends | _____ |

| | |
|---|---|
| Your adult friends | _____ |
| TV and movies | _____ |
| The lives of people in the news | _____ |

These messages may be based on immoral assumptions. For example, the advertising media often tries to sell an item because it will make us more sexually appealing.

➤ **How do you think these immoral assumptions, about sex and sexual identity, affect your ability to relate in healthy ways to other men and women, including your spouse?**

Christians need to evaluate what culture has taught us about being a man or woman. We can ask ourselves what God intends for our roles with each other. Before I became a Christian, I thought being a Christian meant being a sissy. When I accepted Christ, it was at the invitation of a famous athlete who had preached that night. He was one of my sports heroes. He was the first man to model to me that being a Christian and being athletic at the same time was OK.

**KEY POINT**
To be more Christlike we must get support from other Christlike men and women.

A biblical view of our sexual identity must recognize that God created us as sexual beings. Our sexuality is a valid and valuable part of who we are. We can choose to honor God by healthy sexual attitudes and behaviors.

## Assignment for the Lesson

➤ Compare your list of cultural influences with your image of Christ. What are the differences? Discuss them with your *Faithful & True* group.

➤ Practice your Scripture memory verses for all five units of *Faithful & True* you have studied so far.

➤ Say this affirmation.

The way for me to be a real man (or woman) is to be Christlike.

➤ Pray for our culture and the ways it influences us. Ask God to help you understand what it means to be a real man or woman.

LESSON
5

# Being Alone Without Feeling Alone

Gary was an average, normal guy. He grew up in a family, however, that was always busy. They never played, rarely had fun together, and oriented almost all of their time to working. They worked at home, at work, and at church.

Now Gary is married. His wife is a nurse and works a 3-11 p.m. shift. He doesn't like the fact that she's gone, but the family needs the money and she enjoys her work. Gary feels somewhat inadequate that he can't make enough to support the family by himself, but he reassures himself that in this modern world women work.

He does not like being alone. He does not know how to enjoy himself or relax. He feels bored and abandoned, but barely recognizes or accepts these feelings. So, he works around the house or volunteers for everything he can find. Late at night while waiting for his wife to come home he typically grabs a beer and snacks and sits down in front of the TV. He is alarmed by some of the sexually explicit material he sees, but he does not think that it is affecting him. His wife usually responds to his increasing sexual demands when she gets home. She is tired, though, and finds herself being more resistant and angry about it.

You may relate to Gary's feelings of loneliness. Have you felt totally, utterly alone in a room full of people? Feeling alone is not a matter of how many people are around, it is how we feel about being by ourselves. Do we enjoy our own company? Do we know how to re-create ourselves, to relax, to regenerate. In lesson 4 we talked about the importance of relationships. If we do not have healthy intimacy in our lives, we will feel alone no matter what we do or how much we like ourselves.

Gary does not have men friends that he can spend time with. He also does not know how to be alone. He does know how to work. His only form of relaxation is to drink, eat, and watch TV. What he does not know is how sex on TV is affecting him. Through TV he is adding sexual fantasy to his list of ways he copes with being alone.

*When you are alone, what do you feel? Check the following statements that apply:*

❑ afraid              ❑ bored
❑ left out            ❑ useless
❑ abandoned           ❑ sad
❑ angry
❑ other _____

Any of these feelings could be symptoms that you lack healthy relationships in your life and/or that you don't know how to be by yourself and use the time to relax and regenerate.

*What remedy do you use when you feel alone? Check the action that you most often do:*

❑ eat                 ❑ read
❑ work                ❑ sleep
❑ watch TV            ❑ drive around
❑ shop                ❑ sexually fantasize or act out
❑ use drugs
❑ other_____

Our minds and our spirits demand that we relax. They need time to regenerate. If we do not, we get tired, angry, depressed, and irritable. Many of us, as we discussed in unit 3, use various behaviors to escape our feelings. Some of us labor under the idea that if we do not use all of our time productively we are lazy. *The idle mind is the devil's playground,* after all. Or is it? Constantly avoiding being alone and feeling like we must always be productive can also make us feel lonely, angry, and depressed.

I've always enjoyed the picture of Jesus with crowds of Pharisees around Him demanding that He teach, heal, and provide miraculous signs. Jesus was in demand. He experienced lots of pressure. What did Jesus do? He got in the boat and went to the other side of the lake! I think Jesus knew how to be alone. When He prepared for His earthly ministry, He went into the wilderness. In His final hours, He went to Gethsemane and left his disciples to pray while he prayed alone.

About four thousand men were present. And having sent them away, he [Jesus] got into the boat with his disciples and went to the region of Dalmanutha. The Pharisees came and began to question Jesus. To test him, they asked him for a sign from heaven. He sighed deeply and said, "Why does this generation ask for a miraculous sign? I tell you the truth, no sign will be given to it." Then he left them, got back into the boat and crossed to the other side.
–Mark 8:9-13

You may be saying, "Yes that's true, but Jesus was the Christ, the Son of God. His alone times were supposed to be more spiritual." No doubt, as we will see in unit 6, being alone has a spiritual purpose. But being spiritual is not always about praying or Bible study. Part of the spiritual nature of Jesus' activity was to get away for a while from the pressures, the questions, the demands. For Him, this was regeneration. If we are to be more Christlike, we, too, need to learn how to be alone for its own benefit, the purpose of regeneration. If Jesus understood the importance of taking time to be alone, why should we expect any less of ourselves?

Think about this for a moment if you are tempted to say to yourself that being alone is a waste of time. Time alone enabled Jesus to maintain His vision and sense of purpose. If He did not have the strength that came from time alone, would Jesus have been able to go to the cross?

Sometimes, being alone makes us realize what we are missing—that we lack healthy relationships in our lives. We may feel abandoned, that no one likes us. Remember that these feelings may be part of our unhealthy shame. These feelings may point to some old wounds reminding us of being left out and not getting the love and nurture that we needed. If we experience these feelings, we need to talk about them with others.

When Jesus was in the Garden of Gethsemane, His disciples went to sleep. He was alone. He must have felt alone. But being alone differs greatly from feeling lonely. Feeling lonely may be a symptom of our need to develop healthy relationships. You'll remember working on this in unit 4.

When we feel both alone and lonely we may be anxious or frightened. These feelings may come from age-old wounds about previous times we have been alone. When we are not distracted by external activities and other people, some of these feelings come in. These feelings may be very normal. We can benefit from talking to others about how we feel. Anytime we talk to others, share ourselves honestly, and become vulnerable, we create intimacy. This kind of intimacy and relationship creates community, all of which can be antidotes to the feelings that we are having.

Finally, feeling alone may mean that we are feeling bored. We simply don't know how to use our time of being alone. Perhaps no one ever modeled alone activities to us.

✎ Following is a list of some activities you can do by yourself. Check the ones that you have occasionally done and would like to do more. Put an X by the ones that you would like to try for the first time.

❑ listening to music
❑ reading a good book
❑ taking a walk
❑ riding a bike
❑ pursuing a hobby
❑ exercising
❑ keeping a diary or journal
❑ writing a letter
❑ any form of play
❑ doing anything that makes you laugh
❑ other _____

The key to any of these activities is why we do them. What motivates us to be involved in these activities? Relaxation and regeneration is a good reason. Work, competition, escape, or because someone else told us we "should" are all bad reasons. Some of these activities may be combined with our need to exercise, others with our need to discover our true talents, some to express our feelings, and some to learn how to play.

### A NOTE ON LAUGHTER

"[There is] a time to weep and a time to laugh" (Ecclesiastes 3:4). A friend of mine calls laughter "emotional and spiritual jogging." Laughter benefits us emotionally, spiritually, and physically. Laughing helps us take ourselves less seriously and thus decreases the pressures that we put on ourselves. Studies have shown that exposing patients hospitalized for depression to TV shows that make them laugh helps them get better faster. Laughter can give us a sense of spiritual joy. We can laugh at ourselves and our troubles. This reminds us of who is really in control of our lives. Finally, laughter has all kinds of physical benefits. For example, when we laugh our muscles relax (have you ever "fallen over laughing?") and our blood pressure decreases.

Laughter may happen with other people. Sometimes, however, we must be disciplined to laugh by ourselves. Can you think of a TV show, a movie, or a book that makes you laugh? Would it not be nice to regularly schedule alone times in which you can laugh.

## Assignment for the Lesson

➤ You must schedule times to be alone, particularly for those of you who are not used to being alone. Start slow and build a few minutes per day into your daily routine. Pick one of the activities that you have discovered or remembered here. Vary this routine. Don't try to do the same thing every day. Build on the time you do these and the variety of things you do. Report to your *Faithful & True* group how you are doing.

➤ Say the following affirmation to yourself five times.

I can be alone, and enjoy my own company.

➤ Review your Scripture memory verses.

## Discussion Group Questions

- Describe a time when your trust was betrayed or someone disappointed you.
- What did you learn about yourself by completing the expressing-emotions test on page 81?
- Relate a story that was repeated in your family that told what you were or were not good at or what was expected of you.
- In what way did God "make you fast" (p. 86).
- What do you believe to be God's calling in your life?
- Which of the lessons James learned about life (checklist, middle of page 89) did you learn when you were growing up?

# The Spiritual Dimension

## FOCAL PASSAGE

*The mind of sinful man is death, but the mind controlled by the Spirit is life and peace.*

—Romans 8:6

### AARON'S STORY

Aaron was the responsible child in his family. His father was too busy at work to be at home much. When he was home, he drank a lot. Depressed and anxious, Aaron's mother spent much of her time in her room reading. When dad came home she hid from his anger. Someone had to help so Aaron learned to cook and clean and tend to his father. Aaron learned to get his dad to bed when he was drunk. In these ways Aaron grew up to think that he was a wonderful rescuer and great manager, especially with his father.

Aaron became a Christian not so much out of surrender as out of a desire to gain God's approval. He just knew that he could be the best church member who ever lived. God would be so pleased. Aaron took on every job his church had to offer. His pastor was thrilled to have a man like Aaron around. At the church Aaron became as important as the pastor.

Aaron's wife, while outwardly proud of him, was inwardly lonely. They didn't talk very much. She has discovered several men at church who are good listeners. Why can't her husband be like them?

Aaron never took time to be alone or to pray or read the Bible. He was, after all, doing mighty things for God.

## MEMORY VERSE

Test me, O Lord, and try me, examine my heart and my mind; for your love is ever before me, and I walk continually in your truth.
–Psalm 26:2-3

Spiritual

## GROWTH GOAL

In this unit you will learn how your past influences your current level of spirituality. You will assess your level of spiritual maturity, establish a plan for spiritual discipline, and understand how spirituality affects the other dimensions of healthy sexuality. We keep before us constantly the goal of sexuality between a man and a wife as a spiritual moment.

| Your Religious History | Shame and Spirituality | Magical Thinking and Spirituality | Spiritual Discipline | Spirituality as the Center |
|---|---|---|---|---|
| LESSON 1 | LESSON 2 | LESSON 3 | LESSON 4 | LESSON 5 |

# Your Religious History

**By the grace of God I am what I am, and his grace to me was not without effect. No, I worked harder than all of them—yet not I, but the grace of God that was with me.**
–1 Corinthians 15:10

Do you know any Christians like Aaron? Outwardly, they seem like such wonderful believers. When you're with them, however, you don't feel a sense of surrender or humility. One part of you wants to be like them, another part doesn't like being around them. One of the symptoms of Aaron's superficiality is that he has no personal spiritual life. He has a church life. He is active and contributes, but he seems to have no depth to his story. Can you hear Aaron speaking the words of Paul in the passage in the margin?

Yet, Aaron's problem is not really pride or conceit. At an early age, he learned that his role in life was doing things to take care of others. He was the responsible one in his family. He assumed the role of father even though he was a child. While he was doing this, no one modeled to him how to have a spiritual life. As he grew up, he naturally continued to play his caretaker role in all of his relationships. In his marriage, Aaron's behaviors contribute to a profound loneliness. Even though he is strong and successful, his wife is tempted by other, more sensitive men.

Aaron's story demonstrates how a family can influence personal spirituality without ever saying anything about religion. In this unit we seek to help you create a deeper spiritual life. To do that, you need to look at your own history. Perhaps you grew up in a healthy Christian home where the family shared Bible stories and said prayers. People practiced what they preached. What a foundation you received! How have you built on that healthy foundation? Or your religious history may have been primarily influenced by forces outside the home.

## Karl's Story

Karl Barth was a famous theologian. He was a prolific writer and lectured all over the world. At the end of his life, he was lecturing at a major university. When he finished, explaining his theology, a young reporter came up to him and asked, "Dr. Barth, could you summarize your theology in a couple of sentences for my paper?" What a request! How does a man who has written so much and lectured so widely answer that question?

Dr. Barth replied, "Of course I can. My theology is 'Jesus loves me this I know for the Bible tells me so. Little ones to him belong. They are weak but He is strong.'"

Let's retrace the steps of our spiritual journey. What has your spiritual life and history been like?

✎ **In the spaces below think back to the faith of your parents. Give a brief description of your parents' attitude about faith and church.**

Mom _____

_____

Dad _____

_____

In many ways, our parents represent God to us. We call God "Father." Our experience with our parents may influence our ability to think of God as loving, giving, gracious, disciplining, angry, and nurturing. In unit 5 we discussed how messages from parents may affect our attitude about our talents and our mission. Our ability to talk to God in prayer or meditation may be influenced by whether or not we could talk to our parents.

Certainly, our parents may not have been the main religious influence in our lives. Others may have led us in positive and negative ways. Pastors, Sunday School teachers, youth group leaders, other adults, or friends may be part of our spiritual journey.

✎ Think of the one person who most represents a positive example of faith to you. Write that person's name below.

_____

✎ What did that person teach you about God?

_____

_____

✎ How did he or she demonstrate the faith?

_____

_____

➤ Take time to thank God for people who gave you a positive example of faith. Have you tried to be like them in any way? Would you like to be more like them? Would they now be proud of you or disappointed?

Have people in your life represented religion to you, but given you a negative sense of faith or of God? Perhaps they were hypocrites, or possibly they modeled anger, judgment, bigotry, or rigid thinking.

✎ In the margin write the names or initials of those who have given you a negative sense of God or of faith.

Mahatma Ghandi once said that of all the religions in the world he had studied he found that Christianity was the most meaningful. He would choose to become a Christian, he said, if it were not for the example of other Christians.

➤ Have negative Christian influences in your life been a turnoff to you? Discuss these with your *Faithful & True* group.

✎ Karl Barth reverted back to a song to express his faith. Remember the infancy of your faith. Answer the following series of questions out of your early faith.

Who was your favorite Bible character? _____

What was your favorite Bible story? _____

What was your favorite verse of Scripture? _____

What was your favorite hymn or inspirational music? _____

Does God ever smile or laugh? Does He always frown or look angry? When have you felt the most confident about your faith? When have you felt the least confident? Do you ever sit in church on Sunday, like I do, and wish that you could sing some of those songs or hear some of those stories like you did when you were a child? Maybe some of us go to a different kind of church now than we did when we were small. Although we have intellectually chosen our present church, a part of our spirit misses what we knew as a child.

The stories, Bible characters, music, and image of God that you described in the exercise above will give you information to understand how some of your religious feelings and attitudes began. For example, if God never smiles in your experience, is He an angry God who sits in judgment waiting to punish people? Do you feel you must always avoid making Him even angrier?

➤ **Discuss with your *Faithful & True* group some of your findings from this exercise. Ask them to help you interpret what they mean.**

"Little ones to Him belong. They are weak but He is strong." When have you felt weak and that God is strong? When you became a Christian, what was your experience like? Consider the following question.

✎ **When you became a Christian, was it an act of surrender because you felt weak, or were you seeking to control your life and destiny? Did you give in to God no matter what happened or did you bargain with God? If you have a difficult time deciding on this, describe to a friend your salvation experience and how you felt. Ask that person to help you identify what motivated you.**

❏ Surrender          ❏ Control

If you recognize that your surrender to God may have been an attempt to control, what were you trying to control? Were you trying to control Him? your circumstances? your fate? your eternity? What are you still trying to control? Do you sometimes get angry because God doesn't seem to be doing what you would like Him to do?

One way to know if you are self-controlled or surrendered to God's control is to examine the spiritual authorities you follow. To whom do you hold yourself accountable?

✎ **In the margin list the persons who represent spiritual or religious authority to you right now.**

Do you ever have trouble with authority? Do you have difficulty submitting to others? If you do, the problem often involves trust and insecurity. Do you trust anyone else to help you with your needs? If not, you may have a problem trusting God and being in submission to Him.

✎ **Have other persons or events shaped your approach to spiritual matters? List three other significant events in your spiritual history and describe how they impacted your thoughts, feelings, or behavior.**

1. _____

_____

2. _____

_____

3. _____

_____

Test me, O Lord, and try me, examine my heart and my mind; for your love is ever before me, and I walk continually in your truth.
–Psalm 26:2-3

The Scripture memory verses for this unit appear in the margin. **Begin to memorize the passage. Write the verses on a card, and carry the card with you. Whenever you get a drink, review the passage.**

➤ Say the following affirmation five times.

I desire a closer walk with God.

**LESSON 2**

# Shame and Spirituality

*"If anyone is ashamed of me and my words in this adulterous and sinful generation, the Son of Man will be ashamed of him when he comes in his Father's glory with the holy angels."*
–Mark 8:38

### Angie's Story

When Angie was three years old, her parents were having a Bible study meeting at their home with other couples from their church. This was important activity and Angie had been instructed to entertain herself and not bother them. She knew that whatever her parents were doing, it was about church and, therefore, really "serious." To occupy her time, Angie decided to slide down the banister. She fell off, bumped her head, and started to cry. Her mother rushed over, gave her a tight hug, and told her that big girls don't cry. Angie couldn't stop crying, and her mother became increasingly irritated.

Finally, Angie's mother preached Angie a sermon. "I wonder if Jesus wanted you sliding down that banister? I think if He did, He wouldn't let you bump your head." Angie wanted to be a big girl and for Jesus to like her, so she stopped crying. Her mother assured her that Jesus would be so pleased that she had been a big girl.

The next Sunday in Sunday School when they sang "Jesus loves me," Angie was translating it in her head, "Jesus hates me this I know, for my mother tells me so."

In college, when Angie started drinking and became sexually involved with her boyfriend, she was convinced again that Jesus didn't like her and that she could never be forgiven. Attending church was too painful for her so she stopped going. Everyone there would surely ask her to leave if they only knew about her activities.

In the margin read the story from John 8 about a woman caught in adultery. Based on this story, what would you like to say to Angie about her sins?

_____

_____

_____

The teachers of the law and the Pharisees brought in a woman caught in adultery. They made her stand before the group and said to Jesus, "Teacher, this woman was caught in the act of adultery. In the Law Moses commanded us to stone such women. Now what do you say?" They were using this question as a trap, in order to have a basis for accusing him.

But Jesus bent down and started to write on the ground with his finger. When they kept on questioning him, he straightened up and said to them, "If any one of you is without sin, let him be the first to throw a stone at her." Again he stooped down and wrote on the ground.

At this, those who heard began to go away one at a time, the older ones first, until only Jesus was left, with the woman still standing there. Jesus straightened up and asked her, "Woman, where are they? Has no one condemned you?"

"No one, sir," she said.

"Then neither do I condemn you," Jesus declared. "Go now and leave your life of sin."
–John 8:3-11

Angie suffers from that sense of unhealthy shame we have talked about. She is convinced that God's grace does not apply to her. She believes she is a mistake in the sight of God. Angie's story is true; my wife and I were at that Bible study. How does one communicate the experience of grace to such a person? I responded that I wanted Angie to know that Jesus loves her, does not condemn her, and wants to help her find healing and change.

Angie's mother used the image of Jesus and His approval to discipline and control Angie. We can imagine that this particular instance was not the only time Angie received distorted messages about herself and about God. Her example demonstrates one of the ways that early experiences as a child can influence your very nature. Do you feel like a mistake? Do you feel like a mistake in the sight of God? Do you remember the question I asked you in lesson 1 about whether God ever smiles? What did you say?

Feeling shame about yourself prohibits a closer relationship with God and others. It prevents you from being honest about yourself and can cause you to become vulnerable with others. Shame can cause you to look for others to approve of you. What you do to get that approval or how you symbolize that approval can lead you into sexual sin. If the activities we pursue to gain approval cause us to sin, they lead to a perpetual cycle of shame. We continually do things that cause us to feel more shameful.

Thus we need to work on feeling accepted by God—that His grace is sufficient for us. Many of us have committed sins that cause us to believe that God can't forgive us—unpardonable sins. Is God incapable or unwilling to forgive some sins?

✎ **In the margin read Romans 8:38-39. Below check the response that best reflects what the verses say concerning the question of sins God will not forgive.**

> ❑ If you commit certain sins, God will give up on you.
> ❑ Absolutely no sin is powerful enough to defeat the grace of God.
> ❑ No power in life is powerful enough to separate me from Jesus' love and care.

> For I am convinced that neither death nor life, neither angels nor demons, neither the present nor the future, nor any powers, neither height nor depth, nor anything else in all creation, will be able to separate us from the love of God that is in Christ Jesus our Lord.
> –Romans 8:38-39

Romans 8:38-39 clearly states that no power can separate us from the love of our Lord. That certainly means no sin we are willing to turn over to God is powerful enough to defeat God's grace. Yet, something may be lurking in your soul that prevents you from feeling accepted. Have you ever really confessed your sins—all of them. In the 12-step tradition of Alcoholics Anonymous, 2 steps, step 4 and step 5, deal with confession. They talk about making a "fearless and searching" moral inventory of our lives and telling it to at least one other person. Have you ever made such an inventory? Doing so requires courage, fearlessness, and dedication.

✎ **Think back over your life. What behaviors, thoughts, and actions cause you the most shame? Are you willing to make a list of them? Make an attempt now by listing those that readily come to mind. Remember that this is your workbook and no one else should look at it unless you want them to. Be courageous and honest.**

_____

_____

_____

_____

This may just be a partial list and you may need to spend more time working on it. Sometimes as we begin the process of being honest with ourselves, memories and thoughts come back to us. This may happen to you.

✎ **Who is a spiritual authority to you who would be available to you (your pastor, a deacon, an elder, a mentor)? In the margin write his or her name.**

Would you be willing to make an appointment to tell that person about your list? If you are, make the appointment, and in the margin write the time you have made to read your list. Then talk with this person.

If you can complete the last assignment, you will have the experience of confessing your sins to at least one person. This may be a different experience for you than confessing directly to God or confessing as a large group of people in church. Confession is more directly personal when one person is involved. My experience indicates that such personal confession reduces our sense of shame.

People who attend 12-step fellowships, for any addiction, find that they can tell about their worst imaginable behaviors and that others listen and understand. Many of the people there have done the same things. It is an experience of what Paul said in Romans 3:23, "for all have sinned and fall short of the glory of God." Nothing about a 12-step meeting is magical, but it is an experience of grace received at the hands of other people.

➤ Read Psalm 32:2-5 (margin). Silence is the enemy of your spirit. Confession is like a medicine. Take time to pray. Confess to God any sin you have not already confessed.

The ability to confess shows a humble spirit. Humility signals an openness to God and a willingness to rely on Him. Paul was a proud man at the beginning of his ministry. Often, he included himself in the list of original apostles. Listen, however, to what he has to say toward the end of his ministry. "For I am the least of the apostles and do not even deserve to be called an apostle, because I persecuted the church of God" (1 Corinthians 15:9).

To accept my need for God and surrender to His grace are the first steps toward a healthy spiritual journey. Such surrender requires humility—giving up control. Recognizing my need for God demonstrates my healthy shame rather than unhealthy shame.

Where are you in your journey? Are you still trying to control God's love and grace by your actions, your petitions, your prayers? Do you get angry with God because He doesn't do things the way you would like?

✎ Check any of the following statements that express your feelings or desires:

❑ I want God to forgive me now!
❑ I'm angry that He won't give me what I've asked for.
❑ I have a difficult time believing God really loves me.
❑ I'm ready to submit my will to His regardless of what He wants.
❑ I'm ready to confess all of my sins.
❑ I'm not perfect, but I believe that God loves me anyway.

Whatever you learned in your family, whatever put-downs you have experienced, whatever negative views of yourself you hold, God still loves you.

✎ From your Bible, read the story of the Samaritan woman at the well (John 4:5-19) and the story of the prodigal son (Luke 15:11-32). What is Jesus illustrating by His actions and teaching by His words? Remember that the woman certainly was a sexual sinner and probably the prodigal son was too. The older brother said the prodigal had squandered his inheritance on prostitutes.

_____

_____

_____

Blessed is the man whose sin the Lord does not count against him and in whose spirit is no deceit.

When I kept silent, my bones wasted away through my groaning all day long. For day and night your hand was heavy upon me; my strength was sapped as in the heat of summer. Then I acknowledged my sin to you and did not cover up my iniquity. I said, "I will confess my transgressions to the Lord"— and you forgave the guilt of my sin.
–Psalm 32:2-5

You could have stated the teachings of the two Bible passages in one of many ways. Certainly the passages illustrate that Jesus readily forgives and gladly accepts sexual sinners.

### Assignment for the Lesson

➤ Say the following affirmation five times.

Jesus loves me this I know, for the Bible tells me so. To my God I do belong. I am weak but He is strong.

➤ Practice repeating your Scripture memory verse for this unit. Review the Scripture verses from the previous units. Hiding God's Word in your heart is a powerful aid to effective living.

➤ Pray for humility, a sense of God's grace, and the courage to confess all of your sins.

LESSON

3

# Magical Thinking and Spirituality

Michael was first exposed to pornography when he discovered his dad's hidden collection in a closet. He was 11 years old. From that moment he began a lifetime habit of finding it, later buying it, and collecting it. As an adult he kept a box full of it hidden so that his wife and children couldn't find it.

When he was a teenager, Michael went to a revival. The preacher was the type who inspired burning enthusiasm. He talked about all kinds of problems being removed if a person would only dedicate his life to Christ. The preacher healed many people on stage and claimed that many people in the congregation were being healed of emotional and physical problems, including addictions of all kinds.

That night Michael went forward bargaining with God that since he was committing his life, God would heal his mind. Michael hoped and prayed that he would never look at pornography again.

In his adult life Michael searched for the spiritual solution to rid himself of pornography. He prayed and read the Bible. He was baptized in four different denominations. Each time he thought that if he found the right church his problems would be over. Every time he went into a bookstore to buy more his sense of shame told him that he was worthless and that he was not spiritual enough. His shame said he was not a good enough Christian. He kept seeking to do more and to find the right **formula**.

Michael became depressed about his inability to stop. His search for biblical solutions intensified. One passage of Scripture kept coming to him: "If your eye causes you to sin, pluck it out. It is better for you to enter the kingdom of God with one eye than to have two eyes and be thrown into hell" (Mark 9:47).

Michael wondered, *Did Jesus really mean this?* His eyes were causing him to sin. Should he cut them out?

Like all the stories in this book, Michael's story is true. I have changed the names to protect the identities of the people I describe. Michael was referred to me by his ophthalmologist because, in his depression and search for spiritual answers, he plucked out both eyes. Unfortunately, the only solution that this approach offered was that he couldn't look at new pornography. He still had all of the old images stored away in his memory. Now he has added new fuel for his feelings of shame. His drastic strategy brought him no closer to a solution to his problem.

Most people probably haven't thought of doing something this drastic to themselves. Many people have, however, searched for solutions and formulas that will cure all of their problems. If we are not careful, we may repeat a basic part of Michael's mistake. We repeat his error whenever we search for "magical" answers that will take all of our problems away. A solution to Michael's problem with pornography does exist, but that solution involves self-understanding, growth, and discipline.

✎ **Here are some magical solutions you may have tried. Check any you have experienced.**

❑ Bought a lottery ticket thinking that it will solve my financial problems.
❑ Memorized lots of Scripture thinking that God would be so pleased He would give me something I needed.
❑ Joined a different church because it is where the really "successful" people go.
❑ Bargained with God that if I performed a certain action God would do a certain action in return.
❑ Contributed money to the church thinking that God would reward me with more money back.
❑ Believed that when something bad happened to me it was because God was punishing me for some sin.
❑ Tried to prevent God from punishing me for some sin by doing increased amounts of Christian work.
❑ Performed some superstitious ritual like carrying a rabbit's foot.

❑ Your addition to the list: _____

This is just a partial list. You may or may not have checked any of the examples, but do you recognize the pattern of thinking? I call those thought patterns "magical" thinking.

With magical thinking a person believes he or she can affect God's behavior. Magical thinking can be manipulative. A person thinks, *If I do something, God will either do or not do something else.* It can create anxiety about God's reaction. I remember a woman at church being totally anxious because the candles on the altar were taller than the cross. To her this was some kind of violation of a formula. The cross should always be the highest object in church. God would be mad. Bad things would happen.

**KEY POINT**
Magical thinking seeks formulas to appease or please God for selfish purposes— not to serve Him.

Magical thinking is rather juvenile or adolescent—like a little kid wondering how mom or dad will react. *What did I do to cause this? How can I prevent these consequences from occurring? (As if my actions cause everything?)*

Magical thinking is a primitive though process normal to the preschool child. It is the opposite of true spirituality. In the spiritual dimension of healthy sexuality we need truly to—
• surrender to the will of God
• accept God's grace
• refrain from trying to find the magic formulas
• develop strategies for dealing with temptation.

If we have trouble with sexual thinking, we can become like Michael. I have known hundreds of men who try to appease God for sexual sins that they have committed by doing something "good" the next day. One of them I know calls this the "One Day Rule." He figures God will be angry with him for one day after a sexual sin. He tries to atone for the sin on that one day. Once he feels that he has appeased God he sexually sins again, figuring that he can always make up for it later.

## Thinking in Extremes

In addition to a magical view of the world, many people mimic spirituality by thinking in extremes. When we think in extremes we see everything as good or bad—no grey areas. We search for the absolutely "correct" formulas to please God. When we think in extremes, we often become rigid—more concerned with observing the rules than with the meaning or purpose of the rules.

> In the margin read the story of Jesus and the Pharisees. In your own words describe what you think Jesus is teaching us by this example?

_____

_____

The Pharisees were more concerned about observing the letter of the law than living within the reason for and spirit of the law. Concerning the law of the Sabbath, Jesus says rules are made for people and not the other way around. God tells us to rest on the Sabbath. God did not give the command as a test to see how obedient we are. The spirit of this law is that we can rest. The Sabbath is for our rest. Would a comparison with speed limits help? Speed limits are not to delay our arrival but to help us arrive safely at a destination.

Jesus talks about this in another passage. He said: "Do not think that I have come to abolish the Law or the Prophets; I have not come to abolish them but to fulfill them" (Matthew 5:17).

While Jesus reminds us to obey the law, He also reminds us that the spirit is higher than the letter of the law. As sinners we will never get the law so right that we earn our salvation. The purpose of the law is to protect ourselves and others. It reminds us to care for ourselves. The spirit of the law is grace. Jesus, our Savior, is the fulfillment of the law. Only through His grace will we be saved.

In our spiritual lives we need to look more for Christ's spirit and grace and not as much to magical thinking or rules-keeping to manipulate God. We cannot earn our salvation through the law. Salvation comes only through the fulfillment of the law, and His name is Jesus. We must base our spiritual journey on this fact.

> Be courageously honest. What formulas or lists of rules have you used to try to be more spiritual? List at least one of them below.

_____

_____

> Stop and pray. Ask God to show you if you need to abandon any magical or extremes thinking to be more centered in Christ.

One Sabbath Jesus was going through the grainfields, and as his disciples walked along, they began to pick some heads of grain. The Pharisees said to him, "Look, why are they doing what is unlawful on the Sabbath?"

He answered, "Have you never read what David did when he and his companions were hungry and in need? In the days of Abiathar the high priest, he entered the house of God and ate the consecrated bread, which is lawful only for priests to eat. And he also gave some to his companions."

Then he said to them, "The Sabbath was made for man, not man for the Sabbath. So the Son of Man is Lord even of the Sabbath."
–Mark 2:23-28

✎ I have supplied a list of descriptive words about our spiritual journey. Rank the words (1, 2, 3, and so forth) in the order of their importance for your life.

___ surrendering          ___ peace
___ humility              ___ obedience
___ giving up control     ___ unselfishness
___ trust                 ___ study
___ not manipulating      ___ other _____

## Assignment for the Lesson

✎ Below write Psalm 26:2-3, from memory if possible. Check your work on page 94.

_____

_____

➤ Say the following affirmation five times.

I will trust in the Lord with all my heart and forget not all His benefits.

➤ Think back to your own experience of salvation. What was it like? Take a few minutes and go for a walk, in a quiet place if possible. Spend the time in prayer. Talk to God about how you felt when you first got to know Him. Ask God to restore the joy of your salvation (Psalm 51:12). If your early experience with God was distorted through unhealthy shame, ask Him to grant you the joy that He intends to be a part of your salvation.

# Spiritual Discipline

LESSON
4

Kent felt anxious most of the time. Although he was a Christian, he took his faith for granted. He went to church and participated in various activities. He did what others asked him to do. This seemed to please his wife although the two of them never talked about their faith. Kent worried about money. He worked harder and harder. He worried about his status in his company and fretted over every decision. He so much wanted to impress his boss. He needed a promotion with its added salary.

Kent worried about his house. Whenever he had free time, which was seldom, he worked on projects around the home. Kent never really felt everything was OK, but staying busy somewhat relieved his anxieties. Kent worried about his children. He was always asking them what they were doing. He gave them lots of advice whether or not they ever asked for it. He prided himself on being a good father, but his wife often found herself telling him to leave the children alone.

Kent worried about several things. His blood pressure was high. He experienced frequent headaches. His stomach often troubled him. He always felt tired, although he never allowed himself to rest. At night, he often asked his wife for sex just so he could relax.

Kent has many worries, but he doesn't worry about his spiritual life. That he takes for granted. He relies on the fact that he is saved, but he does nothing to help his faith mature. The anxiety that he feels could be the product of many things, but his faith is not helping him find the peace that "transcends all understanding" (Philippians 4:7). Kent needs to find spiritual discipline. If he doesn't, he will continue to live a life of anxiety and stress. He will continue to find unhealthy ways of dealing with his feelings. In our story, we can see that he already has started looking to the act of sex to relieve his feelings.

The ability to have a spiritual life is not something that comes naturally. It must be developed. How many of us take the time to do that? In this lesson, I want to help you see the importance of spiritual discipline and offer you some suggestions about how to develop that discipline.

✎ **Why do you think Adam and Eve ate the forbidden fruit?**

- ❏ They were hungry.
- ❏ They wanted wisdom.
- ❏ They wanted to be like God.
- ❏ They were curious.

This passage describes the original act of sin. Satan, in the form of a serpent, convinced Eve to eat of the fruit of the forbidden tree. The food looked pleasing, but it was also "desirable for gaining wisdom." Two people were placed in a perfect world, the Garden of Eden, and yet they were tempted beyond their ability to withstand. What tempted them?

In part, their human nature with its natural curiosity caused their sin, but, more importantly, they had a control problem. God promised to provide for all their needs, but they weren't sure they needed His help. Why not be gods themselves?

We share a similar challenge to that of Adam and Eve. God promises to meet our needs. Do we really need His help? Can't we make it on our own? Why not be our own god?

Our spiritual journey must begin with the ability to surrender to God's authority as our Creator and Savior. We can't rely on our own strength, ability, or wisdom. We must rely on God. Like Adam and Eve, we daily discover the limits of self-reliance. Spiritual discipline is the vehicle by which we practice giving up control to the One who can be relied upon and who will never fail us. God is absolutely trustworthy.

✎ **You may think you don't have discipline, but you do. The list below contains some areas of your life in which you already practice discipline. Check the ones that apply to you and add any others that you think of.**

- ❏ I get up every day.
- ❏ I go to work regularly.
- ❏ I brush my teeth, comb my hair, and take a bath.
- ❏ I provide for my family.
- ❏ I attend church.
- ❏ I practice a sport or hobby.
- ❏ I obey the law.
- ❏ I take care of my house.
- ❏ I do the laundry and wash the dishes.
- ❏ I go to school and do my homework.
- ❏ Other (be specific) _____.

So you see, you do practice discipline in areas of your life. You regularly do things you know you should do. Perhaps you would suffer very negative consequences if you didn't do some of these things. Others you may do simply because you enjoy how you feel when

> When the woman saw that the fruit of the tree was good for food and pleasing to the eye, and also desirable for gaining wisdom, she took some and ate it. She also gave some to her husband, who was with her, and he ate it.
> –Genesis 3:6

**KEY POINT**
Spiritual discipline is the vehicle by which we learn to trust.

you finish them. The same principles motivate spiritual discipline. You will suffer negative consequences if you fail to practice it, and you will gain very positive benefits when you achieve it.

Certain things you do even when you don't feel like doing them. You may go to work or school on days you do not feel like going. That is discipline. Alcoholics Anonymous has a very popular, if not corny, slogan that says, "Fake it till you make it." Sometimes we must will to do something we don't feel like doing, such as acting in a loving way when we don't feel loving. Usually we find out that the very act of doing something changes our feelings. Spiritual discipline depends not on how we feel but on how we choose to act.

In lessons 2 and 3 you learned the dangers of basing your spiritual life on your sense of shame or on rules and formulas. That does not mean you don't need appropriate patterns and practices of discipline. The challenge is to find spiritual disciplines that are meaningful for you, not just acts others tell you to do.

✎ **Think back to spiritual moments in your life, times when you felt the real presence of God. When were they?**

_____

_____

Where were they? _____

_____

Who, if anyone, were you with? _____

What were you doing? _____

_____

If there has been more than one time, can you detect a pattern? If so, explain.

_____

_____

If you listed places you have felt closer to God, is spending time in those places on a regular basis possible? If not, can you find positive substitute places?

✎ **Does someone in your life model spiritual discipline to you? Think of someone who seems to have a peace and serenity about their relationship with the Lord. Who is that person?**

_____

✎ **Would any of the following be things you might do with the person you listed? Check all that apply.**

❑ Have a conversation about spiritual discipline.
❑ Ask for spiritual guidance or direction from him.
❑ Ask her if you could be accountable to her about spiritual discipline.
❑ Review your own plan for spiritual discipline with him.
❑ Other _____

We all need guides and role models. Having a person in our life who gives spiritual direction can be a tremendous help. Jesus models three principles about spirituality:

**1. Jesus was often alone.** At the beginning of His ministry, He was alone for 40 days. Later, He talked about the simplicity, humility, and aloneness of prayer.

✎ **Evaluate your "aloneness" factor. Do you spend time alone with God—time not consumed with duties and tasks? Place a check mark on the following scale. to rate yourself.**

| | | |
|---|---|---|
| Not enough Aloneness | Healthy Aloneness | Unhealthy Isolation |

**2. Jesus' alone time was often consumed by prayer.** From the time of His stay in the wilderness at the start of His ministry to His struggle in the Garden of Gethsemane, Jesus had a continuing conversation with God. In one of the shortest passages in the Bible, Paul says, "Pray continually" (1 Thessalonians 5:17).

✎ **Evaluate your "continual prayer" factor. Do you have an ongoing conversation with God as you go through the day? If so, is that conversation filled with love, encouragement, and worship? Or is it filled with shame and guilt? Rate yourself on the following scale.**

| | | |
|---|---|---|
| Guilt Ridden Thoughts of God | Positive Conversation | Ignore or Avoid Him |

**3. Jesus was intimately acquainted with Scriptures.** Do you remember the story of Jesus when at age 12 He stayed behind in Jerusalem and talked with the priests at the Temple? In His ministry, Jesus often quoted Scripture. In one of His first appearances after the resurrection, He walked with two men who were grieving His death as they were on their way back to their home in Emmaus. They poured out their hurt to Jesus. In the margin, read what Jesus said to them.

Later in this same story, Jesus stayed with these men and ate with. They finally recognized who He was when He broke the bread. Isn't it interesting that at their time of most profound grief, Jesus helped them by interpreting Scripture?

✎ **Evaluate your relationship to God's Word. Do you have a workable plan for growing in the study and application of Scripture? Rate yourself on the following scale.**

| | |
|---|---|
| Growing in God's Word | Neglect God's Word |

By Jesus' example we can see that we practice spiritual discipline best when our lives include time alone as well as time spent in prayer and study of the Scripture. The example of Elijah in lesson 4 pictures how we hear God in our moments of quiet. You have just done some self-evaluation concerning these areas in your life. We live in a culture that bombards us with constant stimuli. To find times of being alone is not easy. Family, work, church, TV, and many other activities keep our minds occupied.

✎ **Examine your typical day. When could you have time to be alone?**

_____o'clock a.m./p.m.

When you pray, do not be like the hypocrites, for they love to pray standing in the synagogues and on the street corners to be seen by men. I tell you the truth, they have received their reward in full. But when you pray, go into your room, close the door and pray to your Father, who is unseen. Then your Father, who sees what is done in secret, will reward you. And when you pray, do not keep on babbling like pagans, for they think they will be heard because of their many words.
–Matthew 6:5-7

He said to them, "How foolish you are, and how slow of heart to believe all that the prophets have spoken! Did not the Christ have to suffer these things and then enter his glory?" And beginning with Moses and all the Prophets, he explained to them what was said in all the Scriptures concerning himself.
–Luke 24:25-27

Like running races, we may not be able to take on the entire distance right away if we are not in shape, conditioned for the effort. You may want to start with only five minutes of quiet time a day, and build minute by minute until you are more "in shape" to spend more time with the Lord.

➤ **You may not be good at prayer. Many people benefit by reading the prayers and devotions of others. Reading the prayers of others will develop your prayer life so that you will be able to voice your own prayers. Go to your church library, a Christian bookstore, or ask your pastor for devotional resources.**

➤ **Likewise, you may not think you're good at understanding Scripture. Many books, classes, and other resources can help you with this. Find one of these resources. You will find information on the *Step by Step* studies on page 222.**

By completing the work of this lesson you have identified spiritual mentors and leaders, places where you feel closer to God, times designated for spiritual growth, and resources to help you with prayer and Bible study. Spiritual discipline is a matter of practice. All discipline involves goals. Runners, for example, decide what goals they will work to achieve. Remember, the goals of spiritual discipline include—
* humility—acknowledging my need for God
* obedience—surrendering to God's standards
* trust—relying upon God.

Don't be too hard on yourself. We all are imperfect. The Bible is full of great servants of God who had problems with humility, surrender, and trust. This is the challenge of sin and our human nature.

## Assignment for the Lesson

➤ **Read the following passage of Scripture.**

"Be joyful in hope, patient in affliction, faithful in prayer" (Romans 12:12).

➤ **Say the following affirmation five times.**

I can be a person of spiritual discipline.

➤ **Pray by yourself, for yourself, and listen for the whisper of God.**

**LESSON 5**

# Spirituality as the Center

Loren is in recovery because of many sexual sins that he committed. Thankfully, he received good counsel and help and has been free of his sexual acting out for over a year. As part of his care he has begun to take care of himself physically. He exercises, eats better, and makes sure he gets enough rest. Loren has also quit smoking cigarettes. He works less compulsively. He regularly reports to a group of men in his church to whom he is accountable.

Loren and his wife have received counseling together and regularly work on their communication skills. They enjoy times of playing together, just having fun.

Loren has had to work diligently in counseling on some abuse issues from his past. He was sexually abused as a child. He is beginning to heal from these wounds. He is talking with his pastor about some career decisions that he is praying about.

Loren has started a new quiet time of prayer and Bible study. Lately, he has asked his wife to have a daily time of prayer with him. During their last experience of sex, Loren and his wife felt an overwhelming sense of presence with each other. It was a spiritual moment and they both cried tears of joy to be in each other's arms.

In this lesson my goal is to help you understand how the spiritual is the center of the other dimensions. This will be a review of Part 1 of this book. As Loren demonstrates, healthy sexuality experienced in a spiritual sense will result from practicing all of the dimensions of our model.

Go back and review the diagram of Ginger Manley's model on page 26. You will notice again that the spiritual dimension is in the center of the model. In the remaining portion of this lesson you will consider how the spiritual affects the other dimensions.

## 1. The Physical Dimension.

✎ **Compare the two passages from Paul that appear in the margin. Check all the following responses that correctly reflect what he is saying to us about our bodies.**

> Flee from sexual immorality. All other sins a man commits are outside his body, but he who sins sexually sins against his own body. Do you not know that your body is a temple of the Holy Spirit, who is in you, whom you have received from God? You are not your own; you were bought at a price. Therefore honor God with your body.
> –1 Corinthians 6:18-20

- ❏ We need to respect our bodies and take care of them.
- ❏ Our bodies don't make up God's kingdom. His kingdom is about the Spirit inside.
- ❏ Sexual sin defiles the body, God's temple, so sexual morality is part of our care for our bodies.
- ❏ Our bodies are unimportant. Only "spiritual" things matter in life.
- ❏ Our bodies are mortal and perishable, so we should never worship them.
- ❏ Jesus reveals Himself through the very weaknesses and degeneration of our mortal bodies.

> We have this treasure in jars of clay to show that this all-surpassing power is from God and not from us. We are hard pressed on every side, but not crushed; perplexed, but not in despair; persecuted, but not abandoned; struck down, but not destroyed. We always carry around in our body the death of Jesus, so that the life of Jesus may also be revealed in our body. For we who are alive are always being given over to death for Jesus' sake, so that his life may be revealed in our mortal body. So then, death is at work in us, but life is at work in you.
> –2 Corinthians 4:7-12

Second Corinthians 4:7-12 became important to me when I became diabetic. I was 26 years old and to myself seemed indestructible. Suddenly I had a lifetime disease to deal with. Every day I take insulin shots in order to stay alive. Diabetes reminds me that I must eat well, exercise, and otherwise take care of myself that I may honor God by staying alive as long as possible. On the other hand, every day as I take a shot I feel given up to death. My disease is a reminder that something is always more important than my body and that is my spirit. You correctly could have checked all of the responses above except two. Our bodies certainly are important. They are God's temple, and how we care for our bodies is a "spiritual" issue. So the second and fourth responses are wrong.

## 2. Behavioral Dimension

The behavioral dimension commands us to be good stewards of our behaviors. The possibility of sexual sin is only one of many temptations in the world. In lesson 3 we learned that we must examine other areas of our lives to be sure we are not escaping our emotions. We can use any number of behaviors and substances to "medicate" our feelings. If we are not careful this can include our spiritual feelings.

> For the grace of God that brings salvation has appeared to all men. It teaches us to say "No" to ungodliness and worldly passions, and to live self-controlled, upright and godly lives in this present age.
> –Titus 2:11-12

Read the passage from Paul to Titus that appears in the margin. Paul confronted as many worldly sins in his day as we do in ours. He reminds us that we must discipline our behavior in order to live godly lives.

In 1 Peter 5:8, Peter describes the enemy: "Be self-controlled and alert. Your enemy the devil prowls around like a roaring lion looking for someone to devour."

➤ Where are the lions in your life? To live a victorious Christian life, you must know two things about the enemy: 1) he exists (he is real), and 2) he is a defeated spiritual power (Christ has overcome the devil). You must trust and pray for God's protection. Stop and pray. Thank God for the lions He has defeated in your past. Those successes give you strength to face the lions you encounter today. Then name your current lions. Ask God to conquer them—one day at a time—for today.

## 3. Relational Dimension

Paul knew the value of community. He continually encouraged the churches to support and love each other. He provided guidelines on how to do so. Relationship and the ability to love and be intimate with others is a key to staying healthy. Building healthy relationships with our spouses and with healthy believers is a key to sexual wholeness.

## 4. Personal Dimension

Jesus said to His disciples, "You will know the truth, and the truth will set you free" (John 8:32). In the personal dimension, we need to know the truth about ourselves, the past, and the present. The truth includes the wounds we have experienced, the strengths, talents, and abilities we possess, and the vocation to which we are called. We need to learn how to make healthy choices. This truth will help us to be honest with ourselves and others and improve our relationships.

## 5. Spiritual Dimension

Spiritual growth holds all the other dimensions of our lives in balance. Only as we develop our relationship with God do we become capable of fulfilling our capacities in the other four dimensions.

### Assignment for the Lesson

✎ The following list contains possible roadblocks to the journey of sexual and spiritual wholeness—by now you recognize that spiritual wholeness is essential to sexual wholeness. Check the roadblocks you consider issues for your journey.

❑ Perfectionism—I expect to get everything right overnight.
❑ Time management—I fear that I will not use my time well.
❑ Will power—I fear that I don't have enough.
❑ Boredom—I may become bored with the ongoing work of sexual health.
❑ Distraction—I fear getting distracted from the journey.
❑ Support—I'm not sure I will find support along the way.
❑ Accountability—I fear not being accountable to another person.
❑ Isolation—I do not have a mentor.

❑ Other _____

---

Let us not give up meeting together, as some are in the habit of doing, but let us encourage one another—and all the more as you see the Day approaching.
–Hebrews 10:25

"Whoever lives by the truth comes into the light, so that it may be seen plainly that what he has done has been done through God."
–John 3:21

✎ Below write Psalm 26:2-3, your Scripture memory verse for this unit.

_____

_____

**What guidance do you find in the passage to help you deal with the potential roadblocks to your growth?**

_____

_____

➤ Say the following affirmation five times.

I am a person who is disciplined and can apply this to my spirituality.

➤ Pray for guidance and for perseverance.

Congratulations! You have now reached the end of Part 1 of *Faithful & True*. You have done significant work on self-understanding and spiritual growth. If you have completed Part 1 after first working Part 2 as part of your sexual addiction recovery, I encourage you to continue working your program. You will find additional resources on page 221 to aid you in spiritual and personal growth.

If you completed Part 1 as the first part of your study, I invite you to continue with Part 2, even if you do not struggle with sexually compulsive or addictive behaviors. If you do not struggle with such behaviors, you may choose to study Part 2 as a way to better understand and minister to others. Or, you may choose to go on to other areas to develop your life as a disciple. You will find additional resource ideas on page 221. I pray that you will "grow in the grace and knowledge of our Lord and Savior Jesus Christ. To him be glory both now and forever! Amen" (2 Peter 3:18).

**KEY POINT**
All of what you have learned is a matter of discipline and practice.

## Discussion Group Questions

- In the beginning of your faith, what was your favorite Bible story? Bible character? Scripture verse? hymn?
- When you became a Christian, in what ways were you seeking to control? In what ways were you surrendering to God? (p. 97)
- Describe an event that has shaped your approach to spiritual matters.
- What would you like to say to Angie about her sins? (p. 98)
- Can you share one item from your list of behaviors, thoughts, and actions that have caused you shame? (p. 99)
- Describe any magical thinking solutions you have tried. (p. 102)

# PART TWO

# RECOVERING FROM SEXUAL SIN

Part 1 of *Faithful & True* helps you understand and create a plan for healthy sexuality. Part 2 addresses a more difficult situation, restoring those who have become entrapped in sexual sin. Part 2 is written for the person in the lifetime battle with sexual sin. Life change is the goal—to understand how sexual sin happens and become faithful and true again.

Some of you will be working Part 2 before you work on Part 1. Your immediate goal will be to stop sexual sin. Once you have achieved a period of "sobriety" from these behaviors, you then can go back to Part 1. Staying sexually sober is essential to staying sexually healthy.

My prayers are with those who come to this workbook as sexual addicts. I myself am recovering from a pattern of addictive sexual sin. At age 11, I discovered pornography. Through my teenage years I was on fire with sexual thoughts. My sexual sin led me through a destructive path of masturbation, prostitution, pornography, and extramarital affairs. Much of this happened while I was a pastor.

Thanks to the work of the Holy Spirit, someone intervened when I was 37 years old. I went to treatment and counseling. Gradually, I have been able to heal, stay sober, and restore my marriage. I give praise to God for the forgiveness and gift of love from my wife. I have written Part 2 from my clinical experience with hundreds of sex addicts. I have also written from my heart as one who knows God's healing and restoration.

**Regardless of the sexual sins you have committed, HOPE EXISTS.** If you are willing to be rigorously honest and courageous, Part 2 is for you. May God bless you in your work.

# Sexual Sin and Sexual Addiction

## FOCAL PASSAGE

*I do not understand what I do. For what I want to do I do not do, but what I hate I do. And if I do what I do not want to do, I agree that the law is good. As it is, it is no longer I myself who do it, but it is sin living in me. I know that nothing good lives in me, that is, in my sinful nature. For I have the desire to do what is good, but I cannot carry it out. For what I do is not the good I want to do; no, the evil I do not want to do— this I keep on doing.... What a wretched man I am! Who will rescue me from this body of death? Thanks be to God— through Jesus Christ our Lord!*

—Romans 7:15-19, 24

## MEMORY VERSE

The body is not meant for sexual immorality, but for the Lord, and the Lord for the body.
–1 Corinthians 6:13

---

### A SUCCESS STORY

Ben was 11 when he first looked at pornographic magazines. Pornography fascinated him and he kept the magazines for awhile. Later, however, he became bored with them and began to feel guilty for keeping the magazines. He threw them away and vowed never to look at such magazines again. Not too long after that Ben felt tempted to indulge in pornography again. Frightened by the temptation, he confessed his problem to his pastor. His pastor was able to counsel Ben and reassure him that while sexual desire was normal, for him to be involved with these magazines was destructive. The pastor shared Christ's forgiveness with Ben and helped him talk about his feelings. After that, Ben discovered that whenever he felt temptation he could talk to Jesus, his pastor, or his parents and feel forgiven. With these changes, he was able to remain free of pornography.

---

Praise be to God! We start with the answer. We can't save ourselves. Sin is at work in our very human nature. Our natural sexual drives can be at war inside us and we cannot control them. But God has saved us through His son Jesus Christ. Grace, forgiveness, and healthy behaviors kept Ben from the dangers of sexual addiction. In the same way, God delivers persons from sexual addiction through a combination of His grace and a network of healing relationships.

## GROWTH GOAL

In this unit we will define unmanageable sexual sin and learn how it wages war in our bodies. This will include the forms it takes, the cycle of acting out it produces, and how we think and feel when we are in the middle of it.

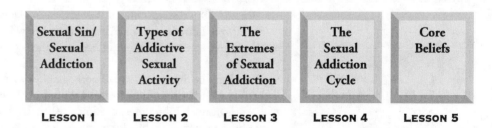

| Sexual Sin/ Sexual Addiction | Types of Addictive Sexual Activity | The Extremes of Sexual Addiction | The Sexual Addiction Cycle | Core Beliefs |
|---|---|---|---|---|
| LESSON 1 | LESSON 2 | LESSON 3 | LESSON 4 | LESSON 5 |

# Sexual Sin/Sexual Addiction

You read Ben's story on the unit page. John was also 11 when he saw his first pornographic magazines. Like Ben, John also kept the magazines. When he became bored with them, however, he started to seek out more. He felt guilty, but his friends convinced him that to look at such things was normal. He didn't dare tell his pastor or his parents. They would be mad at him and punish him. Time and time again he wanted to stop but could not. John even sought out a psychologist to find help. This man told him that looking at pornography was "normal" for a young man and not to worry about it.

Whenever John looks at the pictures, he temporarily feels a high–an excited feeling that relieves his stress. To this day he keeps stacks and stacks of pornography in his house. All of the fantasy of this material led him to a habit of masturbation. Eventually, he became obsessed with seeing a prostitute. When he finally succumbed to this temptation, John's wife found out. Her anger and frustration led her to ask John for a divorce.

✎ **What made the difference between Ben's story and John's?**

_____

_____

_____

Both Ben and John were 11 when they discovered pornography. In many ways their reaction was normal. They were adolescent boys, and their natural sexual desires were developing. To be attracted to the opposite sex and be curious about what a naked body looks like is normal.

**The man and his wife were both naked, and they felt no shame.**
**–Genesis 2:25**

Nakedness is not by itself sinful. Remember that before the fall Adam and Eve were naked and not ashamed. Looking at nakedness with lustful desire is sinful. Lust involves wanting to have something that is not part of God's intention for the relationship between a married man and woman. Lust separates us from God. For this reason looking at pornography is sin. It excites our lustful desires—desires for something we can't have.

Both Ben and John committed sexual sin by looking at pornography. Both of them, appropriately, felt guilty about what they did. Beyond that their stories are very different. They dealt with their guilt in different ways. Ben decided to confess his sin. He sought help and experienced forgiveness. He learned from the experience, grew as a Christian, and stopped the behavior. John felt guilt and shame. He was afraid that he was a bad person for what he had done. Therefore, he didn't confess his sin. He did not learn from the experience, did not grow, and did not experience forgiveness. He remained in sin and continued to repeat it. For John, sexual sin became sexual addiction.

Ben and John reacted differently to their experience of experimenting with pornography. Their reactions differed for many reasons. We will try to understand these reasons. Below is a list of some of the other differences in their stories.

For John, the first experience of pornography developed in several ways. It:
- became repetitive, John returned to sexual behaviors again and again.
- degenerated, John progressed to more serious sexual activities.
- became unmanageable, John wanted to stop but couldn't. He became powerless.

Remember the following
key words. Addictive
behaviors are:

1. Repetitive
2. Degenerative
3. Unmanageable
4. Medicative
5. Destructive

- made John feel better at least temporarily. Without even understanding what he was doing, John used sex to medicate his mood.
- led to destructive consequences.

The five key words in the definition of addiction appear in the margin. Examine the words individually. Compare the key words to the development of sexual addiction in John's life.

 Begin honestly to examine your sexual behaviors by the the five elements of addictive behavior. Place a check mark beside each of the key words that describe your experience with pornography or other shame-producing sexual thoughts and actions.

### Repetitive

I believe to classify a behavior as an addiction requires a pattern of repetitive use for at least two years—however, not necessarily every day. Some alcoholics, for example, only get drunk occasionally. This is known as a "binge" pattern. They may get drunk only on weekends, days off, holidays, or every six months. The pattern is still repetitive. Sinful sexual behavior can be repetitive in the same way. It may occur every day, or it may happen periodically. A person may have one affair a year. He or she is not acting out every day, but the pattern is still repetitive.

### Degenerative

The addiction intensifies over time. The person requires more of the activity to achieve the same effect. This dynamic reflects the experience called "tolerance." Alcoholics, for example, require increasingly more alcohol to achieve the same high. Sex is no different. The addict needs more and more, more frequent or more intense, sexual activity to achieve the same sexual high. The degeneration may mean progression to more dangerous and damaging activities, or it may mean the same behaviors produce increasing shame and decreasing pleasure.

### Unmanageable

Addicts use the word "powerless." An addict wants to stop doing something and can't. In Romans 7:21 Paul says, "When I want to do good, evil is right there with me." Paul also talks of a war between his spirit and his body. Addicts know this war. Over and over again, addicts do things they don't want to do.

Paul was probably not talking about sexual addiction, but the principle is the same. As Christians we know that we can never live the kind of life we desire through our own power. If we could, we wouldn't need God; our lives would be manageable on our own.

*I see another law at work in the members of my body, waging war against the law of my mind and making me a prisoner of the law of sin at work within my members. What a wretched man I am! Who will rescue me from this body of death?*
**–Romans 7:23-24**

### Medicative

We use addictive substances or behaviors to change our feelings. We use the addictive agent to alter our mood. If an addict feels sad, depressed, lonely, tired, angry, abandoned, or a variety of other emotions, he or she may use a substance or behavior (like sex) to achieve a "high." The high may not be a feeling of euphoria but simply a relief from the depression. Substances like alcohol, cocaine, or heroin produce a temporary artificial feeling of well-being. Sexual behaviors produce chemicals in the brain that give us this same high. Many sex addicts consider themselves drug addicts because of the chemical changes sex has on their brain.

### Destructive

Addiction always destroys. Have you ever known an alcoholic who literally drank himself or herself to death? Sexual addiction also leads to a variety of destructive consequences. Divorces, financial cost, ruined vocations, and legal difficulties all result from sexual sin. Sexually transmitted diseases including AIDS lead to many early deaths. Paul says, "For the wages of sin is death, but the gift of God is eternal life in Christ Jesus our Lord" (Romans 6:23). The verse speaks primarily of separation from God, spiritual death, but the wages of sexual sin include the death of dreams, families, and lives.

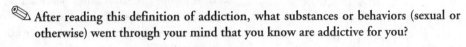 After reading this definition of addiction, what substances or behaviors (sexual or otherwise) went through your mind that you know are addictive for you?

_____

_____

Maybe the Holy Spirit is telling you what you need to work on.

➤ Think about your definition of sin. What qualities of addiction are sinful?

I define sin as anything that—
- separates us from fellowship with God
- keeps us from the salvation given to us in His Son Jesus
- prevents us from experiencing His will for our life.

The healthy sexuality model in Part 1 explains that each of us are sexual beings. We are sexual beings whether we are married or not. We can be sexually whole whether we are married or not, but genital sexuality is designed exclusively for the marriage relationship.

> "For this reason a man will leave his father and mother and be united to his wife, and the two will become one flesh." This is a profound mystery —but I am talking about Christ and the church.
> –Ephesians 5:31-32

As Paul says in Ephesians 5, marriage is a spiritual union that reflects the relationship between Christ and His church. Sexual intercourse is an expression of that union. Any sexual activity that doesn't spiritually honor the sacredness of the marriage union is sin. As I describe in Part 1, healthy sexuality is an expression of healthy spirituality.

Don't confuse sexual sin with sexual addiction. Addiction is a process of repetitive, degenerative, unmanageable, medicating (mood-altering), and destructive sinful behaviors. Sexual addiction is the process, not merely the behaviors. You might explain the difference with the following analogy:

> Joe has coronary artery disease. He has had two heart attacks. His doctor tells him that his cholesterol is too high, and he needs to stop smoking. Joe has two distinct problems. First, he has a disease process at work in his body. His arteries are damaged. Second, he has some destructive behaviors; lack of exercise, smoking, a bad diet. His destructive behaviors are sins. He abuses the body God gave him. The sins add to the disease, but the disease is a process separate and distinct from the behaviors.

I sometimes describe sexual addiction with the language of a disease. Some people misunderstand and think I am saying the addict is not responsible for his or her behaviors. I explain that seeing the disease process helps the addict to take appropriate responsibility for the behavior. The process involved in becoming a sexual addict involves some of the same processes as a developing disease. Thus, by looking at the disease process we can see how the sexual addict can take responsibility for his or her behavior.

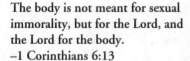 Three elements of a clinical description of a disease appear below. Beside each one write a statement explaining how that element applies to sexual addiction. For example, you might write that the cause of sexual addiction is sinful behavior.

Disease has a known cause. _____

Disease has a known course of development. _____

If left untreated, disease will get worse and sometimes lead to death. _____

_____

Sexual addiction has known causes. We know what path it takes. If left untreated it will get worse. It kills self-worth, relationships, and can lead to physical death.

Sin is not a disease. Sexual addiction, remember, is a *process* of sexual sin. Wrong sexual thoughts and behaviors are sin, but the addiction is the process that drives the behaviors. As such, sexual addiction operates like a disease. The cure for the disease of addiction begins with a relationship with God through Jesus Christ. Sin is unmanageable as long as we reject Christ's salvation. We do have the power to accept God's love in Christ. Sexual addiction is unmanageable only if we don't get help. We get help from God and from healthy relationships with others who can show us how to change behaviors.

## Assignment for the Lesson

➤ Are you willing to take a long and courageous look at your sexual behaviors, family, and current relationships? Are you willing to be honest and take some risks? Are you willing to trust others to help you with your problems?

If you can answer yes to these questions, continue working Part 2.

✏ Write on a card 1 Corinthians 6:13, the Scripture memory verse for this unit. Carry the card with you. Regularly review your memory verses.

➤ Say the following affirmation five times.

I can find sexual sobriety.

➤ Pray for yourself. Remember that right now, as Paul says, the Holy Spirit prays for you "with sighs too deep for words" (Romans 8:26, RSV).

The body is not meant for sexual immorality, but for the Lord, and the Lord for the body.
–1 Corinthians 6:13

LESSON
2

# Types of Addictive Sexual Activity

*For a prostitute is a deep pit and a wayward wife is a narrow well. Like a bandit she lies in wait, and multiplies the unfaithful among men.*

—Proverbs 23:27-28

Any form of sexual activity can become addictive if it meets the criteria described in lesson 1. My purpose in this lesson is not to graphically describe sexual activity, but rather to explain several categories of it. Why is that important? Consider how Jesus dealt with a severely troubled man. Jesus confronted the demon-possessed man. He asked the man what his problem was, making the man admit and face the problem.

*When he saw Jesus from a distance, he ran and fell on his knees in front of him. He shouted at the top of his voice, "What do you want with me, Jesus, Son of the Most High God? Swear to God that you won't torture me!" For Jesus had said to him, "Come out of this man, you evil spirit!"*

*Then Jesus asked him, "What is your name?"*

*"My name is Legion," he replied, "for we are many."*

–Mark 5:6-9

When Jesus cast out the demons in this man, He asked them their names. When a doctor gives you a diagnosis, he calls it by name. We know what we are dealing with as opposed to something ambiguously frightening. The same is true for sexual sin. We need to call it by name.

Pat Carnes, author of *Out of the Shadows*, categorized sexual behaviors into three main groups. We used to call these groups levels I, II, and III. Those labels were misleading; because each of the behaviors are problems in their own right, and it is dangerous to start comparing. I have given different names to these groups. I refer to the behaviors as building block behaviors, sexual addiction behaviors, and offending sexual behaviors.

## BUILDING BLOCK BEHAVIORS

Fantasy
Pornography
Masturbation

**But I tell you that anyone who looks at a woman lustfully has already committed adultery with her in his heart.**
–Matthew 5:28

### 1. Building Block Behaviors

The building block behaviors include: fantasy, pornography, and masturbation. In any particular individual these behaviors may or may not lead to sexual addiction behaviors and offending behaviors.

Fantasy is the cornerstone of sexual sin/addiction. Sexual fantasy, simply, is thinking about sex. It may be thinking about previous experiences, current ones, or imagined ones in the future.

Fantasy is not inherently evil. Sexual thoughts about one's spouse are normal. The writer of the Song of Solomon certainly describes this. Fantasy becomes a problem when we think about sex in inappropriate, sinful ways. Fantasy is a powerful drug. Thinking about sex creates chemicals in the brain that are more powerful than heroin. When we think about sinful sex, we can easily get addicted to these powerful brain chemicals. Because of this effect, sex addicts are actually drug addicts. When sex addicts cease fantasizing they experience a kind of withdrawal, a chemical reaction in some ways similar to the one alcoholics experience when they stop drinking.

Fantasy can be used to raise our mood. However, it has still another and perhaps more powerful effect on us emotionally. Fantasies can create perfect sexual partners and perfect sexual experiences in our imagination. How can any spouse measure up to what can be imagined? This dishonors a spouse and dooms us to perpetual disappointment with our actual sexual experience.

Some sex addicts dream of a "magic" partner, someone who will be all-loving, nurturing, and sexual. This person will give unconditionally to the addict in both emotional and sexual ways. In this dynamic, sex addicts have emotional longing attached to their fantasies. As we will describe more fully later, sex addicts want to be nurtured and loved in their sexual experiences. They are looking for love in all the wrong places.

✎ Have you ever fantasized about a magic partner, a perfect lover? ❑ Yes ❑ No

Did you ever find that partner? ❑ Yes ❑ No

Is finding such a person actually possible? ❑ Yes ❑ No

Pornography is all around us. We can get into much debate trying to define pornography. Some would criticize nudity in art museums as being pornographic. To me, pornography is anything that excites lustful and sinful thoughts. By this definition, many magazines, TV shows, movies, songs, even paintings are obviously pornographic because they excite sinful passions in almost everyone. In other cases, however, pornography may be in the mind of the beholder. Whatever stimulus triggers sinful fantasy could be considered pornographic for that person. A sexually addicted minister told me that, for him, a popular TV game show was pornographic because he fantasized about the female models on the show. Many people fantasize about models in catalogues. Many men tell me that *National Geographic* magazine was the first place that they saw naked women. You wouldn't consider that magazine pornographic, but to them it was.

You can find pornographic magazines dedicated to any imaginable perversion. Child pornography is a billion dollar industry. Some pornographic material is so expensive that sex addicts spend thousands of dollars a month to buy it. Another sad development is the unlimited amounts of pornography available for home computers.

### Esther's Story
Esther was 80 years old when she entered the hospital to have surgery on her genitals. A pastor's wife for 60 years, her husband became impotent in their first year of marriage. Too ashamed to discuss the problem, he never talked about or initiated sex after that. Lonely, but wanting to be faithful in marriage, Esther learned to masturbate. She did this daily for 59 years. The friction had so damaged her, she needed medical intervention.

To be judgmental of a lonely and childless woman like Esther is difficult. Her story is unusual. Masturbation is a common behavior many children and adolescents discover. Most experiment with it, then move on and away from it as they mature and grow. For Esther, however, masturbation became a chronic and destructive habit. She was addicted. It was an escape from her loneliness and anger. Esther's husband, the pastor, could escape to his work. She had her life of fantasy. In her fantasies, she told me, she could imagine the most charming, gentle, kind, and understanding men.

These three building block behaviors form a vicious cycle. They feed on each other. Pornography fuels fantasy while fantasy can turn many different stimuli into pornography. Masturbation uses fantasy and pornography for sexual stimulation and creates a need for more. This cycle gets worse as the addict needs more to achieve the same effect. The person develops tolerance.

The cycle supplies a quick "fix." It provides instant gratification and prevents the person from making the healthy choices that would lead to nurture and fulfillment for his or her deep hunger for love and affection.

## SEXUAL ADDICTION BEHAVIORS

Prostitution
Sex with a consenting partner
Addicted sex in marriage
Voyeurism and Exhibitionism
Phone Sex
Indecent Liberties
Bestiality

### 2. Sexual Addiction Behaviors
I call the second level sexual addiction behaviors. A list of common sexual addiction behaviors appears in the margin.
Prostitution is, in fact, the most ancient of professions. The Bible is full of references to the dangers of prostitution. The only thing different about prostitution today is the various names it is called (escort services, modeling agencies) and creative ways it can be delivered (by phone or computer).

Some people spend thousands of dollars a month on prostitution. One friend is in jail because he robbed banks to pay for his addiction to prostitutes. Many men visit prostitutes looking not only for sexual excitement, but also love and nurture. Perhaps you know the feeling of despair after your encounter with a prostitute. Even though you found sexual excitement, you were emotionally disappointed.

Sex with a consenting partner can include a variety of circumstances and relationships. On the one end are those affairs of long duration involving some degree of emotional attachment. On the other end are those encounters that are quick and may not involve even knowing the other person's name. These encounters are called *anonymous sex.*

Having a sexual encounter outside marriage creates the high of newness. Marriages have difficulty competing with the excitement of an affair. The adrenaline or the dangers of the chase may also factor into the experience. Usually, when an affair moves toward a decision about commitment, the newness wears off. An addict will terminate the experience and look for a new one. Just as with prostitution, the addict is usually looking for the sexual high and the false sense of emotional nurture that the affair symbolizes.

✎ If you are married, have you ever had sex with your spouse while you fantasized about someone else? ❑ Yes ❑ No

Have you ever thought that your relationship with your spouse was OK because you had sex? ❑ Yes ❑ No

Have you ever demanded sex from your partner even though he or she was unwilling? ❑ Yes ❑ No

Have you ever asked your spouse to engage in a form of sexual activity even though he or she was unwilling? ❑ Yes ❑ No

The fact that sexual activity takes place in marriage does not make that activity healthy or appropriate. Sex in marriage can be addictive. Remember, when marital sex becomes an escape from intimacy, rather than an expression of it, a problem exists. When we repetitively use sex to avoid being present with each other, sex destroys intimacy. Sexual activity doesn't have to be adulterous to lead to sexual addiction.

✎ Place a check in the box beside any of the following activities that you have done.

❑ Undressed someone with your eyes.
❑ Positioned yourself someplace to get a look into a bathroom or dressing room.
❑ Worn something revealing.
❑ Hugged someone and felt sexually excited.
❑ Talked to someone on the phone and sexually fantasized about him or her.

These questions reveal that some types of sexual activity occur in ways we don't typically consider expressions of sexual addiction. Exhibitionism can involve more than wearing a raincoat and exposing yourself or being a stripteaser. Voyeurism—the act of watching someone for sexual excitement—is not just looking into bedroom windows at 2:00 a.m. It can be done in the most public of places. Obscene phone sex is not just a matter of heavy breathing or obscene language.

Indecent liberties are a matter of touching someone and getting sexually excited by it. The other person might not even know that you are having this reaction. A friend of mine used to hug everyone at church. It seemed like such a loving thing, but he was constantly getting sexually excited with the women he hugged. Indecent liberties also happen in crowded places, like elevators or buses.

Finally, bestiality—having sex with animals—is one of the most shameful of sexual activities. Bestiality is quite common. Pornography portrays it. I have been shocked when traveling to Amsterdam, for example, to see postcards being sold on the street portraying bestiality.

OFFENDING SEXUAL
BEHAVIORS

Incest
Molestation
Rape
Authority Rape

## 3. Offending Sexual Behaviors

I call the final classification of sexually-addictive behaviors offending sexual behaviors. I don't think I need to explain incest, molestation, or physical rape. They are, unfortunately, quite common. As many as one third of all women and one fourth of all men have been sexually abused. An alarming percentage of women have been raped. Some offenders are sexually addicted and some are not. People commit offensive sexual acts for reasons other than sexual addiction. If you have ever committed any of these offenses, please get professional help. Remember, no sin is so great that it cannot be forgiven. Be of courage and reach out for help.

When we think of rape, we usually think of an attacker who physically overpowers the victim or uses the threat of physical violence. Another, more subtle form of rape also occurs. Authority rape occurs when someone uses the power of his or her role to gain sexual access to another person. A person who becomes dependent on a therapist, for example, may become sexual with the therapist. On the surface this may seem mutual, but the client's dependence on the therapist's authority usually means that the client's trust is childlike. The client's consent to sex, even if he or she is the initiator, makes this an emotionally incestuous situation. Likewise, a doctor, pastor, teacher, boss, lawyer, or any other person in power and authority over someone else can use that power for sexual gain.

➤ Have you ever felt that someone was attracted to you because of your role or position?

In many states this kind of sexual activity is considered criminal in nature. Pastors, for example, have gone to jail for being sexual with consenting members of their congregation.

## Assignment for the Lesson

➤ Repeat your Scripture memory verse for this unit.

➤ This lesson may have caused some deep shame for you. Please talk to your group or someone about how you feel.

➤ Say the following affirmation five times.

No matter what sexual sin I have committed, I can become sexually whole again through Jesus Christ.

➤ Pray for God to give you wisdom and strength to deal with the challenges you have identified in this lesson.

# The Extremes of Sexual Addiction

In this lesson you will examine the diverse ways people act out sexual addictions. Being sexually addicted is not a matter of engaging in sexual sin all the time.

**ACT OUT:**
We refer to any form of practicing an addictive behavior as "acting out."

### Ryan's Story

Ryan couldn't understand himself. As a Christian he was committed to sexual purity. All his life, however, he struggled with periods of sexual sin. Masturbation and pornography were destroying him financially. He went through periods when he would spend hundreds of dollars on pornographic videos, watch them, and masturbate several times a day. After doing this for several weeks, he would get so angry and disgusted with himself that he would throw all of the tapes away, rededicate himself to God, and preach to himself to stop masturbating. Sometimes, he would punish himself by denying himself food, TV, or some other part of his daily routine. He would also deny himself sex with his wife. Sometimes he went for days and weeks free of the sexual sin. Once his wife found the videos in the garbage and confronted him. That time he was able to go several months without buying another video. But he always came back to it.

Ryan is like a lot of sex addicts who are able to stop their sexual behaviors for various periods of time. Some punish themselves in major or minor ways. Several sex addicts I have known have been so desperate they have even cut off their genitals.

Ryan is an example of the extremes of sexual addiction. Sometimes he acts out a lot, sometimes not at all. Pat Carnes, the pioneer in the field of sexual addiction, understood this when he compared sexual addiction to an eating disorder. Carnes compared these two disorders in the following way:

|  |  | **Sexual overeating** |
|---|---|---|
| **Sexual Anorexia** | **Normal Sexuality** | **Sexual bulimia** |
| **Anorexia** | **Normal Eating** | **Overeating** |
|  |  | **Bulimia** |

Food anorexics stop eating, or eat very little. They starve themselves. Usually, they have a very distorted view of themselves and think that they are fat. Stopping their eating is a way of controlling their perception of themselves. Overeaters simply eat a lot. They may have different appetites and metabolism, but most of them eat when they are lonely, bored, angry, or frightened. Food becomes like a nurturing friend. Overeaters may also get a high from shopping for and eating various kinds of food. Bulimics also overeat. When they do, however, they also do something to purge themselves of the food. They may throw up, use laxatives, or exercise excessively. Bulimics are also concerned that they are too fat. Their behaviors are also attempts to control their self-image.

Similar problems underly food addiction and sex addiction. In fact, many sex addicts are also food addicts.

✎ **Review the last two paragraphs. List some of the similarities that you see between food addiction and sex addiction.**

_____

_____

Sexual anorexics may be like Ryan. They turn their sexuality off for periods of time. This is their effort to control their sexuality. (As we will see in unit 9, this need to control sexuality may also be due to memories of sexual traumas in the past.) This phenomenon is sometimes referred to in the addiction community as "white knuckling" or "acting in." Some sexually-addicted Christians I have known even justify turning off their sexuality as a sign of purity—they are more spiritual than others, they don't follow the ways of the "flesh."

✎ **Have you ever tried something to control your sexual behaviors? In the following short list of behaviors, check all that apply. Add to the list any additional behaviors you have tried.**

❑ cold showers
❑ exercise
❑ not talking to the opposite sex
❑ avoiding TV, movies, radio, magazines
❑ prayer
❑ going to lots of church activities
❑ Bible study
❑ making bargains with God, "If you will take away my lust God, I will _____."
❑ harming yourself
❑ denying yourself something you desired
❑ negotiating with your spouse not to initiate sex
❑ always saying no to your spouse
❑ add your own examples _____

Some of the behaviors on the list clearly are wrong. Others are important, normally healthy ways to relieve stress or avoid temptation. When we use anything to avoid dealing with reality, however, the behavior can become damaging. Some people even use prayer as a destructive way to escape reality. For them prayer ceases to be fellowship with God and becomes a way to manipulate self and others.

Sexual bulimics also are like Ryan. They sexually act out and then purge by punishing themselves for what they've done. They may harm themselves physically, or deprive themselves of another form of pleasure. This may be an attempt to control themselves and to control God. They think they can punish themselves so no one else, including God, will have to.

Sexual overeaters simply act out excessively and feel despair and guilt afterwards. They, too, are trying to fill a deep spiritual and emotional void in their lives. They may be bored, lonely, angry, anxious, or stressed out. We will work more specifically on this in unit 8.

✎ **Can you remember the last time that you were denied an opportunity to be sexual? For example, your spouse said no or was unavailable. What were you feeling emotionally or spiritually at that time?**

_____

_____

✎ **Do you recognize yourself in any of these patterns? If so, which?**

❑ sexual anorexia
❑ sexual bulimia
❑ sexual overeating

Two key points exist here: First, frequency of sexual acting out does not determine sexual addiction. Repetitiveness is the distinguishing mark of addiction, but the repetition may be over long periods of time. Between acting-out episodes you may experience periods of no sexual activity at all. In some extreme cases, sex addicts have been known to go for years without being sexual.

Second, these extremes of sexual addiction are, in part, an effort to control. Sexual anorexics and bulimics are trying to control their sexuality. Both may be trying to control memories. Those who sexually act out excessively may be trying to control their emotions and find love and nurture.

✎ **In the light of what you have just read, which of the following methods provide an answer to the question of finding sexual faithfulness?**

❑ More willpower, I just need to try harder.
❑ Surrender, I need to stop trying to control.
❑ Incentive, I need a more effective system of rewards and punishments.

Write your own statement describing the first thing you need to do to develop greater sexual health and faithfulness.

_____

_____

Being out of control usually means that a person is trying to exercise too much control. The answer is to surrender that control to God. You may have answered in one of many ways. I responded that the beginning place is surrender. I must stop trying to control. I need to learn about myself, establish supportive relationships, and become accountable.

## Assignment for the Lesson

➤ **What roadblocks do you experience in surrendering control of your sexuality? What feelings make it difficult for you to give up control?**

➤ **Say the following affirmation five times.**

I am able to trust and give control to God.

➤ **Pray for humility.**

LESSON
4

# The Sexual Addiction Cycle

Leslie was near suicide when she finally got help. A legal professional by day, for years she lived a life of sexual sin at night. Her pattern started when she was small. Her father, brother, and uncle molested her. The pattern continued when she dated sexually aggressive boys. In college Leslie engaged in sex with several of her professors.

In her adult life, Leslie's pattern of sexually acting out continued. She had an elaborate ritual. She dressed in a way she knew would attract certain types of men. Then Leslie would go to a bar and pick up a man. Leslie then took him home, had sex with him, and usually never saw him again. She was known to do this more than once per night. Leslie figured that she had been sexual with more than 500 men.

Each night after her sexual acting out, Leslie felt despair and hopelessness. Many times she vowed to stop. Sometimes she abstained for days, even weeks; however, she consistently returned to this lifestyle. Her sexual behaviors were the only way she knew to be with a man—to be held, to be touched, to be talked to. Leslie became so desperate she began to ask herself: *What good is living anyway?*

## Cycle of addiction

Leslie is now in recovery and has been sober for 15 years. Her story, however, is typical of many others. It illustrates a pattern that is really a cycle. Pat Carnes first described this cycle in his book *Out of the Shadows*. Diagrammed, it looks like this:

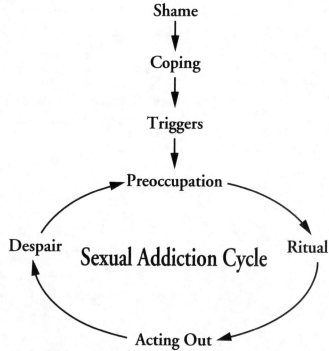

Let's look at each of these stages.

### Shame

Shame is a strong emotion caused by consciousness of guilt, shortcoming, or impropriety. We feel shame when we are exposed physically or emotionally. When our real or imagined faults are exposed, we feel shame. I use shame as a very inclusive word to describe the feeling of utter worthlessness most sex addicts feel. In units 9 and 10 we will try to understand where this feeling originates. The same events that produce shame also may create anger, anxiety, and loneliness. Because these feelings are unpleasant, the mind seeks to avoid them.

✎ **Check the word which describes how often you feel lonely.**

Constantly          Occasionally          Seldom          Often

✎ **In the margin describe the last time you recognized feelings of loneliness.**

## Coping

Coping may simply mean we seek to avoid feelings of shame. Coping can also mean that we try somehow to deal with the sexual stimuli we have experienced. Another way of looking at coping is to understand it as a matter of survival. We survive our feelings. Again, as we will see in later units, our feelings may stem from life experiences. Having sexual thoughts may be our only learned method of surviving those feelings.

## Triggers

Triggers are any stimuli that a person interprets as sexual. This varies from person to person and depends on the person's past experiences and memories. We can interpret as sexual input from any of our senses. For example, looking at certain pictures in the newspaper may trigger one person while the smell of a particular perfume or cologne may trigger someone else.

✎ **What triggers you sexually? List at least five examples.**

_____

_____

## Preoccupation/Fantasy

Preoccupation, in this cycle, means that we get stuck in sexual fantasy. We spend hours fantasizing. We may be distracted from everything else. Remember, we may fantasize for a purpose. We use fantasy either to alter feelings or in an attempt to produce love and nurture.

✎ **Check the one that is most true for you. I fantasize—**

❏ as a way to avoid or alter certain feelings
❏ in a search for love and nurture
❏ but seldom or never engage in sexual fantasy.

Perhaps you fantasize for all of these reasons. For example, if you are trying to avoid the feeling of sadness or loneliness, you may fantasize about someone wonderfully loving and nurturing. Perhaps this fantasy involves the perfect sexual experience or the "magic" partner.

## Ritual

Ritual is a key part of the addiction cycle. Another word for ritual might be "preparation." It means anything that you do to get ready for a sexual encounter. Whatever you do between fantasizing and being sexual can be a part of the ritual.

Consider Scott's example. Something at work triggered Scott to fantasize. The fantasy led to thoughts of pornography. Scott had acted out his ritual many times. He immediately thought of the store where he could purchase pornography.

Scott left work with the excuse that he was going to visit a client. He drove out of the office parking lot in the direction of the client's office. Within a few blocks, however, he stopped at a cash machine.

Scott withdrew enough cash and headed back to the store in his usual indirect route so no one would notice. He purchased his pornography and headed to his favorite viewing location. Scott shuffled through the pornographic magazines and grew more sexually excited. From his car phone, Scott called a woman who worked in the same office complex and with whom he had been having a lunchtime affair for a few weeks. Scott pleaded with her to make up an excuse to leave work so that they could have sex. She gave in, vowing that this was the last time, and they met at their usual spot.

In our example, Scott sought an outlet for his sexual feelings through an affair. Many addicts masturbate, go to a prostitute, or demand sex from their spouses.

Let's look at the elements of Scott's ritual:
- He encountered a sexual thought or trigger.
- The thought brought memories of his past experience with pornography.
- He began to process mental rationalizations about using pornography.
- The rationalizations became the excuses or lies that support his behaviors.
- He maintained a supply list of knowledge—where to buy pornography.
- He acquired the necessary money.
- He made the purchase.
- He secretly viewed the material.
- He acted out sexually.

Notice some of the key words here: trigger, memories, rationalizations, lies, and secrets.

➤ Do you recognize any of these elements for yourself? We will work more on them in unit 8. What might be an antidote to these words? What positive qualities do you need to cultivate to replace memories, rationalizations, lies, and secrets?

_____

One answer would be honesty. When you start getting honest about your triggers, memories, rationalizations, lies, or secrets, the power of your experience will diminish.

Rituals can vary in length. Rituals can be very quick. A trigger may lead you to walk into a bathroom and masturbate. That may take only a few minutes.

Rituals can also take place over a matter of days or even weeks. Take Tim and Donna's story as an example of an extended ritual.

Tim met Donna at the water cooler at work. It was a very brief encounter, but Tim was immediately sexually attracted to her and wondered what an encounter with her would be like.

Tim was married, but his sex life fell far short of his expectations. Donna, too, was married. Her husband's job, however, kept him away for days at a time. Tim and Donna met again, this time the conversation lasted a bit longer. As time passed, their conversations increased in length. At some point, sexual humor entered into the conversations. Both Tim and Donna laughed, neither one was offended. Eventually, they both decided to have lunch together. They developed a regular pattern of having lunch. They began to discuss intimate details of each other's life.

Tim and Donna discovered a mutual loneliness and became "soul" mates. Meanwhile, the sexual humor grew to a deeper level. One day, they decided they were both serious and headed for the nearest place for their sexual encounter.

This whole process evolved over months. If ever discovered or found out, Tim would protest. "We don't know how this happened, it was like a thunderstorm. We just fell into bed with each other." They both were deluded, this feeling of being "soul" mates has convinced Tim and Donna that they have finally found the truly "right" person.

✎ Check the descriptions that seem true of this ritual:

❑ new and romantic          ❑ secretive
❑ exciting                  ❑ no responsibility of commitment.
❑ dangerous

For Tim and Donna, the ritual itself was addicting. The wonderfully exciting feelings of a new relationship were difficult to avoid. Tim and Donna crossed many moral boundaries. They lied to many people. They deluded themselves. They kept many secrets. Tim and Donna offended against two spouses. Their story contains all the ingredients of a romance novel or a soap opera.

Note two points about rituals. First, they are totally unique to you. No one else will perform a ritual the same way that you do. Second, you must understand all of your rituals if you are going to stop sexually sinning. You may have more than one ritual going at the same time. You may have countless rituals going: one to buy pornography, one to see a prostitute, one to masturbate, and several rituals involving people whom you are "recruiting" for affairs.

The third stage of the sexual addiction cycle is acting out. We have already discussed the various forms of this (pages 117-121).

### Despair
The final part of the cycle is despair. In a study, Pat Carnes found that 72% of sex addicts had actively contemplated suicide.[1] This is despair. They tell themselves, I did what I told myself I was not going to do again. I have failed. I am a miserable sinner. Not even God can forgive the multiple times I have done these sinful sexual acts. I am a terrible and worthless person.

You may feel like a victim. You wonder how this could have happened. Why won't God take away your lust? You are angry at God and others. How could that other person have so seduced you? You feel out of control, angry, sad, lonely, and disgusted with yourself. What will you do?

Addicts continually return to the one certain answer—medicate the feelings again.

So, the whole cycle starts all over again. That is why it is a cycle. Perhaps you turn to other behaviors, like drinking, work, gambling, drugs, or anything that medicates and takes away your feeling of despair. If you are a sex addict, however, you will always return to sex—until you experience genuine change.

✎ Review Ben's story on page 113. Ben experienced the early stages of what could have become sexual addiction. Below check each of the elements of Ben's story that helped to rescue him.

❑ Honesty—he admitted the problem.
❑ Confession—he broke the silence.
❑ Shame—he shamed and punished himself into better behavior.
❑ Support—he found people who would accept and encourage him.
❑ Prayer—he discovered he could talk to Jesus about the temptation.

Ben used all but one of these sources of help. He exercised the wisdom of Proverbs 28:13 rather than allowing shame to capture him. The same sources of help that saved a little boy named Ben have helped millions of addicts to find recovery.

**KEY POINT**
Sexual preoccupations and rituals will almost always lead to sexual acting out. In order to stop sexual sin, you must stop the rituals as well.

He who conceals his sins does not prosper, but whoever confesses and renounces them finds mercy.
–Proverbs 28:13

## Assignment for the Lesson

✎ What thoughts and memories came to you while working on this unit? List as many as you can on the lines below. You will need to refer to them in unit 8.

_____

_____

_____

_____

➤ Say the following affirmation five times.

"I can do all things through Christ which strengthens me" (Philippians 4:13, KJV).

➤ Reread the Focal Passage for this unit. Pray for understanding of your own unmanageability.

**LESSON 5**

# Core Beliefs

Those of us who have committed sexual sin have thought about ourselves and about our sin in various ways. In this unit I want you to examine some of those thoughts.

## Larry's Story

Larry grew up in a family that looked good from the outside but was an emotional wasteland. Neither his mother nor his father helped Larry to feel loved and valued. He looked at pornography for the first time at age 13. He discovered it in his father's closet. Secretly, Larry took it to his own bedroom, but he was always careful to put it back. He thought to himself that it must be all right if his father did it. Still, he felt terrible about it. What he was doing seemed against what the church was teaching him. But, looking at pornography gave him such a sense of pleasure and a definite high. Neither of his parents spent much time with him. The women who smiled in the magazines seemed like such friends.

Not long after he discovered pornography, one of the older neighborhood boys showed Larry how to masturbate. When he responded to this, the same boy talked Larry into participating in oral sex. He felt ashamed and frightened. The neighbor boy was older and Larry didn't know what to do. How could he talk to his parents or anyone else about what he had done. Larry was afraid of being called "gay."

A pattern of escalating sexual activity continued in Larry's life. He felt terrible about himself. Every time, Larry would confess his sins to God and feel forgiven for a while. Then he would go back to sexual sin again. Larry was lonely. He never really had a girlfriend until he met his wife. They dated for a short time and then got married. They didn't really know each other well, but their marriage seemed like the right thing to do.

Sex between them was rare after the first few weeks. Larry was disappointed and angry but didn't know how to talk to his wife about his frustration. He was afraid of her, not because of anything she said or did. Larry feared her because she was a woman and he was generally frightened by women. When his wife said no to sex, Larry thought she must not love him.

Larry justified his sexual sins because his sexual needs were not being met at home. Something had to be done to ease his frustration. He thought he wasn't really hurting anyone with pornography and masturbation. Later he began to visit prostitutes.

## CORE BELIEF #1:
### "Sex is equal to love, and sex is my most important need."[2]

Let's look at this story carefully and examine Larry's patterns of thinking. When he first looked at pornography, the women were smiling at him. They seemed friendly. Larry associated this "friendliness" with their nakedness and the sexual content of the pictures. It was one of the first times in Larry's life when sex was associated with "friendliness." Larry never felt that his mother loved him. He felt desperate to get close to a woman to fill that void. Larry later translated his wife's rejection of sex as a personal rejection of himself. Larry believed that because of this rejection, she did not love him. Larry was practicing the first Core Belief. He believed that "sex is equal to love and sex is my most important need."

✎ List any movies, TV shows, magazines, advertising, or life experiences that have taught you that sex is equal to love.

_____

_____

## CORE BELIEF #2:
### "I am a bad and worthless person."

Larry's experience growing up taught him that he wasn't worth much. His parents didn't spend time with him, an older boy sexually abused him, and he started to violate his own values early in life. His pattern of increasing sexual activity convinced him that he was not worthy of even God's forgiveness.

✎ Can you remember a time when you felt utterly worthless? When was it?

_____

## CORE BELIEF #3:
### "No one loves me as I am."

Larry didn't have a base of security in his life. He felt abandoned emotionally by his parents. He married the first girl who showed any interest in him. Then Larry thought his wife didn't love him because she did not meet his sexual needs (Can you see how his thinking is based on the first Core Belief?)

Operating on the first core belief led Larry to experience more rejection. Since he believed sex equals love, and since his need for love was so great, his demands for sex were unrealistic. Thus Larry caused his wife to react in a way he saw as rejection. The rejection and his feelings of worthlessness led to and reinforced the next core belief.

✎ Have you ever felt that you weren't good enough for someone, or that someone didn't like you because of who you are? Who was that person?

_____

## CORE BELIEF #4:
### "No one will take care of me but me."

Larry took it upon himself to meet his own sexual needs. He didn't know how to ask for help or how to admit that he needed help. Larry learned from the beginning that he must meet his own needs. His developed self-sufficiency expressed the fourth core belief of sexual addiction.

✎ Can you think of a time when you felt hurt or angry because you couldn't or wouldn't ask for help? When was that?

_____

_____

➤ Ponder this question. Do your Christian beliefs teach that you are better if you are strong or if you are weak?

When you think about the last two core beliefs—no one loves me as I am and no one will take care of me but me—you may feel a deep sense of anger. Larry was angry at his wife for not meeting his sexual needs. Perhaps you feel angry because you believe no one has ever given you much, that you have always been alone, and that you have always had to do things for yourself. Maybe you're angry at others who have more money, better looking spouses, nicer houses, fancier cars. When you see all the sex rampant in our culture, you may be angry that others are being more sexual than you.

Anger may fuel your thinking. You feel angry that no one has given to you and others have more. This anger may cause you to feel entitlement. You feel you are entitled—that you have a *right* to get your needs met. When your sense of entitlement turns sexual, you think you deserve to be sexual so you're going to go out and get what you want.

✎ Can you remember a time when you felt entitled to something? Below, describe the situation.

_____

_____

Almost every person I know who has committed sexual sin knew what he was doing was sinful. Healthy individuals learn, grow, and stop the sexual sin. Addicted individuals, however, must find some way to justify their behaviors and relieve their feelings of guilt. People use an amazing array of justifications to avoid facing responsibility.

In the addiction/recovery community, we call the two most common forms of justification *denial* and *delusion,* the twin demons of addiction. Practicing denial and delusion means telling lies to myself and others. We get so good at these lies after a while that we're not even aware we're telling them.

✎ Below is a list of some of the forms of justification. Check which ones have applied to you:

❑ Classic Denial—I didn't do it. You must be mistaken. It wasn't me.
❑ Minimizing—It's not really that bad. It's no big deal. Others have a problem with that but I don't. I haven't done such terrible sexual sins like others have.
❑ Rationalization—We Christians are so sexually inhibited. What's the big deal, everyone else is doing it?
❑ Avoidance—I don't want to talk about that now, let's talk later.
❑ Procrastination—I'll stop tomorrow. I have enough strength to do so when I'm ready.
❑ Blame—It wasn't my fault, someone else made me do it. If my spouse had been more sexual with me, I wouldn't have needed to do what I did. Pornography is so available, what am I supposed to do? Culture is so sick, how can a person withstand it?

**KEY POINT**
Anger about abandonment combined with envy about what others possess is one of the major fuels that feeds the fire of sexual sin.

Though she [Potiphar's wife] spoke to Joseph day after day, he refused to go to bed with her or even be with her.

One day he went into the house to attend to his duties, and none of the household servants was inside. She caught him by his cloak and said, "Come to bed with me!" But he left his cloak in her hand and ran out of the house.

–Genesis 39:10-12

The Lord detests lying lips, but he delights in men who are truthful.
–Proverbs 12:22

The Lord abhors dishonest scales, but accurate weights are his delight.
–Proverbs 11:1

The Pharisee stood up and prayed about himself: "God, I thank you that I am not like other men—robbers, evildoers, adulterers—or even like this tax collector. I fast twice a week and give a tenth of all I get."

But the tax collector stood at a distance . He would not even look up to heaven, but beat his breast and said, "God, have mercy on me, a sinner."

–Luke 18:11-13

❏ The Delilah Defense—What was I supposed to do? She was so seductive she took away my strength.

❏ The Potiphar's Wife Strategy—What was I supposed to do? He chased me around the room?

❏ The Caring Delusion—No one is really getting hurt by this. As long as my spouse doesn't know, she won't be hurt. I really care for this other person, she is not getting hurt in this relationship. When I look at pornography I am not hurting anybody. When I seen a prostitute, at least it's not an affair.

❏ The Myth of Special Protection—I won't get caught. I'm a Christian, God wouldn't hurt me that way. No one will (or could ever) find out.

❏ Bargaining—I'll do 15 good things tomorrow to make up for this one bad thing today.

❏ Taking Forgiveness for Granted—God has promised to forgive. He will whenever I decide to stop.

❏ Your Own Delusion— _____.

➤ Ponder this question: How do you break through denial and delusion?

That's right, the answer is *honesty*, which can be difficult if you're lying to yourself or if you are self-deluded. Honesty must always be weighed on a scale to see if it balances. One of the ways to do that is to be honest with someone else. In the case of denial and delusion, tell someone else what you are thinking and get his reaction and feedback. He can tell you if you're fooling even yourself. In a 12-step program, for example, your group and your sponsor provide honest feedback to confront denial.

You have completed some very difficult work in this unit. Possibly you have gained some new insights into issues that have plagued and baffled you for many years. Possibly you feel new hope, or you may feel beaten-up and depressed. Whatever you feel, give yourself credit for the work you have done. As you courageously face the truth and your pain, you are doing the difficult work of recovery. In the next unit you will explore what we mean when we say that we are powerless over addiction, and you will learn how God's power can provide the wisdom and strength you need.

## Assignment for the Lesson

➤ In the margin read Luke 18:11-13. Jesus describes an example of self-delusion and an opposite example of honesty and humility.

➤ Say the following affirmation five times.

I can and will be honest with myself and others.

➤ Pray for humility.

Notes
1. Pat Carnes, *Don't Call it Love*, (New York: Bantam Books, 1991).
2. Adapted from Pat Carnes, *Out of the Shadows*, (Minneapolis: CompCare Pubs., 1983).

# Powerlessness

## FOCAL PASSAGE

*The grace of God that brings salvation has appeared to all men. It teaches us to say "No" to ungodliness and worldly passions, and to live self-controlled, upright and godly lives in this present age.*

—Titus 2:11-12

## MEMORY VERSE

Those who sleep, sleep at night, and those who get drunk, get drunk at night. But since we belong to the day, let us be self-controlled, putting on faith and love as a breastplate, and the hope of salvation as a helmet.
–1 Thessalonians 5:7-8

### DAVID'S STORY

David was influential in his community. He served on the city council and was well-respected by many. His business was very profitable. David volunteered for many civic activities and was an elder in his church.

David's marriage, however, was in trouble. Outwardly, he and his wife seemed like a normal couple, but inwardly they barely tolerated each other. Actually, she frightened David. She was constantly critical of him. He could never seem to do anything right in her opinion. She was generally cold and unavailable in bed.

One night as he walked his dog, he looked into a neighbor's window and saw a woman taking a shower. For a moment he was transfixed, but he kept walking. The next day he continually thought about the experience. That night he guided his dog along the same route in hope of seeing the woman again.

This nightly walk became a regular ritual. David began searching for new houses and other windows. Time and time again, he told himself to stop but couldn't. Several times he was almost spotted by other neighbors. Once a police car drove by. None of this stopped him. David prayed and prayed, but his lust did not go away. He tried many things to stop himself; he even went to a counselor. How could he be honest, however, about what he was doing. The counselor was a member of his church and a resident of the town where he was a council member.

The thought of talking to his pastor never crossed his mind.

## GROWTH GOAL

In this unit you will examine key components of addiction. You will evaluate yourself. Are you powerless over certain behaviors? Does sexual fantasy and ritual lead to repeated acts that cause you to despair? Do you become rigid in your efforts to control yourself?

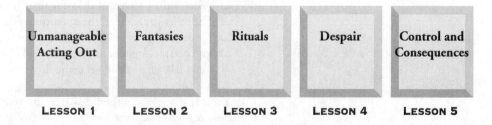

| Unmanageable Acting Out | Fantasies | Rituals | Despair | Control and Consequences |
|---|---|---|---|---|
| **LESSON 1** | **LESSON 2** | **LESSON 3** | **LESSON 4** | **LESSON 5** |

# Unmanageable Acting Out

David is like so many of us—not necessarily in his sexual activities, but in his own powerlessness. While he has tried many ways to free himself of lust, he has not tried honesty and accountability. This unit may be one of the most difficult to complete. I am going to ask you to be totally honest about your own behaviors. Remember, we must call sin by its name. In finding out the exact truth about your life, you will start to know where the true battle needs to be fought.

I remember being at my first church camp when I was 12 years old. At the end of the camp we had a bonfire. The leader invited us to write on a piece of paper what sin concerned us most. I wrote the words *Playboy Magazine*. We then tossed the papers in the fire as a symbol of God taking away the sin and burning it in the fire. I went away thinking I would no longer be tempted by *Playboy*.

Unfortunately, I never talked to anyone about my problem. I was too ashamed and frightened. Besides, I was convinced that the problem was now gone. Imagine my surprise and disappointment when I discovered that the magazine, as well as other forms of pornography, called out to me just as powerfully as before.

✎ **Think back to the first time you knew you had done something sexually sinful. How old were you? What was the nature of the sin?**

_____

How did you feel?_____

_____

Was this your first sexual experience? ❑ Yes ❑ No

For most of us our first experience of pornography, masturbation, prostitution, or sex with a partner is exciting, fascinating, and frightening all rolled into one. We may be surprised that something can feel so good and cause us to feel such guilt at the same time. We become confused. We need to talk to someone. Yet, shame and guilt cause us to refrain from talking.

✎ **You may have tried to talk to someone at some time. Below is a list of possible responses. Which response did you encounter?**

❑ The person was angry at you.
❑ The person did not believe you.
❑ "That's all right, we all do those things."
❑ "Get right with God, and you won't do it again."
❑ "Just say no."
❑ "What's the problem with doing that. It's old-fashioned to think that's sinful."
❑ The other person used the opportunity to try to initiate sex with you.
❑ The person acted as if he or she understood but started avoiding you.
❑ The person listened, understood, and directed you to someone with whom you could talk further and get counsel.

Chances are, if the last response is true for you, you are no longer having problems. However, many sex addicts have run into trouble trying to find help. They have been judged, misbelieved, or given overly simplistic answers. Others, who have sought secular help, have been told their sexual activities are normal human behavior. Many women who have sought help for sexual addiction have then become the object of the counselor's sexual advances.

This kind of experience may remind you of how you were treated in your family. There, too, you may not have been heard or believed; someone judged you, told you not to worry about it, or tried to be sexual with you. We will discuss this further in unit 10.

➤ Remind yourself that as a child you had limited skills, knowledge, and power. No one may have been readily available to help you, even if you were brave enough to try to talk to someone. Maybe you did the best you could under the circumstances.

✎ The three lists below contain the sexual behaviors that we talked about in unit 7. Check those that you've done. This requires courage and honesty.

**Building Block Behaviors**
- ❏ fantasy
- ❏ masturbation
- ❏ pornography

**Offending Behaviors**
- ❏ incest
- ❏ molesting
- ❏ rape
- ❏ authority Rape

**Sexual Addiction Behaviors**
- ❏ prostitution
- ❏ inappropriate sex with a consenting partner
- ❏ addicted sex in marriage
- ❏ voyeurism and exhibitionism
- ❏ phone sex
- ❏ indecent liberties
- ❏ bestiality

The number of boxes you checked may frighten you. You've acted with courage by admitting these behaviors. By being honest you have begun the healing process. If you can share your list with your group, you will also begin to cleanse yourself of the pain of your secrecy and shame about them.

✎ In which of the previous behaviors do you participate most often?

_____

Can you list three examples of how you tried to stop doing this but weren't able to do so? If so, please give these examples on the lines below.

_____

_____

_____

**KEY POINT**
Honesty is the beginning of sexual healing.

These demonstrate how unmanageable your sexual sins have been. In completing the previous exercise you probably felt the sense of shame and despair you have felt so often. You may be tired and discouraged now. Just keep in mind the Key Point that appears in the margin.

➤ God knew of your behaviors long before you were willing to admit them. God wants to free you from sexual sin. Take time now to thank God for His mercy and lovingkindness that are greater than all our sin. You can choose to thank God whether or not you feel grateful.

The teachers of the law and the Pharisees brought in a woman caught in adultery. They made her stand before the group and said to Jesus, "Teacher, this woman was caught in the act of adultery. In the Law Moses commanded us to stone such women. Now what do you say?" They were using this question as a trap, in order to have a basis for accusing him. But Jesus bent down and started to write on the ground with his finger. When they kept on questioning him, he straightened up and said to them, "If any one of you is without sin, let him be the first to throw a stone at her." Again he stooped down and wrote on the ground. At this, those who heard began to go away one at a time, the older ones first, until only Jesus was left, with the woman still standing there. Jesus straightened up and asked her, "Woman, where are they? Has no one condemned you?" "No one, sir," she said. Then neither do I condemn you," Jesus declared. "Go now and leave your life of sin."
–John 8:3-11

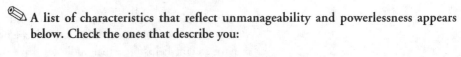 A list of characteristics that reflect unmanageability and powerlessness appears below. Check the ones that describe you:

❑ I went further with a sexual experience than I intended.
❑ I used money for sex that I needed for something else.
❑ I lied about sex to someone I love or to someone who trusts me.
❑ I used work time to be sexual.
❑ I pretended to be someone other than who I am in order to be sexual.
❑ I did something sexual despite the threat of being caught.
❑ I became sexual despite the fear of sexually transmitted diseases.
❑ I did something sexual that I don't like doing in order to please someone else.
❑ I did something that is sexually painful.
❑ I violated my beliefs despite many pledges to stop.
❑ I avoided social or family obligations in order to be sexual.

These, of course, are only a few examples. The point is that your sexual thoughts and actions have taken control. Perhaps some times you can resist sexual temptation. At other times, however, your mind seems to be on "Automatic Pilot." Addicted people often use the term *Automatic Pilot*. We feel as though we are being possessed—like we have no control. In my experience three feelings accompany unmanageability. Those feelings are anger, loneliness, and fear.

➤ Are you ready to look at these feelings? The task will be painful.

➤ Are you ready to live without these sinful sexual behaviors? This may seem like a strange question, but they have given you brief relief from pain for years. Are you ready to live without this form of relief?

## Assignment for the Lesson

➤ Read John 8:3-11 and ask yourself, "Is any sexual sin so bad God can't forgive?"

➤ Say the following affirmation five times:

I want to find sexual sobriety and I will.

➤ Pray for patience as you begin the healing journey.

LESSON
2

# Fantasies

Gary and his high school sweetheart broke up when they went off to college. They missed each other for a while, but gradually became involved with other people. They saw each other during their first Christmas break, but both were distracted with other interests. Eventually Gary settled on his career and married a woman he met during his college days. They were very compatible and things went smoothly in their marriage. Gary had children, a stable job, and a church the whole family enjoyed.

During his forties, Gary began to get rather restless. He felt that something was missing in his life. Maybe it was just mid-life crisis, but Gary longed for more excitement. Everything around him seemed to become dull and boring.

An invitation came for Gary's 25th high school reunion. As he considered attending, thoughts of his old girlfriend began to surface. Gary wondered what life would be like had he stayed with her. He started to compare her with his wife. Maybe his old girlfriend would have been more aggressive in bed. She was attractive in different ways than his wife. This comparison caused Gary to question many things. He began to withdraw from his wife. He became angry and resentful toward his wife for controlling him all these years. Gary began to think about meeting his old girlfriend at the reunion. Would it be the same "magic" between them, just like the night of the Prom? He had thoughts of being sexual with her. Gary's wife had planned to attend the reunion with him, but he found excuses why she shouldn't go.

In this story, Gary is having problems with a fantasy. In his fantasy Gary's former girlfriend becomes the answer to all of his problems. He doesn't know what she is even like today, but that doesn't matter because he has created a perfect image of her in his mind. We don't know whether this will lead to sexual sin in Gary's life, but he is certainly headed in that direction.

Fantasy is the cornerstone of sexual sin and the first stage of the addiction cycle. Being able to manage fantasy will be critical to your ability to stay sexually sober.

✎ **Put a ✓ in the boxes of the statements below that seem to fit you. Do you ever:**

- ❑ think about sex while at work?
- ❑ think about having sex with people that you know?
- ❑ find that movies, TV, or magazines contribute to your images of sex?
- ❑ fantasize about someone else when you're being sexual with your spouse?
- ❑ think about sexual experiences that you've already had?
- ❑ think about sexual experiences that you would like to have?
- ❑ fantasize about sex in order to go to sleep at night?
- ❑ find that thinking about sex relaxes you?

These are just a few of the questions about sexual fantasy. In completing this last exercise did you get a sense of how much time you spend thinking about sex? Time spent fantasizing is certainly an indication of an unmanageable pattern.

Fantasy is like a powerful drug. It causes chemicals to be released in the brain that cause feelings of pleasure. This is God's natural way of preparing the body to engage in the act of reproduction. Sexual attraction to the opposite sex is natural. Without it, the human race would be extinct. Problems occur, however, when we use the power of that drug to escape our feelings. Like any drug, we can get dependent on the pleasure and excitement it creates. We need more and more of it over time to achieve the same effect. Sexual sin occurs when we allow the drug to direct our actions.

The most serious danger of fantasy is that it can create an ideal world. Fantasy creates a world that doesn't really exist—ideal bodies, ideal attractions, ideal sex. You can be the director of your own movie in your imagination. Your leading actor or actress will be "magic," perfectly sexual, perfectly nurturing, perfectly accepting, and perfectly loving.

➤ **Do you remember the first time that you ever looked at a pornographic picture? Since the persons in the picture were smiling at you, did you imagine that they wanted to be with you?**

Like Gary in our opening story, you will compare the ideal world of sexual fantasy to the real world. Did you answer yes to the earlier question of fantasizing about someone else when you're being sexual with your spouse? What spouse can ever compete with the "magic" that we can create in our heads? Since the "magic" lady or man of our fantasies will be all-nurturing and all-loving, how can our spouse compete? Fantasy creates dissatisfaction. It lies to us about many things. It distorts our reality. It fuels loneliness and anger.

➤ **Have you ever told yourself to just say no to sexual fantasy? Did that work?**

If you're like me, the answer to this question reflects that you have been a dismal failure at controlling your fantasies. Maybe you've tried many ways to control your thoughts and ended up totally frustrated. I remember a man who put a rubber band around his wrist and snapped it every time he thought about sex. This approach, however, taught him to associate pain with sexual thought. He became impotent with his wife.

Let's take a different approach. Let's try to understand the feelings that are behind your sexual fantasies. The following is a dangerous exercise in that I'm going to ask you to think about your fantasies. If you find that this causes you to get totally distracted and dangerously close to sexual sin, call a sponsor, counselor, or minister immediately.

✎ **Act as if you are a newspaper reporter, someone who objectively describes information. As objectively as possible, try to determine the theme of your most common sexual fantasy. Don't be graphic; be descriptive of the nature of the activity (for example, "In my fantasy, people respect and honor me.")**

_____

_____

➤ Take a gentleness break. The sexual shame that you feel at having described your most common fantasy is one of the ways Satan has kept you in the cycle of sexual sin. Remind yourself that there is no temptation that is not common to man and that your worst thoughts can't separate you from the love of God in Christ Jesus.

Do you remember Joseph in the Old Testament? At one point in his life, he was the victim of a woman (Potiphar's wife) who sexually fantasized about him (Genesis 39). Recovering from sexual fantasy will require that you become an interpreter of your sexual fantasies. However sexually perverse they may be, they have meaning. By analyzing them, you may discover that you are using sex inappropriately to try to meet legitimate needs.

Consider Gary's story again. He is bored with life. In mid-life he wondered, as most of us do, if he has been successful. His fantasy of his high school girlfriend took him back to the days when he was full of confidence and youthful enthusiasm. Obviously Gary and his wife experienced the normal problems that any couple does. By comparing his marriage with his former relationship (and an active imagination), his high school sweetheart appears more desirable.

The meaning of Gary's fantasy is very basic. The fantasy is an attempt to recapture youth and feel powerful. Many sexual fantasies become more detailed, advanced, and perverse than Gary's. All, however, still have meaning. Consider a man, for example, who always fantasizes about sex with older women. He could be searching for the love and nurture that he didn't get from his mother. How about a person who fantasizes about sexual acts that his or her spouse refuses to perform? These fantasies can come to symbolize acceptance. The spouse, in comparison, doesn't seem to be as accepting as the fantasized sexual partner. The person who fantasizes about a partner who is always available or aggressive could simply want to be desirable and acceptable.

So, if you think you are standing firm, be careful that you don't fall! No temptation has seized you except what is common to man. And God is faithful; he will not let you be tempted beyond what you can bear. But when you are tempted, he will also provide a way out so that you can stand up under it.
–1 Corinthians 10:12-13

I am convinced that neither death nor life, neither angels nor demons, neither the present nor the future, nor any powers, neither height nor depth, nor anything else in all creation, will be able to separate us from the love of God that is in Christ Jesus our Lord.
–Romans 8:38-39

✎ Go back to the previous exercise where you listed your most common sexual fantasy. Ask yourself, "What am I feeling underneath the sexual thoughts?" Below is a feeling list to use as a guide.

- ❑ I am lonely, I fear that my spouse doesn't really love me or that no one loves me.
- ❑ I have been abandoned in my life, no one really takes care of me.
- ❑ I am bored with life, I need excitement.
- ❑ I am angry, I deserve to get some of my needs met.
- ❑ I am angry, people (even my spouse) have mistreated me.
- ❑ I am frightened, I need someone to hold me.
- ❑ I am frightened, I need someone to listen to me.
- ❑ No one touches me, I need something physical.

If you are having trouble understanding the feeling underneath your sexual thoughts, you may need to see a pastor or a counselor who can help you with them. This may sound like an embarrassing thing to do. You will find, however, that when you talk about your fantasies in a responsible and humble way, you take some of their power over you away.

All of us, of course, can be "triggered" into sexual fantasy by the increasing amounts of sexual stimuli in our culture. We would have to be hermits to avoid that. Fantasies become unmanageable, however, when we can't turn them off. Some underlying emotion or need usually fuels these fantasies.

➢ **If emotions or needs usually fuel fantasies, what can we do about the problem?**

Several years ago I was in Amsterdam to give a series of talks about sexual addiction. Amsterdam is home to one of the largest and most perverse red-light districts in the world. I can't begin to describe it. That year I was doing a very good job of taking care of my emotional needs. I maintained many healthy friendships, my wife and I were doing well, my work was fulfilling. In short, things were going well. I was able to walk through that red-light district, with friends, and not feel the power of any lasting sexual fantasy.

The very next year I was asked to come back to Amsterdam to speak. This time, however, stress held a presence in my life for a number of reasons. I had not taken care of my emotional and relational needs. I didn't have to walk through the red-light district, it seemed to call out to my fantasies. I was able to maintain my sobriety, but the experience did remind me that when I feel lonely, tired, discouraged, or angry, I am much more vulnerable to fantasy. When I returned home I knew I had to take the initiative to talk about my feelings and renew healthy relationships with my wife and friends.

**KEY POINT**
Making healthy choices about meeting underlying emotional feelings and needs will take the power of sexual fantasy away.

Part 1 of this workbook will help you take care of yourself. You can't simply deny your feelings. If you just try to turn off your fantasies, you may compound the problem by denying your underlying emotional needs. When you take care of those emotional needs, sexual fantasy will decrease.

## Assignment for the Lesson

➢ Tell at least one person about your most common sexual fantasy. Describe the fantasy briefly and simply. You do not need to go into detail. Ask him to pray for you. Describe what you think is your underlying emotional need.

➢ Say the following affirmation five times.

I am worthy of support and affection from others.

➤ **Pray for cleansing from the sexual fantasies that exist in your mind. Ask God to remove the computer-like storage of images you have there.**

# Rituals

Carl's job demanded a lot of travel. In each town he usually stayed at the same motel chain where pornography was available through the TV. Although he tries to resist, Carl usually pays the money and pushes the buttons to see the movies. The pornography sexually stimulates him and he gives in to masturbation. Many times he looks through the yellow pages and calls massage parlors, finding out the beginning prices of the available "services." Again he tries to resist but is now so excited that he gets in his rental car, finds an instant teller machine, and makes a withdrawal. He engages in acts of prostitution at the massage parlor as he does over and over again in cities all over the country.

Carl's form of acting out is to engage in masturbation and prostitution. He is caught in an unmanageable cycle. An important part of that cycle is the ritual that leads to the acting out. In Carl's case the ritual is very simple. It starts when he plans his next business trip. He reserves a room at a motel that has pornographic channels on the TV, and he reminds himself of the massage parlors available. Carl thinks about all of these things while preparing for his trip. When he arrives at his destination, the ritual becomes very basic: pushing the TV button, looking through the yellow pages, getting in his car, getting instant cash, driving to the massage parlor. It could be, if Carl is going to recover, he may need to evaluate whether or not he can continue to travel because staying in motels may also be a part of the ritual.

Rituals have several qualities that make them powerful in themselves:
- They are done in secret.
- They may be dangerous.
- They may involve a chase, quest, or pursuit.
- They are done in anticipation of something "rewarding."

**KEY POINT**
Engaging in a ritual will almost always lead to acting out.

These elements get a person's adrenaline going. Fantasy and its chemical effect on the brain kick in. A person's mood has already been altered even when nothing overtly sexual has happened. However, the person has set a process in motion. The energy of the ritual demands expression.

As I said in unit 7, one way of looking at ritual is to consider it as preparation for acting out. Anything that prepares you for a sexual act can be part of a ritual. Like so many aspects of addiction, rituals are not inherently bad. Husbands and wives can engage in rituals leading to sex. This can be creative, fun, and romantic. But, when rituals lead to sexual sin, they must be stopped. Your job in this lesson is to begin to figure out how to stop rituals that lead to sin.

✎ **Remembering the work that you did in unit 7, write down the most common form of sexual sin that you have been involved in. This may not be your most serious sexual sin, but it should be the one that you feel is the most unmanageable.**

_____

✎ **When is the last time that you did this?** 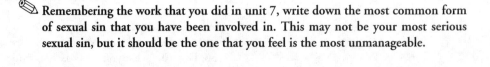 _____

This righteousness from God comes through faith in Jesus Christ to all who believe. There is no difference, for all have sinned and fall short of the glory of God, and are justified freely by his grace through the redemption that came by Christ Jesus.
–Romans 3:22-24

When I called, you answered me; you made me bold and stouthearted.
–Psalm 138:3

➤ Pause, take a break, and read the verses in the margin. Praise God for sending His Son so that you may be both "justified freely by His grace" and "bold and stouthearted."

✎ Can you remember when you first became preoccupied with doing this sexual act? What stimulus triggered you?

_____

_____

You must learn to be comfortable with those things that cause you to think about sex. To be stimulated sexually is normal. How you choose to react to sexual stimulation separates sexual sin from sexual wholeness. You will also learn that you can avoid some sexual stimuli.

✎ Describe how your thoughts and actions developed from the time you first started thinking about this sexual sin to the time when you actually started acting out.

_____

_____

Remember that rituals can be short or long. The time frame that you described may have been several minutes or it may have been several years. Don't leave anything out. Sometimes even the little details are important. You will find that as you grow in recovery, some of these details will become clearer to you.

The previous exercise is for your most common form of sexually acting out. This form may, for example, involve pornography. You may have other rituals for other forms of acting out, such as a ritual that precedes participation in prostitution. You may have several rituals in process at the same time, particularly if they are longer ones.

Let's say, for another example, that you have had a number of affairs. A ritual of several months of getting to "know" each other has been involved. You may have several of these rituals going at the same time in various stages—acting out with one person, almost ready with another, and in the early stages with others.

➤ Review your list of activities above that lead you to one form of sexual acting out. Does any of it surprise you?

As you look at your ritual you will need to start thinking about prohibitions, sometimes called boundaries, that you will enforce on yourself so that you can stop the ritual.

Let's look, for example, at a list of prohibitions that Carl (from our opening story) may have to put in place:
• Don't stay in motels that offer access to pornographic movies.
• Ask the front desk to turn off the pay movies.
• Ask the motel to take out the TV.
• Don't carry an instant cash card.
• Remove the yellow pages.
• Have a member of your accountability group call the motel at a certain time, or arrange to call them.
• Carry a phone list of people to call.
• Don't travel.

Some of these possibilities, like not traveling, may sound extreme. If he is serious about his recovery, however, Carl will do what he needs to do in order to stay sexually whole.

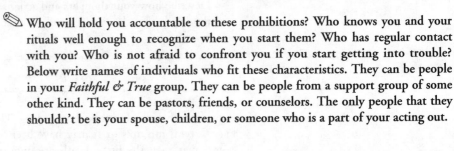 As you have reviewed your rituals, what prohibitions or boundaries will you have to enforce on yourself?

_____

_____

You may be wondering how you will find the strength to follow through with these prohibitions, such as denying yourself certain privileges. You may feel angry, sad, or anxious. These feelings are normal. Old lies are speaking to you, saying you need these things to survive. Other voices may be telling you that you need these things because no one else takes care of you. A part of you is calling out for the instant fix. Don't believe any of these lies. You will survive. You deserve better. Long term rewards are worth the effort.

Who will hold you accountable to these prohibitions? Who knows you and your rituals well enough to recognize when you start them? Who has regular contact with you? Who is not afraid to confront you if you start getting into trouble? Below write names of individuals who fit these characteristics. They can be people in your *Faithful & True* group. They can be people from a support group of some other kind. They can be pastors, friends, or counselors. The only people that they shouldn't be is your spouse, children, or someone who is a part of your acting out.

_____

_____

Your spouse and children must learn that they have no power over you. What they do and how they act must not affect whether or not you stay sexually faithful. For example, you can't say to your spouse, "If we only had sex more often, I would be able to stop sexually sinning." You alone can put the support into place that you will need to stay whole.

Part 1 of this book deals with accountability in greater detail. Part 1 also presents a healthy sexuality plan. If you have not completed Part 1 already, you can use it to begin healthy rituals in your life in order to avoid unhealthy ones. You may discover, for example, that you are more likely to sexually act out when you are tired. Going to bed on time and getting rest is a very basic and simple healthy ritual that will help you. For another example, you may notice that when you are angry at someone, like your spouse, you are in greater danger of acting out. Having healthy rituals about maintaining relationships will be an important part of avoiding unhealthy rituals.

Let's look at Carl's story one more time. Healthy rituals for him may include:

• Call a friend from the motel every night.
• Get lots of rest, schedule a less hectic pace.
• Stay at motels that are nice but which don't have pornography.
• Attend support groups or churches while on the road. (This may have to be researched before leaving.)
• Exercise while on the road.
• Call home every night and have a conversation with his wife.
• Eat at nice restaurants.
• Schedule positive activities.

Therefore put on the full armor of God, so that when the day of evil comes, you may be able to stand your ground, and after you have done everything, to stand. Stand firm then, with the belt of truth buckled around your waist, with the breastplate of righteousness in place, and with your feet fitted with the readiness that comes from the gospel of peace. In addition to all this, take up the shield of faith, with which you can extinguish all the flaming arrows of the evil one. Take the helmet of salvation and the sword of the Spirit, which is the word of God.
–Ephesians 6:13-17

LESSON
4

Healthy rituals are unique to everyone. You may have to experiment with what works for you. Keep in mind, the prohibitions that you put in place for one kind of ritual may be just the beginning. If you have many different rituals, you will need to be creative and courageous about all of them.

➤ Pray and invite God into your decision-making process for new rituals.

## Assignment for the Lesson

➤ Read Ephesians 6:13-17, appearing in the margin:

➤ Say the following affirmation five times.

I will build healthy rituals into my life.

➤ Pray for patience and courage.

# Despair

Sandra is a gifted school teacher. She works with learning-disabled children. She is loving and sincerely cares for her students. All of them love her and her colleagues respect her, sometimes being jealous of how gifted she is. Sandra was sexually abused by her father, and several teachers when she was in school. She has never had a truly intimate relationship with a man.

After her school preparation is completed, Sandra puts on provocative clothing and frequents bars and nightclubs. When she drinks her inhibitions lower and she becomes very flirtatious with men. Each night she takes one of them home and is sexual with him. She may not even know his name and probably won't see him again.

Sandra is becoming increasingly desperate. She grew up in a religious home. Her father was an elder in the church. She loves and hates her father and wonders about a God that would let an elder do the things he did. She loves and hates God. She has prayed to be delivered from this type of living; but she can't stop herself, and God doesn't seem to want to help. At least, He won't take her lust away. Sandra is thinking of the only way she knows to get out of this vicious cycle. She is thinking of killing herself.

Like 72% of all sex addicts, Sandra has thought about suicide.[1] Notice the cycle of addiction in her life. As an abuse victim she feels intense shame about herself. The only way men have ever paid attention to her has been in sexual ways. She fantasizes about a man's love and her thoughts always turn sexual. The way she dressed, the alcohol, the bars, and her flirtations are all part of her ritual. Sandra has been sexual with over 300 men in her life. To Sandra, the only way to deal with her loneliness is to fantasize, which leads her back into the cycle.

I would not tell her story if it did not end with hope. Sandra has now been sexually sober for over 15 years. Her recovery began one day when she discovered another woman, also desperate and depressed, and they began talking. Neither of them had anything to lose. They both had thoughts of suicide. As they began sharing their stories, they discovered how much they had in common and how their sharing dispelled the loneliness.

Honestly sharing ourselves is a key. Whenever I have shared my story, I have received healing, and it often results in healing for others. I have sometimes encountered angry or disappointed reactions, but even those reactions can begin the journey to understanding and forgiveness. Sometimes others have identified with my story and found hope in it. For me sharing my story always lifts the loneliness and brings support.

➤ In your Bible read the story of the Samaritan woman at the well (John 4:4-18).

This Samaritan woman, like Sandra, was an adulteress. She didn't even have to tell her story, Jesus already knew it. She was at the well during the sixth hour, when no respectable woman would be there. We are again confronted with the fact that Jesus chose to associate with and meet the needs of sinners, in this case with sexual sinners.

✎ What do you think Jesus meant by "living water" in this story?

_____

_____

If you had trouble defining this, you're like me. I used to have trouble with it. The phrase seemed rather mystical to me. Now that I'm in recovery for sexual sin, what strikes me about this story is that Jesus gave this woman the gift of fellowship with Himself. Despite her status and despite her sexual sins, Jesus talked to her. He didn't condemn her even though He knew about her. What does that thought do to your feelings of sexual shame about yourself?

This lesson is about the despair of addiction. You, too, may have wanted to kill yourself. You may have been so desperate that you have wanted to leave loved ones or give up things that are important to you. Two key antidotes to despair appear in the margin.

## Telling your story

In unit 7, you began detailing the nature of your sexual sins. Recognizing your inability to control these sins without help resembles the first step in the 12-step process of Alcoholics Anonymous. The fourth step says, "Made a searching and fearless moral inventory." This is another way of saying that you will make a complete and courageous accounting of your sins, sexual and otherwise. This is your story.

The fifth step says, "Admitted to God, to ourselves, and to another human being the exact nature of our wrongs." Another way of saying this is that you will confess your sins. What a novel concept! I think that the 12-steps are really a reminder of what we Christians have known all along (James 5:16, 1 John 1:9). Our shame, however, makes us forget the power of confession. We think that not even God will love us if we confess, but He already knows. So what's the deal?

The fifth step is clear, also, that we must confess to another person. We must tell our story to someone else. As James 5:16 states: "Therefore confess your sins to each other and pray for each other so that you may be healed. The prayer of a righteous man is powerful and effective."

Confession to another person is courageous and humble and it gives the listener the chance to symbolically represent to us God's forgiveness. Confession to another person makes grace more tangible, more real.

### TWO ANTIDOTES TO DESPAIR

- Telling the story of your sexual sins;
- Finding community in those who will understand, accept you, and support you.

### KEY POINT
The road out of despair begins with being honest about your story.

### KEY POINT
The power of confession is not that we will tell God something that He doesn't already know, but that we will accept what we've done as sinful and admit it.

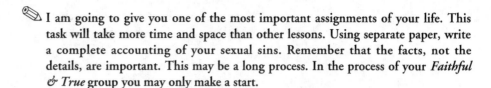 I am going to give you one of the most important assignments of your life. This task will take more time and space than other lessons. Using separate paper, write a complete accounting of your sexual sins. Remember that the facts, not the details, are important. This may be a long process. In the process of your *Faithful & True* group you may only make a start.

My fourth step fills many pages, going back to when I was a child and step-by-step going forward. My first attempt left many things out; maybe I wasn't courageous enough, maybe I forgot some things. Yours doesn't have to be perfect, just get started.

Who represents spiritual authority to you?

_____

I suggest that you make your confession to this person if possible. This person symbolizes God's grace and acceptance to you. Do not confess to this person if a family member or an inappropriate choice for any reason. Some people make an appointment with a counselor or other appropriate stranger to make their fifth-step confession.

❑ Check here when you have shared your history of sexual addiction with the person you have chosen.

➤ Stop work in your workbook here until you write your fourth-step inventory and share your fifth-step confession. If you feel "stuck" and unable to complete this difficult assignment, enlist the aid of your group facilitator or a counselor.

Congratulations! You have taken a courageous step.

➤ How do you feel to have this secret burden off your chest?

## Building a community of acceptance

The second antidote to despair is building a community of acceptance and support around you. By confessing your sins to someone else, you have already begun this process. Notice the three key words: community, acceptance, and support.

Community is one reason 12-step groups have been so popular. They give people the opportunity to tell their whole story to a community of others. All the people in the group have committed the same kind of sins. The group demonstrates acceptance and support by listening and offering helpful feedback on how to overcome the problems. The 12-step process reminds us of what the church has known for centuries.

Your *Faithful & True* group will provide you with early opportunity to tell your whole story. Such confession is powerfully healing. Begin now making plans to attend groups for support after this group is finished. Perhaps you will contract with each other to continue your *Faithful & True* group. As you grow you may find a significant ministry through sharing your recovery with others. Perhaps you will find a 12-step group for sexual addiction. Phone numbers of various support groups are listed in the resource section of this workbook on page 224.

Finding another group may be a process of trial and error. I sometimes refer to it as "shopping." You must find people with whom you are comfortable and who hold the same moral or Christian values that you do.

Your community of acceptance and support will also include family, friends, co-workers, and fellow church members. You will need to get feedback on when it is appropriate to tell your story to them and how to do so. Unit 4 of Part 1 gives guidelines for this process. Sex addicts, in general, are a rather depressed group. Many have had thoughts of suicide.

If the work of this lesson does not help lift your sense of despair, or if you are still having thoughts of suicide, seek professional help.

 **Sign the following commitment:**

*I promise that if I remain depressed, or if I have thoughts of suicide, I will get help.*

*Signed*_____ *Date*_____

## Assignment for the Lesson

➤ Read Philippians 1:19-20, appearing in the margin.

➤ Say the following affirmation five times.

I am worthy of God's grace and of being happy.

➤ Pray to find those who will listen and model God's grace to you.

I know that through your prayers and the help given by the Spirit of Jesus Christ, what has happened to me will turn out for my deliverance. I eagerly expect and hope that I will in no way be ashamed, but will have sufficient courage so that now as always Christ will be exalted in my body, whether by life or by death.
–Philippians 1:19-20

LESSON
5

# Control and Consequences

Richard knew that his sexual acting out was sinful. When he became a Christian, he thought it would automatically stop him from sin. The minister promised deliverance. Richard was a little angry about that. Sexual sin was such a part of Richard's life and he was so lonely and angry. He wanted God to take away his lust in such a way that he wouldn't even miss it. Richard wanted God to take it away without any trouble or consequences to himself.

He thought that maybe he had been baptized in the wrong church so he tried several others. He searched for answers. He thought that reading through the whole Bible would be the answer. He went on retreats. He found little ways to punish himself, such as fasting. Nothing seemed to change him.

Richard was desperate. His acting out became increasingly dangerous. He became bolder and more daring. Finally, his wife found out. She didn't get any counseling or support. She was just angry. She tried to forgive him but couldn't. She stayed in the marriage for a while, but left and filed for a divorce when Richard acted out again.

Richard's boss found out and fired Richard, but he still couldn't stop acting out. One day Richard was arrested for soliciting prostitution. He didn't get any jail time, but his story made the newspapers. All of his friends knew. His children were embarrassed at school.

Richard had spent thousands of dollars on sex. He was broke, divorced, publicly humiliated, and without a job. Where would he get help?

Thousands of addicts can instantly relate to situations like Richard's. They tried to stop but couldn't. They have experienced painful consequences. Strangely enough, those who found recovery look back at such moments and remember that it was finally the time when they became humble enough to seek help. Like the prodigal son, they finally "came to themselves." In the margin read the words of the prodigal son.

"I will set out and go back to my father and say to him: Father, I have sinned against heaven and against you. I am no longer worthy to be called your son; make me like one of your hired men."
–Luke 15:18-19

✎ The list of words below describe the son in the parable. Check the words with which you can identify:

❏ ashamed
❏ broken
❏ repentant
❏ humble
❏ needing a father
❏ reaching out
❏ all of the above

If you checked any of the these words, congratulations! Your response indicates your readiness for God's healing. You remember, of course, the reaction of the father. He received his son home with great joy.

One small catch exists; you must be ready to give up sexual sin—one day at a time—for the rest of your life. Perhaps you need to remind yourself of the efforts you have tried to stop your sexual behaviors.

✎ Like Richard, how have you tried on your own to stop sexual sin? List several ways you have attempted to stop.

_____

_____

Did any of these come close to working? Probably not. Like Richard, maybe you need to remember and accept what consequences you have experienced.

✎ Answer the following questions:

How much money have you spent on sexual sin? _____

How many relationships have you damaged or lost in sexual sin? List every name: Use more paper if you need to.

_____

_____

Have you ever had legal difficulty because of your sexual sin? ❏ Yes ❏ No

Have you ever had physical effects from sexual sin? ❏ Yes ❏ No. If so, what:

_____

_____

Have you ever lost a job or a career because of sexual sin? ❏ Yes ❏ No

Have you ever had to leave a church because of sexual sin? ❏ Yes ❏ No

Have you ever had to move because of sexual sin? ❏ Yes ❏ No

List any consequences to your family:

_____

_____

Other consequences:

_____

_____

➤ Take a time-out and do something nice for yourself. You may be feeling lots of sadness. That's OK. Talk to a friend. Take a walk. Do something pleasant that does not trigger your sexual patterns.

If you look at all of your answers to the questions above, you will see that you have lost a lot. Richard's list would be quite significant. He lost:

- His family
- His work
- Money
- His status
- Friends
- The trust of others

✎ Write a summary statement describing your losses:

_____

_____

**KEY POINT**
Being in recovery means that you will have to grieve.

We can't heal quickly from losses like this. Healing may include a lifetime process of feeling our sadness and expressing our feelings. This is called grieving. Only by walking through the grief does the pain decrease.

I lost the ability to be a pastor because of my sexual sin. Every Sunday that I go to church I am sad because it reminds me of what I've lost. I need to accept that and move on with my life. It is OK to be sad and tell appropriate others about it.

The process of grief is basic. The following are some basic stages we go through in the grieving process. These phases are natural and normal. They only become destructive when we stay stuck in one or more of them.
- Recognize the loss.
- Be angry about it.
- Be frightened. How will I get by without ÷... .
- Try to get it back. Bargain with God to do so.
- Feel sadness about not being able to get back what you have lost.
- Accept the loss.
- Search for ways to find God's will for your life.

I have accepted that I won't be a pastor. I'm still sad about it. In the midst of all of this God has allowed me to speak all over the world. God can do marvelous works with our brokenness.

✎ Did you put sexual sin on your list of losses? ❏ Yes ❏ No

**KEY POINT**
You will heal from your feelings of despair if you are honest with others about your feelings of loss.

What a strange question. How can it be a loss to give up something that caused you so much pain? You will find, however, that if you are really ready to give up sexual sin, it will feel like a loss. Sexual acting out is one of the ways you have coped. Some of your sexual acting out has been like a friend to you in times of fear, sadness, anger, and loneliness. What will you do without these friends? Some of you who have had affairs may have to grieve over people that you thought you really loved. Don't be afraid to express this to those who support you. Other addicts in recovery will understand. God understands.

### Assignment for the Lesson

➤ Read Romans 8:28.

*We know that in all things God works for the good of those who love him, who have been called according to his purpose.*

–Romans 8:28

➤ Say the following affirmation five times.

I am worthy of my Father's banquet.

➤ Ask God to fulfill His word from Titus 2:11-12 in you—that His grace will teach you to say no to all ungodliness and worldly passions and to live a self-controlled, upright, and godly life.

_____

Notes

1. Pat Carnes, *Don't Call it Love*, (New York: Bantam Books, 1991).

# Families (Part 1)

## FOCAL PASSAGE

*The overseer must be above reproach, the husband of but one wife, temperate, self-controlled, respectable, hospitable, able to teach, not given to drunkenness, not violent but gentle, not quarrelsome, not a lover of money. He must manage his own family well and see that his children obey him with proper respect. (If anyone does not know how to manage his own family, how can he take care of God's church?)*

—1 Timothy 3:2-5

## MEMORY VERSE

Peter came to Jesus and asked, "Lord, how many times shall I forgive my brother when he sins against me? Up to seven times?" Jesus answered, "I tell you, not seven times, but seventy-seven times."
–Matthew 18:21-22

### ADAM'S STORY

Adam is in trouble in a number of areas of his life. For years he has been jealous of those around him who had more "stuff" than he did. He bought things with his credit card that he thought he deserved until his credit card maxed out.

Adam has always been restless. He doesn't know how to be calm. He drinks and smokes in an effort to curb his hyperactivity. He has a difficult time sitting still. Adam's wife is always aggravated with him for getting up and going someplace. He can hardly sit still at church, social gatherings, or anyplace else.

Work is a real problem. For years he has been using sexual humor to tease the women in the office. He thought it was normal, but now one of them has reported him for sexual harassment. Adam's boss clearly is upset with him.

With all of this, Adam is a nice guy—always ready to help someone. He is the strong, silent type. Many people ask him to do things because he is so competent. Adam is a good listener, and many people pour out their hearts to him. Inside, Adam is angry that no one ever did anything for him. He is tired of always being strong. Now he wonders, *who is going to help me with my problems?* He has no idea of how to ask for help. Adam does not know how to talk to his wife or anyone else.

## GROWTH GOAL

In this unit you will learn about your family and the rules, roles, and patterns of behavior that you learned as a child. You will determine how these patterns have affected your relationships and your lifestyle today.

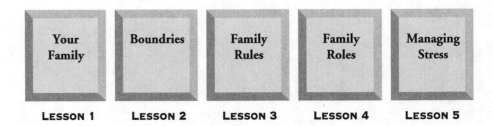

| Your Family | Boundries | Family Rules | Family Roles | Managing Stress |
|:---:|:---:|:---:|:---:|:---:|
| **LESSON 1** | **LESSON 2** | **LESSON 3** | **LESSON 4** | **LESSON 5** |

# LESSON 1

# Your Family

Much has been written about healthy and unhealthy families. Many have described the dynamics of unhealthy families and, unfortunately, have placed a great deal of blame on families. Some people get defensive, not wanting their family to be considered unhealthy. I believe comparing families is unfair. No family is totally unhealthy nor is any family totally healthy. All families have different dynamics. Some of these patterns of relating are good and some of them aren't.

In this unit, don't get hung up wondering whether or not your family is healthy. Accept yours for what it is. Many terrible things may have happened to you, but also many wonderful things. As you grow you will be able to discern the difference.

Focusing on the dynamics—good or bad—of your family is not for the purpose of blaming your parents for whatever sins you have committed. The purpose is not to be angry with them or to not love them. You may be angry about some things that happened. You may wonder why things happened the way they did. Mainly, however, we are about the task of understanding what happened to us and how that has affected us over the years. Your family is the most powerful influence on you emotionally, physically, sexually, and spiritually.

➤ Pray that God will allow you to understand the things that you need to understand about your family.

In this lesson I will ask you to draw a "map" of your family. Having something visual to better understand your heritage will be important later. In order to draw your map you will need some symbols. You can use whichever ones you like for various members of your family, but let me suggest some that have become rather universal among counselors and therapists:

Note: This family diagram will be a key part of your work on this unit. Because I will ask you to include some personal and sensitive information, you may want to write in a private journal or develop your own code to protect yourself and others.

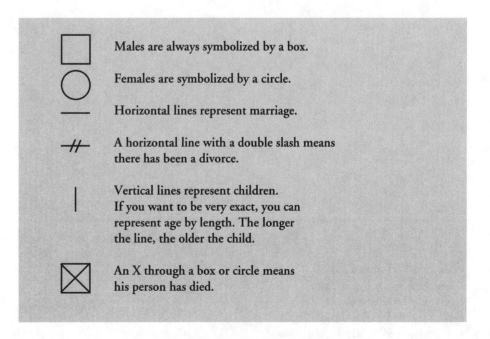

Males are always symbolized by a box.

Females are symbolized by a circle.

Horizontal lines represent marriage.

A horizontal line with a double slash means there has been a divorce.

Vertical lines represent children.
If you want to be very exact, you can represent age by length. The longer the line, the older the child.

An X through a box or circle means his person has died.

Below I have drawn the map of my family just to give you an idea of what a family looks like.

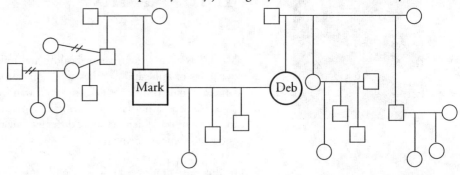

You don't have to label your diagram. The symbols at the top left represent my father and mother, still married and living. My younger brother is represented by the shorter vertical line extending down from the horizontal line that connects my parents. By the diagram you can see my brother has been divorced once. His current wife was also divorced and has two daughters from that marriage. My brother and his wife also have one son from their marriage.

Deb's parents are represented by the symbols at the top right. Deb has a twin sister and an older brother. You will notice that they each are married and have children.

Finally, in the middle of the diagram you will see that Deb and I have three children: Sarah, our oldest; Jonathan, our middle child; and Benjamin, our youngest.

✎ Now it is time for you to diagram your family. You may want to make several rough drafts to get the spacing right before you make a more permanent map in the space below. Don't worry if this is not perfect. Remember that this workbook is for your eyes only. In my diagram, I did not include my grandparents' generation, but you may want to include yours.

Now that you have your diagram of your family, we will refer to it in the remaining lessons of units 9 and 10.

## Assignment for the Lesson

✎ The Scripture memory verses for this unit appear in the margin. Begin to memorize the passage. Write the verses on a card and carry the card with you. Whenever you get a drink, review the passage.

Peter came to Jesus and asked, "Lord, how many times shall I forgive my brother when he sins against me? Up to seven times?" Jesus answered, "I tell you, not seven times, but seventy-seven times."
–Matthew 18:21-22

➤ Say the following affirmation five times.

I accept my family for who they are.

➤ Pray for all families, that they may live in peace and harmony.

LESSON 2

# Boundaries

Hannah's family was rather chaotic. She never really felt she had any privacy. She had two brothers whose job seemed to be to "bug" her. It was more than that, though. Hannah had her own room, but no one ever knocked before entering. Her dad and brothers often just walked in, even when she was getting dressed. The bathroom doors did not have locks and she was frequently embarrassed by others coming in.

Hannah's mother wanted desperately to be her friend. She would incessantly ask Hannah questions about what she was thinking and feeling. When Hannah had a difficult time answering, her mom would accuse her of being too quiet. Her dad would ask her questions about faith, making sure she was believing the correct things. Her brothers teased her often about her dates and the boys in her life.

When Hannah did have questions or feelings, she didn't know who to talk to. No one in her family really ever talked about their feelings. Even though she had a father and two brothers, men were a mystery to her. The only reaction that she ever seemed to get from the men in her family was about dating, sexual teasing, or when she was undressed.

Today, Hannah is married to a quiet man who doesn't bug her too much for sex. She secretly likes to wear revealing clothes and is often embarrassed and yet excited when other men seem to notice her. Hannah's family is not uncommon in many ways. Their boundaries were totally confused. Although she has learned some rather rigid boundaries at church, she has learned some rather loose ones at home.

In this lesson, you will begin to identify the nature of the boundaries that you learned at home. The boundaries you learned affected all of your current relationships.

✎ Boundaries generally refer to the invisible line marking the difference between two different kinds of territory. Do you think that boundaries refer to:

❑ geographic territory          ❑ sexual territory
❑ emotional territory          ❑ spiritual territory
❑ bodily territory

Did you check all of the above? Like lines on a geographic map, boundaries refer to invisible lines between people. These lines separate one person emotionally, physically, sexually, and spiritually from another.

## Force Fields

In science fiction movies, spaceships raise the force fields to deflect enemy fire. The force field is an invisible barrier to keep danger out. When the danger is past, the crew lowers the force fields to conserve energy, to allow friendly forces to come in, or for the ship to be resupplied. Only the ship's captain has the knowledge, skill, and authority to raise and lower the force field.

The force field is a boundary. It keeps bad things out and good things in. We humans are like the spaceship. We need boundaries to keep us safe and allow good things to come in.

➤ **Who is the captain of your ship?**

When we are small, our parents are the captain. They establish the boundaries. They raise and lower the force field. Our parents must make sure that damaging invasions don't occur. They must also make sure that we get the love, training, and support we need. We must be resupplied. We need food and rest, to be held and touched. Did you know that babies who don't get enough touching and holding actually don't grow? Their condition is called "failure to thrive."

✎ **The following list contains some examples of boundaries parents may establish as children grow up. Check those your parents provided for you.**

- ❏ going to bed on time
- ❏ taking your vitamins
- ❏ combing your hair
- ❏ going to school
- ❏ never telling lies
- ❏ not talking to strangers

- ❏ finishing all the food on your plate
- ❏ not playing in the street
- ❏ wearing clothes that match
- ❏ going to church
- ❏ doing your homework
- ❏ coming home on time

This list could go on. Parents are the captains of these boundaries. They model to children how to take care of themselves.

Growing up, developing, is a process of learning to be captain. All of us must learn to have healthy boundaries for ourselves. Our parents need gradually to turn control of boundaries over to us. Some parents are skilled at teaching and then surrendering control of boundaries; some aren't. For example, when we learn to walk, we must learn the boundary between falling and walking. If our parents never let go of our hands, we would never learn to walk.

✎ **Here are some examples of transition times in everybody's life. How successful were your parents in relinquishing control and allowing you to take charge of your boundaries? Check the ones for which they were able to let go of control.**

- ❏ going to school
- ❏ going on your first date
- ❏ finding a marriage partner
- ❏ selecting a career

- ❏ getting your first job
- ❏ driving a car
- ❏ sticking to a curfew
- ❏ deciding about your faith

➤ **What are you discovering? Did your parents let you have responsibility? Did they give you affirmation for making good choices? Were they critical of the things that you did? Did they say nothing? Did you perform so that you wouldn't disappoint them?**

Even though you are an adult, you may still hear your parent's opinions echoing in your head. You may still be searching for their approval.

➤ **Do you still have conversations with your parents in your mind? Are they still the captain of your boundaries, or are you?**

Sometimes, when we feel like we don't have control, we do things to test our boundaries or rebel against those who seek to control us. Two- and three-year-olds have temper-tantrums and refuse to get dressed or go to bed. Teenagers experiment with alcohol, drugs, and sex. They may test their curfews or refuse to go to church.

➤ **Do you do anything to test or rebel against the boundaries in your head?**

Being healthy involves establishing boundaries for yourself. You are able to keep bad things out and let good things in. Later we will discuss healthy sexual boundaries.

Families model how to choose healthy boundaries by maintaining healthy boundaries. We know, however, that many families are not particularly good at this. Remember Hannah in our opening story. Her family, for example, was not able to maintain a healthy boundary about privacy. The men in her family were always coming into her bedroom or the bathroom. She learned little about the privacy of her body. She also learned that her nakedness did get attention. Hannah's mother was not able to maintain a healthy boundary about emotional privacy. She tried to invade Hannah's thoughts. Hannah learned to be secretive.

While Hannah was learning about being invaded, she was also learning that no one talked about feelings. No one really gave her attention in a healthy way. She was also being abandoned. In short, bad things were getting in and good things weren't.

In this kind of situation, can you see that the boundaries are too loose on one hand—invasion is happening, and too rigid on the other—nurturing is not happening. Thankfully, for Hannah, she wasn't invaded sexually in a more destructive way. Neither her father nor her brothers actually molested her. Hannah must learn, however, that her sexual boundaries were violated. She will also have to learn that exposing her body is not a positive way to get male attention.

## Loose Versus Rigid Boundaries

Some examples of the difference between loose and rigid boundaries appear below:

| Loose | Rigid |
|---|---|
| No privacy | No healthy touching |
| Constant questioning | Not listening |
| Unhealthy touching | No affirmations |
| Constant criticism | Love is not expressed |
| Yelling and screaming | Silence |
| Hitting | Avoiding |
| Giving constant advice | Giving no advice |
| Sexual teasing | No sexual information |
| Breaking rules | No rules |

In unit 10, we will learn a lot more about boundary violations.

✎ **List one example from your family of how boundaries were violated in each category:**

Loose _____

_____

Rigid _____

_____

Your examples do not have to be major violations. Boundary violations can be subtle. My father, a minister, at times felt rules were for others and not for him. My favorite example is going to baseball games. Whatever seats he paid for, he always felt entitled to something better. Sooner or later we would wind up in the box seats closer to the action. This is very subtle, but it teaches that rules can be broken if you feel entitled to something better.

At times boundaries may be simultaneously too loose in one way and too rigid in another. If, for example, Hannah tried to tell her mother about her lack of privacy and her mother refused to listen, she would simultaneously experience both invasion (loose boundary) and abandonment (rigid—no talk—boundary).

Some of us grow up confused about boundaries. One part of us knows about appropriate boundaries, but we don't know how to follow them or may even refuse to follow them. This was true for me about sexual boundaries. I knew about sexual sin, but I allowed myself to participate in it over and over again. I could not observe healthy sexual boundaries for myself, my wife, or for others.

➤ Start thinking about how your own sexual boundaries have been confused.

➤ Look back at your family diagram in lesson one. Can you begin to see problems with the modeling of healthy boundaries between members of your family?

## Assignment for the Lesson

✎ Read the following passage of Scripture. In the margin write your own paraphrase of these boundaries God gave to us.

> *"You shall have no other gods before me.*
> *"You shall not make for yourself an idol in the form of anything in heaven above or on the earth beneath or in the waters below. You shall not bow down to them or worship them; for I, the Lord your God, am a jealous God, punishing the children for the sin of the fathers to the third and fourth generation of those who hate me, but showing love to a thousand generations of those who love me and keep my commandments.*
> *"You shall not misuse the name of the Lord your God, for the Lord will not hold anyone guiltless who misuses his name.*
> *"Remember the Sabbath day by keeping it holy. Six days you shall labor and do all your work, but the seventh day is a Sabbath to the Lord your God. On it you shall not do any work ....*
> *"Honor your father and your mother, so that you may live long in the land the Lord your God is giving you.*
> *"You shall not murder.*
> *"You shall not commit adultery.*
> *"You shall not steal.*
> *"You shall not give false testimony against your neighbor.*
> *"You shall not covet your neighbor's house. You shall not covet your neighbor's wife, or his manservant or maidservant, his ox or donkey, or anything that belongs to your neighbor."*
>
> —Exodus 20:3-17

➤ Read also these boundaries, stated in a more positive way.

> *If you, then, though you are evil, know how to give good gifts to your children, how much more will your Father in heaven give good gifts to those who ask him! So in*

*everything, do to others what you would have them do to you, for this sums up the Law and the Prophets.*

—Matthew 7:11-12

➢ Say the following affirmation five times.

I can have healthy boundaries in my life.

➢ Pray for the ability to love others and yourself.

LESSON
3

# Family Rules

When Zachary was growing up his father was very "tough." He never admitted to having any problems. He was a strict disciplinarian. The belt hanging on the door in the kitchen told what happened if rules were broken. Zach often was beaten with that belt. Over the years he learned that the harder he cried, the more hits he received, so Zach learned not to cry. "Big boys don't cry," his father would say. As he grew up Zach learned that real men don't show their emotions. For example, during a championship baseball game, Zach was hit by a line drive. His coach told him to "get tough" and stay in the game.

Zach's mother was a saint of their church. She was always smiling and acting as if nothing ever bothered her. Whenever Zach had a problem, she would always smile and ask him if it was anything too big for God. Sometimes she would use comparisons to tell him it wasn't all right to complain, "You don't like what we're having for dinner," she would say. "Just think of those poor starving children in China." Zachary also learned to be prejudiced. His parents always blamed someone for their problems. The democrats were to blame for taxes, lazy poor people for the welfare state, northerners for taking jobs away from the south, and so on. Zach's dad even blamed Zach's bad grades on his teacher being a Catholic.

Later in life, Zach's marriage was in trouble. He married a woman very much like his mother. They never really talked about anything serious. When Zach had an affair, he blamed his wife for being sexually cold.

As is typical of many families, Zachary's family observed many unwritten rules about communication and responsibility. They communicated both verbal and nonverbal messages about feelings, strength, maturity, other people, and the roles of men and women. Zachary carried these messages into his adult life and they have a destructive effect on his marriage.

Zachary's story contains these five rules:

- Don't Talk
- Minimize
- Deny
- Don't Feel
- Blame

Let's look at them closely and try to understand how they apply.

## Don't Talk

The "don't talk" rule may be overtly stated, "In our family we don't talk about that" (for example, sex). Family members may use shame to tell a person not to talk about something, "That's a terrible way to talk," or, "Mature (or strong) people don't talk like that." Parents may bring religion into the equation, "God doesn't like listening to that kind of talk." Of course, a more subtly powerful way of stating the rule is simply to never talk. Certain subjects, like sex, are not talked about. How easily we talk about the weather, sports, or politics, but not something more serious.

Shame fuels this rule. A person may feel that he doesn't know how to talk (remember Moses before God at the burning bush) without being embarrassed, bad things happening, or someone getting mad at him. He may even feel that by speaking out the situation will be worse.

✎ What was talking like in your family? Can you think of one example of how the don't talk rule was verbally or nonverbally communicated to you?

_____

## Don't Feel

Some of the people who live here in Minnesota can give the impression that these rugged types don't believe in feelings. Sometimes their quietness is referred to as being stoic, or strong. Like talking, feelings can be avoided in many ways. Someone might say, "Don't feel that way," "It's not nice to feel that way," "It's not Christian to feel that way," or "Shame on you for feeling like that." Perhaps someone in your family told you to grow up, be more mature, stop feeling sorry for yourself, or to just be happy. Maybe you were preached at, yelled at, or put down for your feelings.

Your family may definitely have given you the impression that certain feelings are acceptable–joy, happiness, contentment. Other feelings such as anger, fear, and loneliness are unacceptable. Of course, the most common way that most of us learn not to talk about feelings is that no one around us ever does.

✎ Check the feelings below that you remember your family talking about.

❑ anger          ❑ anxiety          ❑ shame
❑ fear           ❑ loneliness       ❑ guilt

Maybe you can recall talking about some of these things with one member of your family and not the others. Did you learn that women talk about certain things and men don't, or vice versa?

✎ Write down one example of how you felt you were taught not to feel your feelings.

_____

## Deny

Denial is a classic strategy of most addicts—they say they don't really have a problem. "That's not really a problem for me, I don't do it that much, I can quit tomorrow." In its most serious form, denial is outright lying. People claim simply not to have done something. "That wasn't me that you saw doing that," "Those aren't my cigarettes," "I wasn't drinking," or "I never said any such thing," are classic denial statements.

Denial is an avoidance behavior. For example, think of the families who put up with alcoholism. Everyone knows the problem exists, but no one chooses to confront it. Family members may fear creating an even more difficult situation, so they do nothing.

Moses said to the Lord, "O Lord, I have never been eloquent, neither in the past nor since you have spoken to your servant. I am slow of speech and tongue."
–Exodus 4:10

✎ What problems or issues were ignored or avoided in your family?

_____

_____

✎ Which of these are still a problem for you in some way?

_____

_____

✎ What other strategies did your family use to deny problems? Write specific statements that members of your family—including yourself—have made to deny problems.

_____

_____

## Minimize

Minimizing is another form of avoidance closely related to denial. One form is to minimize the importance of the feeling or situation. "It really didn't hurt that bad." "That's not a big deal." Authority figures use shame to teach minimizing, "Why are you making such a big thing about that? Why are you getting so excited about such a trivial thing?" Such shaming can be very subtle, "Gee, your reaction surprises me, I didn't think you would be so concerned. It's really not that important." Like Zachary's mother in this lesson's opening story, people can use comparison to minimize. Generally, whatever the family problem is, it can be compared to somebody else who has a bigger problem. "At least we're not as bad as them," is a common statement. This type of statement can make you feel guilty for taking something seriously. A statement such as this is also judgmental toward someone else, in that it allows us to put them down.

One of the most subtle, and destructive, forms is religious minimizing. This strategy suggests that whatever the problem is, God will take care of it in His time. Theologically I agree that God can solve all problems in His own time. Minimizing is when this correct theology prevents us from taking something seriously. It helps us avoid whatever constructive actions we might take on our own to confront or solve something. I call this, "Correct theology, incorrectly timed." What this form of minimizing does is allow us to say that in God's grand scheme of things, this is really not such a big deal. God will take care of it, we don't have to worry about it.

✎ What minimizing strategies did your family use?

_____

_____

## Blame

Blaming avoids responsibility. When a family makes mistakes or experiences problems, they can either own up to their part in the problem, or they can blame it on someone or something else. In Zachary's family any problem could be blamed on some other person or group.

Blaming is a frequent human response. Family members fear that if they say they are sorry for what they've done, or admit their guilt, others won't like them. To blame seems a much safer solution than to honestly and courageously face problems.

➤ **Think about how your family dealt with making mistakes and feeling guilty. What were their strategies for dealing with responsibility?**

Blaming fosters negative feelings for others. It can create a form of prejudice. Women, men, ethnic groups, political groups, and religious groups are popular targets. Such prejudice grows in subtle ways. If the family blames individuals in certain groups for something, we begin to generalize about all members of that group. Zachary's father blamed a Catholic teacher for being unfair. Zachary may generalize this blame to all Catholics. When certain women, even those in the family, are blamed for something all the time, others may generalize that all women have these problems.

✎ **What specific groups were spoken of negatively in your family?**

_____

_____

You may want to consult your family diagram in lesson 1 as you answer these questions.

✎ **What individuals got blamed in your family?**

_____

_____

✎ **Who did the major blaming or criticism?**

_____

_____

## Assignment for the Lesson

➤ **With which of the rules from today's lesson do you still have problems? How have you denied, minimized, or blamed, others for your sexual sins?**

➤ **Say the following affirmation five times.**

I can talk, feel, and accept my problems as being my own.

➤ **Pray for one of those groups that you have learned to dislike as a result of the blaming in your family.**

# Family Roles

**LESSON 4**

Andy was the firstborn in his family. He was long-awaited and the son his father always wanted. He was named after his great-grandfather who had come from another country and been a pioneer and rugged individual. The family treated Andy like royalty. He could do nothing wrong. If he made a mistake, someone explained it away. He was expected to be a scholar, a social star, and an athlete. His father secretly hoped that he would follow his footsteps and become a doctor. While his dad never seemed to have much time for church, Andy was always expected to be there.

Andy, a quiet boy, never caused the family problems. He spent much time in his room, read books, listened to the radio, or played games by himself. When he was small he often talked to his imaginary friends. He became successful at many things. Andy married his high school sweetheart, became a doctor and earned lots of money in his large practice. Everyone was shocked when Andy was arrested for soliciting prostitution.

Andy is a product of the roles that his family assigned to him from birth. These roles were never handed to him in written form, they were just expected of him in conscious and unconscious ways. To complain about all the adulation he received seems difficult, but down deep Andy was lonely, lost, and had no one to talk to. He had to be perfect. When Andy went to see prostitutes, he was seeking someone he could talk to.

Many writers have discussed family roles. Roles are like characters in the script of a play. The family writes the script, assigns the roles, and expects the members to act out the parts. Though different lists and descriptions exist, the following eight names describe common roles that occur in families.

 **You will have an opportunity to read more about the roles, but in the list below circle the roles you imagine might apply to Andy. Underline the roles you imagine might apply to you.**

- hero
- scapegoat
- lost child
- enabler
- doer
- little prince/princess
- mascot
- saint

## Hero

Hero was one of the roles Andy played. Members expect the hero to be the shining star of the family. The hero solves all problems and never makes mistakes. He is expected to excel and represents the family to the outside world. Sometimes the endeavors at which the hero is expected to excel may be prescribed by spoken and unspoken communication. Andy, for example, was expected to be a doctor.

## Scapegoat

The scapegoat is the reverse of the hero. The scapegoat is blamed for family problems. He is expected to make mistakes and amount to very little. The scapegoat learns his role, like all the others, from birth. Unconsciously he fulfills his role by making mistakes and wrong choices. Later in life the scapegoat will feel like a dismal failure. The scapegoat must learn that many of his mistakes are learned behaviors, and he can succeed if he chooses to.

## Lost Child

Andy also played the lost child. The lost child never makes waves. She learns how to be independent and take care of herself. She spends lots of time alone entertaining herself with books, TV, games, and even imaginary friends. The lost child gets lots of affirmation for being so independent and trouble-free. Parents never have to discipline the lost child because she is always behaving well. This child is lost, however, in that she has no one to talk to. Later in life, she might confront her parents about being so lonely. Her parents may respond with, "You never talked to us or seemed to need anything."

## Mascot

The mascot is the comedian of the family. Whenever the tension in the family gets to a certain point, like a thermostat the mascot will turn on and tell a joke or somehow get everyone to laugh. The mascot learns to do silly things, tell jokes, and distract everyone from problems. Everyone likes the mascot because he is so funny and will always be included in activities for that reason. The mascot has long forgotten the passage from Ecclesiastes 3:4, "There is a time to weep and a time to laugh." He has effectively turned off an entire range of his God-given emotions.

## Enabler

The fifth role is the enabler. Enabling is not always a negative thing. To enable is to provide someone with the means or opportunity. Healthy parents enable their children's growth. Enabling becomes destructive when the enabler provides someone with the opportunity to be irresponsible or participate in negative behavior. This can happen in many ways. One way is when the enabler does not confront problems. Enablers make excuses for the person participating in the negative behavior. If an alcoholic, for example, is having a hangover and can't go to work, the enabler will call the alcoholic's boss and say the alcoholic has the flu. The enabler will do his best to keep the outside world from knowing about problems within the family. Thus enablers make continued irresponsible or destructive behavior easier.

## Doer

The doer likes doing things. If she did 10 things today, she will try to do 11 things tomorrow. She thrives on accomplishment. She does the laundry, cooks the meals, pays the bills, does the chores, makes the money, and chauffeurs the kids. In adult life doers may turn into workaholics. Doing may also be a form of enabling if the doer is taking over the responsibilities of other family members because of the members' negative behavior.

## Little Prince/Princess

The main task of the little prince/princess role is to be cute, wonderful, warm, and cuddly. It's the Shirley Temple role. Girls will have frilly dresses and ribbons in their hair. Boys will wear nice outfits and always have their hair combed. The little prince/princess may be expected to perform by song, dance, or impromptu piano recital. This role represents the cuteness and wonderfulness of the family to the outside world. In adult life this role will allow the little prince/princess to perform or somehow be on stage. One danger of this role is that the person will become an approval addict.

## Saint

The saint is the person in the family who is expected to be religious. Like Andy, he may be required to go to church even if other members of the family don't. This role is closely related to the hero, and is expected to solve all spiritual problems. The saint may enter a religious vocation in adult life. One of my minister friends, who played this role, claims, "I was ordained first by my mother and later by the church."

✎ Now, with a more complete explanation of the roles, complete the following chart to indicate how you relate to each of the roles.

| | Not me at all | Sometimes I played this role | That's me |
|---|---|---|---|
| • Hero | ❏ | ❏ | ❏ |
| • Scapegoat | ❏ | ❏ | ❏ |
| • Lost Child | ❏ | ❏ | ❏ |
| • Mascot | ❏ | ❏ | ❏ |
| • Enabler | ❏ | ❏ | ❏ |
| • Doer | ❏ | ❏ | ❏ |
| • Little Prince/Princess | ❏ | ❏ | ❏ |
| • Saint | ❏ | ❏ | ❏ |

One way to understand the roles you played is to remember back to the stories your family told about you. At family gatherings, on your birthday, or on special occasions what stories do they tell about your life? Were they tales of heroic deeds, or miserable failures? Were they about the great things you were going to do or the things that you would never do? Were they about the funny things you said or did, all the things you do, or your performances?

My dad often tells of standing at the window of the newborn nursery looking at me for the first time. He had a feeling that God had something special for me to do. I believe that and claim it, but to live up to that has been a struggle. I have often wondered if my motivation behind my actions is to please God or to please dad. In any event, as oldest child and a son of a minister, two of my roles were to be the hero and the saint.

You have probably noticed that a person can play more than one role. Several people in a family can also play the same role.

✎ Go to your family diagram in lesson 1 and label the various roles you and members of your family of origin played.

✎ What is your personal combination of roles:

_____

➤ Do you still play them?

In some form, most of us play the roles that we learned in our homes. Some of us may be secretly tired, angry, or resentful about the roles we have been assigned, but we don't know how to stop playing them. Our roles are what we know, how we function in life. If you play the hero role, for example, you may be tired of having to be perfect all the time, but can't seem to live without all the adulation you receive for being so wonderful. A lot of ministers I know, for example, play the hero/saint/lost child combination. They are spiritual heroes and everyone expects them to be right. At the same time they are lonely. Who ministers to or listens to the minister?

✎ Now look at your current family situation. In your diagram, label the roles that you, your spouse, and your children play (if you have them).

Notice, for those of you who are married, how you and your spouse match up. A hero, for example, may need a doer to get things done while he is off riding his white horse saving the world.

➤ Consider what roles people play at your workplace, church, and in your community.

## Assignment for the Lesson

➤ What do your sexual sins say about the roles you play in life? Have you been secretly or unconsciously trying to sabotage one of your roles? What roles would you like to change about yourself?

➤ Say the following affirmation five times.

I can be the person I want to be; I don't have to perform for anybody else's expectations.

➤ Pray for strength and the courage to change.

**LESSON 5**

# Managing Stress

In William's family extreme emotions were never tolerated. The "don't talk" and "don't feel" rules were strictly enforced. Feelings were experienced, but they were not expressed.

William's father smoked cigarettes and drank a lot. He never seemed to get drunk and out of control, but an ample supply of alcohol was always available. William's mother liked to read a lot, particularly romance novels. She shopped often, and the credit cards were always stretched to the limit.

In the morning coffee was always brewing. During the day, William's mother was quick to fix him whatever snack he wanted. When his dad got home they usually went to buy sodas and candy. Evening activities were common, mainly sports related and usually involving William and his dad. Late at night, the family watched TV and ate until everyone was tired enough to go to sleep.

Today, William has more TV cable channels than he can watch. After his wife has gone to bed he eats, smokes, and channel surfs until he finds pornography. He usually is not ready to go to bed until one or two o'clock in the morning. During the day William wonders why he needs so much coffee just to keep going.

William's family is a good example of a collective stress management strategy. Drinking, smoking, eating, watching TV, reading, and sports are all activities that they use to keep the collective mood relatively calm. The family didn't want to talk about feelings, so they do various things to distract themselves from their feelings or to alter the mood.

I used to teach stress management seminars. We discussed relaxation techniques for dealing with anxiety and fear. What I didn't realize then is many of us grew up in a stress management seminar. When the feeling level got to a certain point, someone was there to model changing the mood or avoiding the feeling. By the time we went to school, we had a stable of techniques that we could use to change how we feel.

Stress management strategies within the family are not necessarily bad. At times, we need to manage feelings so we can accomplish normal everyday activities. At others times, however, we need to allow feelings to be present so that the family can deal with them in appropriate ways.

In unit 3 I talked about the importance of allowing your feelings to be present so that you can understand them and make healthy choices about expressing them. To continually avoid facing your feelings is extremely destructive. Avoidance is called repression and is often a contributing cause of depression. The substances or behaviors you use to change or avoid feeling can become an addiction. (Remember my definition of addiction in unit 7. A behavior or substance becomes addictive when it is repetitive, unmanageable, degenerative, and destructive.) Notice in the diagram below from unit 3 that addictions can be divided into several categories. Substances can be addictive as well as behaviors. Some substances and behaviors can raise your mood, some can lower your mood.

|  | Substances | Behaviors |
|---|---|---|
| Elevate Mood | caffeine<br>amphetamine<br>sugar<br>cocaine | work<br>shopping<br>cleaning<br>danger<br>sex |
| Depress Mood | alcohol<br>heroin<br>narcotics<br>nicotine | eating<br>watching TV<br>sex |

Sexual thinking and activity is a behavior that can raise or lower your mood. The thrill of fantasy and danger of pursuit elevate mood. Sex as a loving and nurturing experience can be soothing and calming. Your family may have modeled one or several of these behaviors to you.

✎ **Several common emotions or feelings are listed below. After each one describe substances or behaviors that your family used to deal with that particular emotion.**

Anger _____

Fear _____

Sadness _____

Loneliness _____

Boredom _____

✎ **Would you consider that any members of your family used these behaviors addictively? You may think so even if they didn't believe that they had a problem. If so, go back to your family diagram and label those family members as addicts.**

✎ **How did your family deal with sexual feelings, information, or tension? Below is a list of possibilities, check the ones that apply:**

❏ Didn't talk about sex ever.
❏ Sexual humor and teasing.
❏ Sexual acting out in inappropriate or sinful ways.
❏ Healthy discussions of sexuality.

✎ Would you consider that any member of your family is a sexual addict? If so, label your diagram appropriately.

Remember the work you did in lesson 4 on family roles. The role of the enabler is one that often exists in the face of addictions. An enabler "enables" someone else to continue his or her dysfunctional or addictive behavior. The enabler makes excuses, tells lies, and gets things done while the addict is being irresponsible. Sometimes, we refer to this type of enabler as a "co-addict." He "co-exists" with the addict. Enablers who are co-addicts have also led to the use of the term "codependent." The codependent of an addict finds the addict's approval more important than confronting the problem behavior.

✎ Look at your family diagram again. You have already labeled those whom you consider to be enablers. If you have also discovered some addicts in your family, who were codependent or co-addicted to them?

Hopefully in this unit you are discovering how your family dealt with conflict, anger, anxiety, fear, loneliness, or boredom. You may have practiced strategies to avoid feelings due to the modeling you received in your home. Although you may consider yourself primarily a sexual addict, you may also be a codependent to other dysfunctional behavior. You may be afraid to face conflict, confront problems, or face feelings.

➤ In your current family situation, are there addictions or problems that you are not confronting or dealing with? What feelings are inside you that you don't express?

Perhaps you and your sexual problems have been blamed for some other person's problems. Perhaps you think if you get well everything else in the family will be fine. Life is an ongoing process of developing healthy, Christ-honoring behaviors and overcoming unhealthy, sinful ones. When you first understand some of the dynamics of families, you may feel angry and betrayed, or you may think: "Wow! Now I have the ultimate answer to everything. This will solve all my problems." Understanding how family shapes our lives is only a part of the process. As you see and understand the forces that contribute to your behavior, you can more effectively assume responsibility for your actions. You can choose to become the captain of your ship, exercising good boundaries.

## Assignment for the Lesson

➤ Begin thinking now about the entire system of the family in which you now live. Besides your sexual problems, what other problems will need to be addressed as you recover?

➤ Say the following affirmation five times.

I can recover, and I can live in a healthy family.

➤ Pray for the addicts in your family who still suffer and who need to find help.

# UNIT 10

# Families (Part 2)

## FOCAL PASSAGE:

*But you, O God, do see trouble and grief; you consider it to take it in hand. The victim commits himself to you; you are the helper of the fatherless.*
—Psalm 10:14

### MEMORY VERSE

Though my father and mother forsake me, the Lord will receive me.
–Psalm 27:10

---

### JOHN'S STORY

John's father was rarely home. When he was home he was too tired to have any time for John. John's mother was very possessive of John and treated him like the man of the house, particularly when his dad wasn't there. She was often lonely. She frequently asked John to sleep in her bedroom just to keep her company.

When he was 5, John's 13-year-old cousin Ted taught him to play "doctor." Over the years this "game" turned into more serious sexual activity. An older man lived up the street from John. He was nice to all the boys and John enjoyed going to his house. The man always had treats and let the boys play games. One day this man asked John if he would like to take some pictures. This became a frequent activity and John even agreed several times to take off his clothes for the pictures. The older man also began fondling him and being sexual with him.

When John became a teenager he stopped going to this man's house and Ted moved away. John started dating girls. The girls he dated were thankful for a boy like John who respected them sexually. At home, John started masturbating. He often did this to fantasies of girls, but occasionally he also thought of other boys.

John grew up and married a girl he met at a Christian college. They had several children. Everything seemed normal with this family, yet John continued to masturbate and the fantasies of men grew more serious. He discovered a park where men met for sexual encounters with each other. John was distraught. He wanted to remain faithful to his marriage, yet his mind raged with desires to meet men at the park. He was afraid to talk to his pastor or anyone else for fear of being called a homosexual.

---

### GROWTH GOAL

In this unit you will learn about many different forms of abuse and the effect that abuse may have had on your feelings, attitudes, and behaviors.

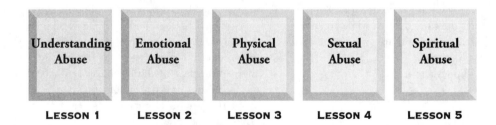

| Understanding Abuse | Emotional Abuse | Physical Abuse | Sexual Abuse | Spiritual Abuse |
|---|---|---|---|---|
| LESSON 1 | LESSON 2 | LESSON 3 | LESSON 4 | LESSON 5 |

# Understanding Abuse

*Honor your father and your mother, so that you may live long in the land the Lord your God is giving you.*

—Exodus 20:12

John's story is a tragic example of how common sexual abuse is. Sexual abuse could lead John into a life of homosexuality. He has confused homosexual acts with being a homosexual. The story illustrates how sexual abuse can lead to a life of sexual sin. This can be true heterosexually or homosexually for either men or women. Many persons struggle as John does with homosexual thoughts, feelings, and fears caused by sexual abuse.

Research indicates that many persons with sexual-addiction problems are themselves the survivors of sexual abuse. Therefore I have written some of the material in this unit directly to the survivor of sexual abuse. If you are not such a survivor, please study this unit to help you understand the struggles of those who have been subjected to sexual abuse.

**This unit may be the most intensely painful part of this workbook for you. If you get in touch with emotions with which you just don't think you can cope, call a pastor or professional counselor immediately. Stop working this workbook until you have received some help for the deep pain that you feel. If sexual abuse has been an issue for you, another workbook, *Shelter from the Storm,* may be the book you need to be working on.**

We appropriately began this lesson with Exodus 20:12—the commandment to honor our parents. We don't want to lose sight of this verse as we study the painful effects of abuse. Perhaps some of you have resisted looking at pain in your life because of this commandment. You haven't wanted to dishonor your parents.

Your memories and your pain are important. You can do this work, not to assign blame but to better understand yourself. We don't want you to stop loving or honoring parents or any other family members.

✎ **Does your attempt to understand the past and your own pain dishonor your parents or others?** ❏ Yes ❏ No

**If someone specific is at the root of your pain, do you dishonor him by telling him how much he has hurt you?** ❏ Yes ❏ No

Many survivors of sexual abuse seek to deal with the pain by avoiding the issue. They either deny the reality of the past, or they try to avoid the person who hurt them. Honoring does not include denial or avoidance. To understand the hurt and appropriately communicate that hurt—sometimes even to confront the offender—may be the way to show genuine honor. I believe the answer to both of the questions above is an emphatic "No." Honesty expressed through love is the way to show genuine honor. In the margin read what the apostle Paul wrote about speaking the truth.

Each of you must put off falsehood and speak truthfully to his neighbor, for we are all members of one body. "In your anger do not sin": Do not let the sun go down while you are still angry, and do not give the devil a foothold.
–Ephesians 4:25-27

When we do not accept our hurts and seek to heal them, we will—sometimes unconsciously—allow them to fester as resentment. We may become inappropriately angry at the person who has hurt us. We become angry over small things, or we displace our anger and direct it at someone else. Thus we practice dishonest anger. Or we may avoid the person altogether. Neither course of action leads to growth, healing, or responsible behavior.

The Christian community has much to offer the secular world. One of those offerings is a proper understanding of forgiveness. We seek to understand our pain, not so that we can be angry forever, but to heal and move on to forgiveness.

✎ **Below are some reasons why survivors of abuse often do not deal with their abuse. Check the ones that apply to your situation:**

❏ I don't remember all or parts of my childhood.
❏ I considered the things that happened to me to be normal, I didn't realize how hurtful they were.
❏ I want to honor my family.
❏ If I accept my pain, and feel sorry for myself, God won't think I'm a Christian.
❏ I'm afraid that someone will get mad at me if I remember certain things.
❏ If I deal with those feelings, I will just get sad and depressed.
❏ Jesus says to forgive. I just want to move on with my life.
❏ It was no big deal. I'm alive and have so many things to be thankful for.
❏ I believe in deliverance, God is going to cure me of this.
❏ If I forgive, I lose my primary defense of keeping the offender at a distance.

**KEY POINT**
If you are unable to heal the pain from your past, you won't recover from sexual sin.

Looking at any of our pains from the past is not only hurtful but also frightening. Many of us have used many excuses and rationalizations to avoid objectively looking at past experiences. A famous philosopher once said that those who forget the past are doomed to repeat it. Many survivors of sexual abuse do exactly that.

We don't want to blame others for our sins. We are responsible for all of our actions. By understanding our pain, however, we will be better able to know why we made some of the choices that we did. In the future, we can then be aware of how this pain has influenced us. We can search for resources to help us make better decisions in the future.

In the next four lessons I will describe the four areas of your life that can be violated: emotional, physical, sexual, and spiritual. In lesson 2 of unit 9 you worked on recognizing the boundaries in your family. Two kinds of boundary violations exist— invasion and abandonment. In invasion something breaks through the invisible barrier of protection that should exist around you. Abandonment occurs when you do not get the love and nurture you need.

Either invasion or abandonment create deep and damaging wounds. For many people, the invasions are easier to remember. They happened. They can be remembered. They are tangible. Abandonment is much more difficult to understand. How do you know what you missed if you never had it in the first place? A songwriter friend told me about a song entitled, "If Your Record Doesn't Have the Grooves, You Can't Play the Song." Abandonment wounds are like that. You may not have the grooves in the record of your mind to even know what you missed. That is why many of us grew up thinking everything was normal. We didn't know what real love and nurture was.

In the opening story of this unit, John was abandoned emotionally by his father. In therapy, John revealed his anger toward his mother for her dominating attitude. His therapist asked him, "John, you have never talked about your father." Surprised, John said, "I don't need to talk about him; he was never around. What's there to talk about?"

➤ How would you have answered John's question?

What's to talk about is the lack of a father in John's life. He never really knew a strong male presence. The attention he got from men involved inappropriate sexual behaviors. John has looked for men in a sexual way. That is all he knew. John will have to heal from this deep wound. He will need to recognize his father's abandonment as a factor in his quest for male attention through homosexual encounters.

Abandonment is even more powerful because it is so difficult to grasp. In my extensive work with sexual addicts, I have never known a sex addict who didn't suffer some kind of abandonment abuse. In many ways we who are sexually addicted have searched for something we missed.

### Assignment for the Lesson

➤ Read the following Scripture.

*I tell you the truth, anyone who will not receive the kingdom of God like a little child will never enter it." And he took the children in his arms, put his hands on them and blessed them.*

—Mark 10:15-16

✎ Write on a card Psalm 27:10, the Scripture memory verse for this unit. Carry the card with you.

➤ Say the following affirmation five times.

I am ready to sit on Jesus' lap and give Him my pain.

➤ Pray for the healing of your memories.

Though my father and mother forsake me, the Lord will receive me.
–Psalm 27:10

LESSON

2

# Emotional Abuse

Philip's dad was a busy man. He worked constantly. Whenever he was home he was so stressed out he didn't have much time for talking. He was critical of most things Philip did and thought. He never really yelled, but he had few good things to say. Philip can't remember when he stopped trying to talk to his father. Philip's mom was long-suffering. She always said Philip's dad was such a good provider. She worked hard and counted on Philip to get things done around the house. She talked to Philip all the time. He was her "Little Man." The two of them spent long hours together. She was lonely. When she talked to Philip, she would often pour her heart out to him about her problems. Philip grew to feel responsible for her. This made him feel proud that he was such a good son.

Philip grew up to be a diligent worker like his dad. He had many male acquaintances, but no real friends. By the time he was 40, he had been married twice and was thinking of marrying again. He always seemed to find emotionally weak women who wouldn't open up to him. Philip thought he was pleasing women when he was "strong" for them, but he became angry if they wanted him to be vulnerable with his feelings. Both his marriages ended because of his numerous affairs.

Both his parents emotionally wounded Philip. What he learned growing up has affected his relationships with women. In this lesson you will take a look at your own family. In lesson one you learned the two types of emotional wounds—invasion and abandonment. In lessons 2-5 you will examine four areas of life in which wounds occur: emotional, physical, sexual, and spiritual.

## Eight Boxes

I have often found that people have an easier time understanding emotional issues if they can first conceptualize or "see" the issues. Here is a diagram that outlines the two types of wounds and the four parts of a person:

|  | Emotional | Physical | Sexual | Spiritual |
|---|---|---|---|---|
| **Invasion** | | | | |
| **Abandonment** | | | | |

You can see that this diagram creates eight boxes. A person can be invaded emotionally, physically, sexually, and spiritually. He or she can also be abandoned in any or all of these areas.

 **When you work through these lessons, check the boxes for the types of abuse or wounds that you suffered. At the end of this unit, you will have a chart indicating where your healing needs to begin.**

## Emotional Invasion

How does emotional invasion occur? One of the most obvious ways is through "put downs" and verbal abuse. These messages can be yelled or screamed, sometimes with profanity. "You are a _____!" The message can be direct, as in: "You're dumb, stupid, and/or ugly!" Sometimes the message can be indirect, as in when you overhear, "I regret the day she was born; he was a pain then, and he's always been a pain." Emotional invasion can come in the form of a question, "Did you screw up again? You're always screwing up! Do it right this time, if you can."

The message doesn't have to be yelled or screamed. It can be said seemingly without emotion, "You got a C on your report card? That doesn't surprise me, you've never done well in school." Often the more subtle put-down can be comparative, "Your sister always got A's, I guess you're not as smart as she was," or, "Your brother made the varsity team, but then he always was more coordinated."

Emotional invasion can occur through non-verbal communication as well. Disapproving looks can leave a child wondering what he or she did wrong. Sighs can be in anger and disgust and be just as harsh as words.

The other day my daughter said to me, "Dad, I know when you're angry at me." This surprised me because I couldn't remember telling her so recently. Then to show me what she meant, she sighed, just like my mom and dad did, and just like I must have learned. Expressions of anger can be healthy with children, but only if they are verbalized in constructive ways. I need to develop the skill to say to my daughter: "I love you. The fact that I am angry does not mean I love you any less, but I need to tell you that I am angry at you right now because … ."

✎ **How did you know when your parents were angry with you?**

- ❑ yelling and screaming
- ❑ comparisons
- ❑ pointed fingers
- ❑ sighs

- ❑ put-downs
- ❑ profanity
- ❑ looks
- ❑ other _____

All of us would have benefited from parents who offered constructive expressions of what we did to make them angry, along with suggestions on how to improve the problem.

Do you remember the story of Jacob tricking Esau out of Isaac's blessing (Genesis 27:1-40)? A father's blessing was a vital thing for a child.

**KEY POINT**
Some people search for
approval from others
through sexual acts.

A parent's blessing is a deep and lasting need. Do you feel you have the blessing, or do you feel like one or both of your parents have never approved of you? Do you feel like a mistake in their eyes? If you don't feel blessed or approved of by your parents, the wound is deep. You may try to heal by finding approval in any way you can. You may feel a deep sense of shame.

To recognize the powerful impact your parents have made on your life does not mean blaming them. Remember that your parents probably did the best they could with the understanding, parenting skills, and resources they had. You can work to understand yourself and your development so you can take charge and avoid being a victim of the past.

Our families can also wound us through a form of mind control. Some have even called it "mind rape." Remember the "Don't Talk, Don't Feel" rules (from unit 9)? That is the way many families deal with emotions. The phrase *mind rape* comes from the fact that someone else controlled your mind. Your family disqualified your opinions and ideas, ignoring your questions and curiosities. They told you or modeled to you that feeling pain or talking about problems was not OK. You learned to shut down for your own protection. If you learned these rules well, the training damaged your ability to talk about or express your thoughts and emotions. You can heal from this disability; but it takes time, and you may need help.

➤ Has anyone ever told you that you needed to open up more, to be more honest with your feelings, or to be more vulnerable? Has anyone ever been angry with you for being so quiet or distant?

If you answered yes to either of these questions, you may be a mind-rape victim. You need to heal from this impairment in order to have healthy relationships. Recognize that you will have to face old fears about being honest and expressing your feelings.

Another form of emotional invasion has been called "emotional incest." The word *incest* implies that a family member, probably a parent, has had an inappropriate emotional relationship with you. Emotional incest happens when a family member tries to have an emotional relationship with you that should exist between a husband and wife.

➤ Do you still hear the voice of one of your parent's in your head? Do you continually talk to them in your mind, wondering what they are thinking?

Emotional incest usually happens because one parent is lonely. Philip's story illustrates a father who was always gone and a mother who depended on Philip. She treated him like an adult—her "little man." Philip's mom needed a surrogate husband to make up for her loneliness. Even though he was small, Philip learned that his job was to care for and nurture her. Although Philip was physically a child, he was being treated like an adult, which gave him a feeling of power. Do you see the reversal of the parent-child roles? At a time when she needed to be a mother to a lonely boy with an absent father, Philip's mom wasn't able to provide the love and nurturing Philip needed. She needed him to be strong for her.

Your mom or dad may have seemed like your best friend. You did everything together, you talked about everything. Their interests were your interests. Was this, however, for your nurture or for your parent's? Did they encourage you to be the person you wanted to be or the person they wanted you to be? In your preadolescent years did you become an adult so that you could be a companion to them? Did you stop being a child so that you could fulfill adult responsibilities?

Emotional incest is so powerful because it seems so innocent. The child is robbed of childhood and deprived of the love and nurture of a parent. The child learns a role and how to fulfill it. That child may play the learned role for the rest of his or her life.

> **Do you find that the only way you can relate to another person is to be the caregiver?**

If you said yes, you may not know how to be child-like. You have problems trusting others to take care of you. You can't be vulnerable and ask for what you need. Your job is to be strong.

The problem with always needing to be strong is that you learn to rely upon yourself. You never learn to trust appropriate people or to trust God. If your own strength was enough to get you well, you wouldn't be where you are. In order to get well, you must allow others to give you help.

> **Are you willing to learn how to trust others to help you? Are you willing to let go of trying to be strong all the time? Can you accept that others may love you or like you even though you're not the strongest person around?**

If you can't learn to trust, find help, and accept other people's love you will find recovery impossible. Remember the words of Jesus in Matthew 18:3-4, appearing in the margin. We need to develop a child-like faith and trust.

## Emotional Abandonment

Sometimes emotional abandonment can work like invasion. If a parent is not good at sending affirmations, what is the child expected to think? If a child does something she is really proud of and a parent says nothing, what is the message? If a parent never tells a child he is smart, attractive, or competent, is this child going to have a lot of confidence?

Emotional abandonment is more difficult to understand because, unlike forms of invasion, abandonment is about what did *not* happen. How do you know what you missed if you never had it in the first place? A void that exists in your spirit may cause you to feel so lonely it takes your breath away. If you were asked to define what makes you so lonely, however, you couldn't.

For Christians, feeling the void of emotional abandonment is especially painful. We believe that God through Christ can meet our needs, so if we still feel lonely we become discouraged, doubt, and look for our own solutions. God does indeed fill this void, but not until we recognize it and bring it to Him.

I tell you the truth, unless you change and become like little children, you will never enter the kingdom of heaven. Therefore, whoever humbles himself like this child is the greatest in the kingdom of heaven.
–Matthew 18:3-4

Often we only come to recognize issues of emotional abandonment through a study of our own behavior. We can see the needs in our lives as we look at the ways we have tried to fill the void.

Jack's mom never talked to him about emotional or spiritual things, but she was a great cook and she always did the laundry. He never "knew" his mother. She emotionally abandoned him. The only attention Jack knows from a woman is through food and laundry.

For Jack love means food and clean clothes, but now Jack's wife, a working mother, wants him to help with the laundry. Her request spells rejection to him. If he were to start doing the laundry, it would take away one of the few ways he knows to relate to a woman. Jack also has problems with overeating. Food is another way he has tried to fill the void. For Jack food is a substitute for his mother's attention.

Perhaps you have tried to fill your emotional void with sex. The only way you know how to relate is through sexual behaviors. Whether or not our mother or father, or both, abandoned us, we have thought that sex is equal to love and that is how we fill the void. Remember, again, the powerful messages that culture teaches about this equation—be sexual and be happy.

➤ **Think of your last sexually sinful experience. You may think that you were just lustful. Were you lonely before the experience? Were you attempting to fill a void in your life?**

Many of us who struggle with abandonment issues have created a mythical or "magic" person in our mind. This person personifies perfect nurturing to us. Somehow we would like to take that person inside of us and fill the empty void. Since we don't know how to really connect on an emotional and spiritual level, we start to sexually fantasize instead.

In Part 1 of this workbook we discuss the healthier ways to find emotional and spiritual nurture for yourself. One of the first steps on the road to emotional healing is to accept that you can't return to the past and get the love and nurture that you needed when you were small. Even if the people who abandoned you are more able today to give nurture, it can't make up for what you missed. Accepting that means that you must grieve the loss.

✐ **Below write the names of those whose blessing, approval, or love you didn't receive when you were younger.**

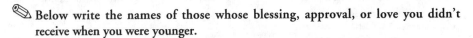

A part of your recovery will involve grieving your losses in those relationships. You can grieve, forgive those who hurt you, and move on with your life.

## Assignment for the Lesson

➤ **Can you accept the losses you experienced? Are you ready to grieve and move on with your life, looking for healthier ways to replace them?**

➤ **Say the following affirmation five times.**

I am worthy of love and nurture, from God and from others.

➤ **Pray for the peace of mind to know that you are loved.**

# Physical Abuse

Ted remembers being afraid since he was a small boy. His father was a good man who worked hard and took his family to church. A terrible secret, however, loomed over the family. Sometimes on weekends, Ted's father would drink. He couldn't stop until he was drunk. At those times his temper went out of control.

Ted doesn't remember his father ever hitting him during those times. He does remember his mom and dad arguing violently. These fights always ended with his mom crying because his dad had hit her. She never was injured to the point of having to go to the hospital. She became skilled at covering up her black eyes and bruises with makeup.

Ted's mom always told him not to worry, dad would be OK as soon as he slept it off. Once or twice when Ted cried and wanted his dad to stop, his father took off his belt, pulled down Ted's pants, and whipped him. Ted learned not to cry anymore.

Ted tried to hide all of his dad's liquor; however, there was always more. When he was 16, Ted intervened when his dad was hitting his mom. Ted threatened his dad.

After Ted left home his dad finally went for treatment of his alcoholism. He has apologized to the family for all of the violence. Still, especially at night, Ted wakes up frightened and doesn't always know why.

Unfortunately, Ted's story is not uncommon. As we know, domestic abuse is on the rise in our violent culture. On the surface, Ted seems to have escaped the harm himself. Or did he?

Researchers indicate that 74% of all sex addicts were physically abused as children.[1] Some were spanked or whipped for no good reason just because one of their parents was angry. The Bible teaches that parents have a responsibility to discipline their children, but discipline does not mean abuse. Discipline means teaching and training. Spanking out of anger is never healthy discipline. In the margin read what the apostle Paul said about how fathers should deal with their children.

> Are you a veteran who was involved in battle or do you know someone who is? What do you think it must be like to live through a time of violence?

**Fathers, do not provoke your children to anger; but bring them up in the discipline and instruction of the Lord.**
**–Ephesians 6:4**

Many veterans have come home mentally, emotionally, and spiritually wounded by the violence they witnessed, even though they may not have been physically wounded. When a Vietnam veteran friend of mine first returned home from the war he woke up in the middle of the night with his heart racing, and he could hardly breathe. He rushed to the hospital thinking he was having a heart attack. Physically, his heart was fine. To this day he sometimes has feelings of panic and doesn't know how to explain it. He is the victim of the violence he lived through in Vietnam. Growing up in a violent home produces much the same results as warfare. The results occur whether you were ever abused or, like Ted, you witnessed violence.

Check the following responses that apply to you.

❑ I have anxieties that I can't explain.
❑ I wake up in the middle of the night afraid.
❑ I experience anger, sometimes rage, that doesn't seem warranted.
❑ I have physical problems, like stomach disorders, that have no physical cause.

❑ I lose my temper.
❑ I am physically violent.
❑ I fantasize about or experience sex that is violent.
❑ I have an especially high tolerance for pain.

If you have any of these symptoms, you may have been physically abused as a child. Perhaps you have buried these experiences or believed that they were not significant.

If you have problems with your temper or with being violent, you can consult with a professional counselor who can help you work through your anger. Be of good courage—now is the time to stop the cycle of anger that you experienced when you were younger.

A friend of mine was repeatedly beaten with a belt when he was a boy. His father told him the more he cried, the worse his beating was going to be. Like Ted, he learned not to cry. He now has a high tolerance for pain. He can even go to the dentist and have a tooth filled without asking for anesthetic.

Another friend of mine was curious about girls when he was in kindergarten. When a girl walked by his desk, he pulled up her skirt. Of course his action was not appropriate, but he could have had appropriate boundaries explained to him. Instead his teacher beat him with a ruler and his father beat him with a belt. To this day he has a difficult time with any sexual thoughts and is virtually impotent.

I know another woman who was sexually and physically abused by both her mother and father. As an adult, she became addicted to physically painful sex. Physical abuse can be powerful and, in combination with other forms of abuse, can lead to sexual problems.

✎ If you were physically abused as a child, write the name(s) or initials of the person(s) who abused you.

_____

_____

✎ How has this abuse affected your life?

_____

_____

_____

Physical abandonment means being left alone. It can include a range of experiences from being accidentally left in a store to being abandoned alone to die. This is one of our first fears in life. We leave the protective environment of the womb and come into the relative coldness of the world. Of course our parents and others quickly hold and nurture us. We never lose our need to be held and nurtured, physically touched and comforted.

**KEY POINT**
Your sexual sin may have been, in part, driven by the human need to be touched.

➤ What was physical touching like in your home? Do you remember being touched in healthy ways?

Like babies, we may fail to thrive if we don't get enough touch from other human beings. People commit many sexual sins because they simply want to be touched or held.

Another form of physical abandonment is to be left alone on a regular basis. Sometimes parents or guardians aren't home because they have to work, or maybe they just aren't there. Many children are given too much responsibility and left to their own resources at too early an age.

➤ When you were growing up were you left alone? Did you feel afraid? Do you sometimes still feel afraid?

For some of you, being left alone creates a rather deep wound of loneliness. Simply wanting to connect with people in any way that we can, even sexually, is the result of this loneliness wound. Remember that the point of this work is not to blame your parents. The point is to understand how past events have shaped your life so that you can take responsibility for your life and actions.

In unit 2 we discuss the physical dimension of healthy sexuality. In order to be sexually whole we must like and take care of our bodies. Did your parents or guardians teach and model to you how to care for your physical needs such as cleanliness and grooming?

✎ In the following list of lessons, check those that you learned from your parents.

❏ going to bed on time
❏ eating right
❏ getting exercise
❏ wearing the right clothes
❏ brushing your teeth
❏ going to the doctor

✎ Did anyone in your family ever tell you that you were attractive? ❏ Yes ❏ No

If your lessons, modeling, and affirmations were limited or non-existent, you may be wounded in your ability to like yourself and take care of your body. Be sure to pay attention to the work of unit 2 in Part 1 of this workbook.

## Assignment for the Lesson

➤ Read the following passage of Scripture.

*Do not fear, for I am with you; do not be dismayed, for I am your God. I will strengthen you and help you; I will uphold you with my righteous right hand.*

—Isaiah 41:10

➤ Read Psalm 23.

➤ Pray for a sense of physical well being.

LESSON
4

# Sexual Abuse

Many experts believe that one third of all women and one fourth of all men were sexually abused as children. Many of us don't like to think about that statistic. In a church congregation of 500 members equally divided between men and women, this would mean roughly 83 women and 62 men have been sexually abused.

➤ From your Bible read 2 Samuel 13:1-22.

Her brother Absalom said to her, "Has that Amnon, your brother, been with you? Be quiet now, my sister; he is your brother. Don't take this thing to heart." And Tamar lived in her brother Absalom's house, a desolate woman.
–2 Samuel 13:20

Second Samuel 13:1-22 tells the story of Tamar and the sexual abuse she experienced. The Bible is not shy about the topic of incest. Almost a dozen references to incest occur in the Old Testament. Perhaps this story of Tamar is the saddest. She was raped by one of her brothers and then told by another brother not to talk about it. The effect on her was profound. As in the case of Tamar, sexual abuse can desolate a person. To overcome the devastating results, we must allow ourselves to talk about it.

Many kinds of sexual abuse exist. It does not always involve rape. It may also involve touching sexually sensitive areas. This may occur above or beneath clothing. Even hugging, kissing, or other contact can be sexually abusive if the person doing it is feeling sexual excitement from it.

✎ Did you feel uncomfortable with touch from someone in your family or some other person? ❑ Yes ❑ No

Sexual abuse occurs when there is no consent or mutuality to the sexual expression. Children are not old enough to consent to sex with anyone, much less an older person. Any sexual activity by a child with an older child or adult is sexually abusive.

Sex with anyone who has physical, emotional, or spiritual power over you is abuse. Even if you are an adult and have given consent, you may have done so due to the emotional or spiritual influence the other person has over you. Here are some examples of people who have that kind of power:

- doctors
- counselors
- employers
- pastors
- lawyers
- teachers

If we have been emotionally or physically abandoned by one of our parents, we may be lonely and looking for a parent figure in our lives. Authority figures like the ones listed above can take on a parent-like quality for us. We trust them, look up to them, and are extremely vulnerable to them. If we become sexual with them, it is really like being sexual with a parent and is therefore the psychological equivalent of incest.

✎ How old were you when you had your first sexual experience? _____

Who was it with? _____

Did you feel in any way pressured, forced? _____

I talked to a man who had his first sexual experience at 11 years old, when his older cousin showed him how to masturbate. His cousin told him everyone did it. The effect on him over the years has been devastating.

In considering this issue, men must consider if they have been sexual with an older woman who had emotional or spiritual power over them. One man I know had sex when he was 16 with his high school history teacher. At the time, this was an exciting experience for him. He thought he was "lucky" as a young male being "initiated" into the joys of sex with an older female. Such initiation is a theme of many pornographic movies. Yet such experiences are examples of sexual abuse.

✎ Check if any of the following experiences have been true for you:

❑ I was teased about my body.
❑ I was teased about puberty and the changing nature of my body (menstruation, wearing a bra, developing hair, or genital size).
❑ Sexual humor was used in my home.

❑ I was teased about sexual attractiveness or availability (women).
❑ I was teased about being sexually aggressive (men).
❑ I was judged by my peer group about my sexual experiences.
❑ I was exposed to pornography at an early age by a friend or relative.
❑ In my home I witnessed sexual behavior that was age-inappropriate.
❑ I was brought into my parent's bedroom because my other parent was gone.
❑ In my home people walked around nude or inappropriately dressed.
❑ I was put down for expressing a sexual attraction to someone else.

None of these experiences are invasive in a genital way, but they are invasive in an emotional way. They may teach us messages about sexuality that are sinful or just incorrect. One or more of them may have taught you to be ashamed of your body or ashamed of your sexual feelings.

The American Family Association, a Christian organization that fights pornography, reports that the average age men are first exposed to pornography is 11 years of age, and the most common source is their fathers' collection.

Recently a man told me that his sexual fantasies were always about watching women get undressed. He remembered that his mother undressed in front of him and then had him sit on her lap. This mother may never have been reported for sexual abuse, but the effect on her son was very damaging.

✎ **When you were growing up, what sexual messages did you receive from each of the following sources?**

Parents _____

_____

Peer Group _____

_____

Movies, TV _____

_____

Music _____

_____

Magazines (pornographic or otherwise) _____

_____

Church _____

_____

Any of these sources may have been sexually abusive to you if they taught that sex outside marriage was OK, or that sex is a shameful issue. You may need to evaluate some of the messages you grew up with.

One of the most destructive messages that sexual abuse can teach us is that we are only valuable when we are sexual. Closely related to this is the message that the only way we can get attention, love, or nurture is to be sexual. For example, if a father never affirms his daughter and never touches her in non-sexual ways, but he does commit incest with her, what does she learn? She learns the only way to get the attention of a man is with her body. Think of how our culture reinforces that message by telling women how seductively attractive they need to be. What will be the effect on the intimacy of this woman's marriage? Will she be a willing sexual partner, or will she be inwardly angry with her husband? Might withholding sex be the only way that she has any control over a man?

For both men and women, sexual abuse may be the source of the false core belief that sex equals love.

## Abuse by Abandonment

When we think of sexual abuse, we most often think of invasive actions. We may not appreciate the damage done by forms of abuse through abandonment. Being abandoned sexually simply means that we don't get accurate information about sexuality physically, emotionally, or spiritually. Many of us were given a list of don'ts about sexuality, but received no positive messages about healthy sexuality.

➤ When you went through puberty did anyone talk to you about the emotional and physical changes that you were experiencing?

➤ Think about what you learned about healthy sexuality emotionally, physically, and spiritually at home, church, or school. What modeling did you receive? If you are married, what did you learn about healthy sexuality in marriage based on what your parents modeled to you?

✏ Check the attitudes that you saw modeled in your family.

- ❑ We don't talk about sex.
- ❑ Sex is dangerous.
- ❑ Sex is dirty.
- ❑ Feelings of sexual attraction are perverted.
- ❑ Sex is only for the purpose of producing children and not to be enjoyed.
- ❑ Men enjoy sex, women don't.
- ❑ Men are sexually aggressive and can't control themselves; therefore, women must prevent sexual behavior.

The most powerful effect of sexual abandonment on you may be that whenever you have a sexual thought or a sexual problem, you think you are alone. No one ever talks about these things. This aloneness causes feelings of sexual shame and sexual fear that usually work to make things worse.

**For this reason a man will leave his father and mother and be united to his wife, and they will become one flesh. The man and his wife were both naked, and they felt no shame.**
**–Genesis 2:24-25**

According to Genesis 2:24-25, sex is a beautiful expression of the sacred union of man and woman in marriage. In 1 Corinthians 10:13 Paul says that any temptation you experience is "common" to humans. By honestly and bravely participating in your group you can overcome the shame of feeling alone in sexual matters.

## Assignment for the Lesson

➤ This lesson may have dredged up many painful memories for you. If so, talk to your sponsor, pastor, or a professional Christian counselor. If you are married, together seek out a Christian marriage counselor.

➤ Say the following affirmation five times.

The guilt for sexual abuse belongs absolutely and only to the abuser.

➤ Pray that abuse victims will find understanding and healing in their groups, churches, and families.

# Spiritual Abuse

When my grandma died, I drove a long way to be at her funeral. I was new into recovery and my emotions were pretty raw. Although I hadn't known my grandma all that well, I felt very sad, and I cried a lot. Others of my family were doing the same.

Our family was moved into another room to spare us the pain that accompanies the closing of the casket. We all sat crying. My grandma's pastor was a wonderful older man, gentle and kind. He visited his members in the nursing home. He came into the room and saw us crying. I'll never forget what he said: "Now stop it, your mother and grandmother is in heaven with Jesus. She has found her reward. Wouldn't it be better if we went back out with smiles on our faces, reflecting the joy of her salvation?"

I didn't know whether to say "Amen," or "Go away and let me cry!" This pastor's heart was in the right place, he had the right theology, but his timing and application were bad. We needed to express our sorrow. The pastor's words show how even well-intentioned and kind people can cause harm.

Today's lesson is difficult because we need to be careful theologically. Even correct theology incorrectly timed or misused can be harmful. As you study this lesson, allow yourself to examine your spiritual wounds. Remember that doing so is not about judging those who have hurt you. This work is about healing and changing your life patterns.

➤ Read this passage from Luke 13.

> On a Sabbath Jesus was teaching in one of the synagogues, and a woman was there who had been crippled by a spirit for eighteen years. She was bent over and could not straighten up at all. When Jesus saw her, he called her forward and said to her, "Woman, you are set free from your infirmity." Then he put his hands on her, and immediately she straightened up and praised God.
> Indignant because Jesus had healed on the Sabbath, the synagogue ruler said to the people, "There are six days for work. So come and be healed on those days, not on the Sabbath."
> The Lord answered him, "You hypocrites! Doesn't each of you on the Sabbath untie his ox or donkey from the stall and lead it out to give it water? Then should not this woman, a daughter of Abraham, whom Satan has kept bound for eighteen long years, be set free on the Sabbath day from what bound her?"
>
> —Luke 13:10-16

Here is an example of correct theology—the commandment to remember the Sabbath and keep it holy—that is misused. The synagogue ruler was maintaining a rigid boundary: Nothing happens on the Sabbath. Jesus reminded him about the spirit of the law, not the letter of it.

LESSON 5

Correct theology incorrectly timed or misused is a form of spiritual abuse. Whether the person is well-meaning or malicious, our boundaries are trampled. We are taught that God considers wrong what we are feeling or doing. We are, therefore, bad for feeling or doing it. This may be a form of spiritual mind control, even if it is well-intentioned.

✎ **What passages of Scripture have been quoted to you, by yourself or someone else, to talk you out of feeling...**

Sad _____

Lonely _____

Angry _____

Afraid _____

Doubtful _____

➤ Are these feelings really unacceptable to God?

Spiritual encouragement, biblical reminders, and reminders of our faith are appropriate at some times. Listening and just being present without trying to talk someone out of what they feel is appropriate at other times.

In the garden of Gethsemane, Jesus experienced intense anxiety, fear, and loneliness. Later on the cross, He felt forsaken by God. He experienced our humanity as He took on our sins. Did He ask the disciples to talk Him out of what He was feeling, or did He ask them just to be with Him?

On another occasion, Jesus talked with the disciples about His impending death. Peter reprimanded Jesus. "Never, Lord!" he said. "This shall never happen to you!" (Matthew 16:22). In the margin read how Jesus responded. Jesus is our role model for dealing with those who seek to control us. He did not allow others to manipulate Him.

Spiritual abuse causes us to believe our feelings are unacceptable to God. It causes us to push back feelings and feel shameful for having them in the first place.

Another form of spiritual abuse that invades our boundaries occurs when we are led to believe that God's love is conditional. In unit 6 I told the story of a little girl whose mother told her that Jesus didn't like how she was playing. This little girl had fallen down and bumped her head. She felt pain. The mother said that Jesus had allowed this pain to punish her for playing. This little girl did not hear that she was a good girl or that she had done things well. She was left to believe she was bad and a mistake in the sight of God. The concept of a loving God will be difficult for her to grasp.

As a sexual sinner, you may think that your sins are unpardonable, that you are a mistake in God's sight. Does that message really come from God or from someone in your past?

✎ **List the people you can think of in the Bible who were sexual sinners. If you have difficulty thinking of any, check Joshua 2:1; Judges 16:1; 2 Samuel 11:1-17; 1 Kings 11:1-4.**

_____

_____

**Jesus turned and said to Peter, "Get behind me, Satan! You are a stumbling block to me; you do not have in mind the things of God, but the things of men."**
**–Matthew 16:23**

What makes you think that you are more sinful than some of these people, all of whom God forgave and continued to use as His leaders or prophets? If you have a difficult time accepting God's forgiveness, you may need to examine your past. Did you learn to be angry and unforgiving toward yourself from some angry and unforgiving people?

Finally, spiritual abuse can occur if you learned distorted theology, morals, or beliefs about right and wrong. For example, pornography teaches many destructive messages. I believe that pornography is destructive for persons of any age, but when minors are exposed to pornography the experience is particularly spiritually destructive.

✎ **Think about the first time you were exposed to pornography. Check the messages about sex you learned.**

    ❑ Sex is for recreation.
    ❑ If it feels good do it.
    ❑ Lots of people are having more fun than me.
    ❑ An ideal woman or man exists out there somewhere.
    ❑ Only "bad" women enjoy sex.
    ❑ The more sex the better.
    ❑ Sexual behaviors bring no negative consequences.
    ❑ Sex is only physical—not emotional or spiritual.
    ❑ Other _____

Pornography is just one way you may have been spiritually invaded. Every time you use pornography, you invade yourself.

## Abandonment by Spiritual Default

Spiritual abandonment occurs when no one models or teaches healthy spirituality. Just because someone took you to church or made you go to religious activities doesn't mean that you had healthy modeling.

I know a man whose mother took him to church and Sunday School. She taught in Sunday School for years, she sang in the choir, she served on every committee, and baked more potluck dishes that you would care to imagine. She never talked to her son, however, about God or Jesus or her personal faith. In the midst of all her religious activity, she spiritually abandoned her son. This man became a minister, married a woman very much like his mother, and today wonders why they can't talk about their faith. Unfortunately, many other women in the church were willing to talk about spiritual matters. They would do anything for him. His quest to fill the void left by his childhood made him vulnerable to sexual sin.

➤ **Think about your mom and dad. What spiritual modeling did they give you.**

Have you been alone in your faith journey? Do you think more church activities increase your faith? Maybe you also think more religious activities will cause God to take away your lust. Your lust is about spiritual loneliness, not lack of religious activity. As you fill your deep need for spiritual meaning you will weaken the power of lust in your life. You will develop spiritual maturity and meaning as you practice honesty and develop relationships with God and others.

If you have experienced emotional, physical, or sexual abuse at the hands of a person who represented religious authority to you, that abuse carries over to the spiritual area as well. It affects your thoughts and feelings about God and spirituality.
Examples of such abuse include:

**KEY POINT**
You need to find spiritual fellowship and encouragement, but this won't happen as long as you lead a double life sexually. You must be honest with yourself and with others.

- the father who preached God's love and never affirmed his son
- the mother who went to church every Sunday but never talked to her daughter
- the father who was an elder of the church and expected his daughter to take care of him emotionally
- the father and mother, a pastor and his wife, who physically beat their children
- the father who attended church regularly and yet molested his daughter
- the pastor who became sexual with women he counseled
- the church that never talks about healthy sexuality.

These forms of abuse create spiritual damage. In addition to whatever other damage they do, they give us the wrong message about church, God, Jesus, and morality.

Because any church is made up of imperfect people, all churches do a less than perfect job of modeling God's character. We need to practice grace as we forgive each other for our failures, and we need to look to God as our perfect example. Only in God's love, portrayed to us in Jesus life, death, and resurrection, will we find unfailing and unconditional love.

## Assignment for the Lesson

➤ Say the following affirmation five times. If you have a difficult time feeling loved by your Heavenly Father, substitute God for Jesus.

Jesus loves me this I know, for the Bible tells me so. Little ones to Him belong. I am weak but He is strong.

➤ Pray for those who hurt you. Your abuse was a result of their behavior. Only they can be responsible for their behavior.

➤ If this unit has been particularly difficult for you, consider participating in a group study of *Shelter from the Storm: Hope for Survivors of Sexual Abuse.* You will find more information on page 221.

**KEY POINT**
The fault for any form of spiritual abuse belongs to the abuser. These forms of abuse are about the abuser, not about God and not about you.

---

Notes
1. Pat Carnes, *Don't Call It Love,* (New York: Bantam Books, 1991).

# UNIT 11

## MEMORY VERSE

Do not conform any longer to the pattern of this world, but be transformed by the renewing of your mind. Then you will be able to test and approve what God's will is— his good, pleasing and perfect will.

–Romans 12:2

# Tools for Recovery

## FOCAL PASSAGE

*Be strong in the Lord and in his mighty power. Put on the full armor of God so that you can take your stand against the devil's schemes.*

—Ephesians 6:10-11

### BILL'S STORY

Bill had been secretly engaging in sexual sin for many years. He knew that he needed to stop these behaviors. He even wanted to stop. One day in church he felt inspired to change. This time he was confident because the Holy Spirit had convicted him. He didn't think he needed to tell anyone; he was just going to stop.

Bill was ashamed of the things he had done. He thought: *If I only stop, no one need know.* He certainly couldn't tell his wife and family. Bill didn't have close friends, so he didn't have to worry about them finding out. For several weeks Bill was able to stay sexually "sober." He stayed away from the things he needed to avoid. Everything seemed fine, but in the back of his mind Bill worried that his wife would find out. What would she think of him? When an argument with his wife triggered Bill's old feeling of loneliness, he worked harder, ate more, and occasionally drank a little too much, but at least he remained sexually sober.

Then one of the secretaries at work seemed to be really friendly. She was nice in ways that his wife hadn't been in years. Bill felt a sense of comfort and, strangely, a sense of sexual excitement. He began to think about her often. They began to joke around at the office. She didn't seem to mind working the extra hours Bill was putting in. They began having quick lunches and started getting to know each other better. In the evening at home, Bill found himself thinking of her.

After another night of his wife saying no to his sexual advances, Bill went downstairs and masturbated. Bill kept doing this, occasionally finding something on TV sexually stimulating. Soon he was buying pornographic videos. At the Christmas party the next year, Bill surprised himself when he suggested to his secretary they go off somewhere by themselves.

## GROWTH GOAL

In this unit, you will learn how to find help and support and how to build the community you will need to help you stay sexually sober.

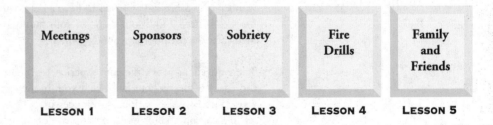

| Meetings | Sponsors | Sobriety | Fire Drills | Family and Friends |
|----------|----------|----------|-------------|--------------------|
| LESSON 1 | LESSON 2 | LESSON 3 | LESSON 4 | LESSON 5 |

185

# Meetings

*If we walk in the light, as he is in the light, we have fellowship with one another, and the blood of Jesus, his Son, purifies us from all sin.*

—1 John 1:7

He who conceals his sins does not prosper, but whoever confesses and renounces them finds mercy.
–Proverbs 28:13

Two are better than one, because they have a good return for their work: If one falls down, his friend can help him up. But pity the man who falls and has no one to help him up! Also, if two lie down together, they will keep warm. But how can one keep warm alone? Though one may be overpowered, two can defend themselves. A cord of three strands is not quickly broken.
–Ecclesiastes 4:9-13

You met Bill in the unit story. Bill's problem was not that he lacked desire to stay sexually sober. His problem was not even that he needed the power of the Holy Spirit. His problem was that he disobeyed a basic biblical principle. He chose to conceal his sin. Read what Proverbs 28:13 and Ecclesiastes 4:9–13 (margin) teach about confession and about depending on others.

Being out of control with sexual sin means we have tried to control our behaviors alone. If you are going to recover you must find fellowship with others. In the early days of your recovery this most likely will be with others who have suffered from similar sexual sins. To experience fellowship you will have to combat some well-practiced isolation habits.

✎ Check which of the following apply to you.

❑ I was a lost child in my family.
❑ I am afraid of people really knowing me.
❑ I don't trust others.
❑ My sexual sins are too perverse; no one else has ever done them.
❑ No one understands me.
❑ No one has ever cared.
❑ I don't know how to talk to others.
❑ I hate crowds.

This is just a partial list you may be using to avoid fellowship with others.

➤ **Are you ready to try something different, to take some risks? If so, you are getting ready to get well. If not, you will continue your sexual sins.**

In units 9 and 10 you completed difficult work related to your family. You may have discovered many painful things about your past. You may have also discovered some of the reasons behind your thought patterns. In lesson 5 of unit 7, you learned about the core beliefs of sexual addiction. Those core beliefs appear in the margin.

## CORE BELIEFS OF SEXUAL ADDICTION:

Sex is equal to love, and sex is my most important need.

I am a bad and worthless person

No one loves me as I am.

No one will take care of me but me.

Can you now see how these core beliefs may have originated in your family? A child cannot always think rationally. An invaded or abandoned child tends to blame himself or herself for the wounds inflicted by other family members. The child may wonder, *If I were a good person, these things would not happen to me. If I were not a bad person, I would get the love and nurture I need.*

Was this your experience? Did you believe that something was wrong with you? Did you wonder why other kids seemed to have a better life? Did you learn to rely on yourself to meet your needs? Did something in your family or in your experience teach you that sex medicates the pain of the wounds you felt?

These questions probe the core experience of shame. For years, you may have coped with the legacy of shame your family left you. In my experience, many of us cope in one of two ways. First, we use various substances or behaviors to avoid the pain of the shameful feelings. Second, since we don't approve of ourselves, we seek approval from others. We think if others like us, we must be OK. One of the reasons I went to graduate school to get my Ph.D. was so I would have the title of "doctor." I thought, *if people call me doctor, I must be OK.*

✎ Here are some approval seeking strategies you may have tried. Check the ones with which you identify.

- ❑ having money
- ❑ having the right house in the right neighborhood
- ❑ having a nice car
- ❑ having the right job or profession
- ❑ having the right degree
- ❑ doing so much for others
- ❑ being wise and wonderful
- ❑ going along with others even if you disagree with what they're doing
- ❑ being athletic
- ❑ being talented
- ❑ knowing the right people
- ❑ going to the right church

If you have equated sex with love, you may also have thought if others will be sexual with you, you must be lovable. That is why sex addiction is so powerful—it both medicates or helps to avoid painful feelings, and provides feelings of love and approval. Sex seems to satisfy both survival strategies.

Diagrammed, this dynamic looks like this:

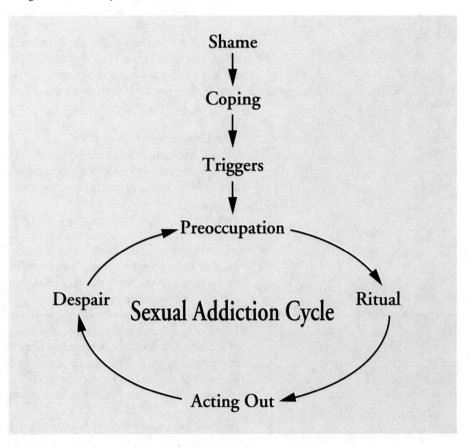

As the key point in the margin indicates, shame is a barrier to healing. If you desire genuine life change, you must attack the real problem. You must get to the root of the problem—the false beliefs empowered by the sense of shame.

To heal from a deeply-rooted sense of shame you must address old wounds. You can take two important actions to address those unhealed hurts. First, you can study your own history. You study the past not to blame but to understand. Second, you need to find a source for the unconditional love and acceptance every person needs to grow and develop.

 In the following passage *righteous* means to be accepted by God. Underline the statement that indicates how we are *not* made righteous. Then circle the statements that describe how we *are* made righteous.

*No one will be declared righteous in his sight by observing the law; rather, through the law we become conscious of sin. But now a righteousness from God, apart from law, has been made known, to which the Law and the Prophets testify. This righteousness from God comes through faith in Jesus Christ to all who believe. There is no difference, for all have sinned and fall short of the glory of God, and are justified freely by his grace through the redemption that came by Christ Jesus.*

—Romans 3:20-24

Shame tells us that we are unacceptable, that we are worth less than others, that neither God nor others will love us. Our degree of shame may be small so we only feel unacceptable part of the time or in certain situations. Or our shame may be an ugly charred brand burned across the fabric of our lives. The cure for shame begins by allowing God's acceptance to soak deeply into our minds and hearts.

You have sinned and fallen short, as we all have. Grace, unconditional love, and acceptance comes from God through Christ. Did you underline *observing the law?* And did you circle such words as *through faith in Jesus Christ, justified freely by his grace,* and *through the redemption that came by Jesus Christ?*

## The Community of Faith

One of your core beliefs may be that no one loves you as you are. You may believe if others know you they will hate you and leave you. This belief prevents you from being honest. How do you share your story without the fear of being rejected?

The answer, I think, is practice. You must begin by being honest with trustworthy people. You may need to find a group of persons who have already been where you are but who are further along in the healing and recovery process. With such acceptance and support you can learn how to tell the truth even about your worst sins. As you find loving, trustworthy people with whom you can practice honest sharing, you can begin to confront and overcome your shame.

Twelve-step fellowships have been successful because much of the meeting time is spent telling the truth about ourselves. Most of us have lived a lie. Now we are learning how to be truthful. Strangely, no one finds the life stories we hear to be bizarre or unrealistic. When we share, no one goes screaming out of the room. Everyone there has sinned and fallen short of the glory of God. In such groups we experience love and acceptance.

You, too, must find a group where you can tell the truth. Hopefully, your *Faithful &True* group has become such a place. If you have done the work of the previous units, you will have practiced honesty and experienced grace from other group members. This honesty reverses the silence and shaming judgments that you may have received from your family and others.

You may develop a deeper bond of fellowship with the people in your support group than you have with anyone else. The challenge is to expand your ability to be honest to other groups and relationships . One of the slogans of a popular 12-step group may be appropriate for you. They say that if you are having a difficult time maintaining sobriety you should attend 90 meetings in 90 days. This is sometimes referred to as 90/90. Your *Faithful & True* group probably meets only once a week, but you can take steps to find more fellowship and support. Arrange to meet with members of your group during the week. Find other group meetings you can attend. Find an accountability group such as Promise Keepers.

As you are seeking life change, be realistic about groups. Some groups are wonderful, accepting and trustworthy; some are not. No group is perfect. I have gotten some bad meals in restaurants. I probably do not go back to a bad restaurant again, but I don't give up eating out. Don't place unrealistic expectations on groups or people. You can learn to trust people appropriately.

In the resource section on page 224 you will find phone numbers of various 12-step fellowships for sexual addiction. Use these sources to find the meeting times, place, and contact people for your area. You may live in an area that doesn't have many of these groups and you will have to travel some distance to find one. You don't necessarily have to attend one of these groups. Other support groups may be in your area. You will benefit from attending any support group with which you share a common addiction.

In whatever groups you choose to attend, you will find you are beginning to reverse the cycle of shame. You will be creating a new "family" of like-minded and dedicated people.

### Assignment for the Lesson

✎ When you have discovered the meetings you will try in your area, write in the margin those times and your commitment to participate in them.

➤ Say the following affirmation five times.

I can stop my sexual sins with the support of others.

➤ Pray for your group and the members in it.

# Sponsors

*The things you have heard me say in the presence of many witnesses entrust to reliable men who will also be qualified to teach others.*

—2 Timothy 2:2

Jeff was a small boy when his father died. Jeff's mom did the best she could to rear him and his sisters. Jeff didn't really know what he missed in his dad because he never really knew him.

As he was growing up, Jeff liked to be around older boys. He was always looking for their attention and doing just about anything to get it. He ran errands for them and did anything else they needed.

One day, one of the older boys started asking Jeff some sexual questions. Jeff didn't really know what the questions were about, but he pretended he did. The older boy didn't make fun of him and Jeff liked that. Gradually, their sexual conversations graduated to "demonstrations." Before he knew it, Jeff was committing sexual acts with this boy. Jeff didn't like it, but was afraid to tell the older boy.

These past incidents still bother Jeff, even now that he is married. Jeff believes something must have been wrong with him for the older boy to commit such acts with him. Jeff fears that if his wife found out, she might think he is homosexual. Who could he talk to about what has happened? Jeff's doubts and fears create anxieties. He also cannot stop watching pornography. He wants to quit, but hasn't been able to.

Jeff's experience is not uncommon. The loss of Jeff's dad left him needy and vulnerable to the approval of men and older boys. He was seeking attention from a man and didn't know how to get it in a healthy way. Jeff has carried this secret with him for a long time. He is a victim of an older boy but has not learned to stop blaming himself. His original need, combined with the abuse he experienced, and his own immature and sinful choices have resulted in an addictive sexual behavior. That addiction has now taken on a life of its own. On his own he cannot overcome his addiction to pornography. [Note that many people seem to overcome an addiction through sheer force of will. But without genuine healing they continue to fight an inner battle. As a result, they become exhausted and angry people. Many groups call this the "dry-drunk" syndrome.]

As you learned in lesson 1, Jeff can find comfort in a group where he can honestly share and know that he is not alone. The grace of having someone else understand and accept him would be a wonderful relief.

As part of his recovery, Jeff will also need a sponsor. *Sponsor* refers to a person who has some length of time in recovery and has been successful in staying sober. A sponsor will be a guide in the process of recovery. A sponsor provides encouragement, affirmation, and accountability. A Christian sponsor will help Jeff work through his problem to a life that will glorify God.

When I think of a sponsor, I think of the relationship that Paul must have had with Timothy. As you read the communication that Paul writes to Timothy, it sounds very much like a father to a son. Paul cared for Timothy, encouraged him, taught him, and continually challenged him to fulfill God's plan for his life.

Timothy, my son, I give you this instruction in keeping with the prophecies once made about you, so that by following them you may fight the good fight.
–1 Timothy 1:18

But you, man of God, flee from all this, and pursue righteousness, godliness, faith, love, endurance and gentleness.
–1 Timothy 6:11

✎ **Below are some of the characteristics of a sponsor. Check the ones you recognize that you need in your life.**

❑ A sponsor will hold you *accountable.* You can share with this person all of your past sexual sins, acting-out behaviors, rituals, and fantasies. With your sponsor's help you will develop a plan for staying sober from all of these. If your sponsor ever sees you coming close to returning to a behavior, he or she will directly confront you about them.

❑ A sponsor is someone who will give you *encouragement.* As you slowly make progress a sponsor will celebrate with you.

❑ A sponsor is someone who will *listen.* Whenever you feel tempted, lonely, frightened, sad, or angry, you can call a sponsor to discuss your difficulties. Sometimes your sponsor will meet with you until the crisis passes.

❑ A sponsor is someone with whom you can *pray.* The two of you can seek the Lord's guidance together. You may also share Bible study.

❑ A sponsor is a *model.* He or she should be someone with at least one year of successful sobriety from addictive behaviors. His or her success will serve as an inspiration to you.

❑ A sponsor is a *guide.* He or she will help you find the resources you need in recovery and show you the path to success.

If you checked any or all of these characteristics, you are ready to find a sponsor. In many ways a sponsor is like a surrogate parent. A sponsor must be tough, wise, and loving. If you were abandoned emotionally, physically, or spiritually by one of your own parents, the idea of having a sponsor may seem very strange. You may even resist it. Addicts, after all, prefer isolation and self-reliance. On the other hand, you may also find a wonderful relationship you have never experienced before.

✎ How will you find a sponsor? Select from the following list of possible actions.

❑ 1. Put an ad in the newspaper.
❑ 2. Look "needy" at the next meeting you go to so that someone will offer.
❑ 3. Ask for volunteers.
❑ 4. Ask someone else to recommend someone.
❑ 5. Ask your group leader to suggest someone.
❑ 6. Ask the first person with enough sobriety that you meet.
❑ 7. Pray about it.
❑ 8. Take your time, get to know people in your groups, and ask the person you most admire and respect.

The Lord is my shepherd, I shall not be in want. He makes me lie down in green pastures, he leads me beside quiet waters, he restores my soul. He guides me in paths of righteousness for his name's sake. Even though I walk through the valley of the shadow of death, I will fear no evil, for you are with me; your rod and your staff, they comfort me. You prepare a table before me in the presence of my enemies. You anoint my head with oil; my cup overflows. Surely goodness and love will follow me all the days of my life, and I will dwell in the house of the Lord forever.

–Psalm 23:1-6

You need a sponsor of the same sex with whom you are comfortable and have respect. Pray about your decision and seek the Lord's guidance. You may have a number of sponsors over the course of time. In the early days you may have a temporary sponsor, someone who agrees to help you until you get to know more people in recovery. Responses five, seven, and eight have merit. Avoid the other approaches.

Ultimately, we turn to God our Father as the source of strength. No more powerful image shows His care for us than Psalm 23. The psalm appears in the margin. I have paraphrased a portion of the psalm as follows:

*The Lord is my sponsor, I shall not be alone. He leads me to a support group where I find those who understand and where I can be honest. He restores my self-worth. He guides me in paths of healthy sexuality. Even though I live in a world of temptation, I will not yield to it, for He strengthens me.*

## Assignment for the Lesson

➤ Pray that the Lord will show you a sponsor to choose.

✎ Write the name of your first choice to be your sponsor.

_____

➤ Say the following affirmation five times.

I can be humble and submit myself to the care of a sponsor.

# Sobriety

*Do not conform any longer to the pattern of this world, but be transformed by the renewing of your mind. Then you will be able to test and approve what God's will is— his good, pleasing and perfect will. For by the grace given me I say to every one of you: Do not think of yourself more highly than you ought, but rather think of yourself with sober judgment, in accordance with the measure of faith God has given you.*

—Romans 12:2-3

The Bible talks often of living a self-controlled life and guarding against various temptations. In Romans 12 Paul talks about evaluating yourself with sober judgment. Even in Paul's time, with no photographs, TV, movies, or radio, he talked about not conforming to the pattern of the world. Living a disciplined life was a challenge then as it is now. The word *sobriety* describes a life of self-control, free from bondage to addictive chemicals or behaviors.

➤ **In what ways is recovery from sexual addiction like recovery from alcoholism? How is it different?**

Recovery from sexual addiction is different from that of chemical addiction. Some of the practices and principles are the same, but sexual addiction and chemical addiction have different definitions of sobriety. For most alcoholics, sobriety is a matter of total abstinence from alcohol and other chemicals. A person can completely stop using a drug like alcohol. Abstinence is a black and white issue.

Total abstinence in sexual matters is problematic. You cannot abstain totally from sexuality because sexuality describes who we are, not simply what we do. You can stop a specific sexual behavior, but you must continue to deal with yourself as a sexual being. If you are married, abstinence is probably not what either you or your spouse has in mind. Even if you are single, you must still deal with the sexual feelings and implications of many relationships.

Recovering from sexual sin is more like recovering from a food addiction. Eating is an essential daily activity. A person can't stop eating and live. Food addicts are taught to eat for the nutritional value of food. They also learn to discern between actual hunger and using food to medicate their emotions. Addicts may totally avoid some foods. Sobriety from sexual addiction is very similar.

Notice the definition of sexual sobriety in the margin. If you attend a secular 12-step meeting for sexual addiction, you may not find all members adhering to this strict definition. Some may have different morals. For example, some members of these groups may accept that masturbation is acceptable for singles. You will have to be careful what you choose to accept as your own guidelines. An old Alcoholics Anonymous slogan states, "Take what you like and leave the rest." You may have to carefully examine your beliefs and convictions if you continue with some secular meetings. In my experience, members of any of the 12-step fellowships will be respectful of your moral convictions and seek to encourage you in them.

The definition of sobriety—that sobriety excludes any behaviors which are not a part of healthy, biblically-based sexuality—is particularly difficult for singles. Singles who have been sexually active will have the most difficulty maintaining sobriety. Total abstinence, which is clearly consistent with a Christian sexual ethic, will be a shock to their systems, and they will experience a detoxification-like experience. Symptoms can include agitation,

**KEY POINT**
Sexual sobriety excludes any behaviors which are not a part of healthy, biblically-based sexuality.

mood swings, intensity of feelings, and sleeping problems. On the positive side, singles who choose total abstinence may have an easier time maintaining sobriety than married persons.

For all of you who wish to recover from sexual sin and who are married, I recommend that you mutually commit to a temporary period of total abstinence. This commitment means no sex with yourself or with your spouse. Abstinence could be for any period of time. I recommend 90 days.

I recommend abstinence for three reasons. First, by abstaining from genital sex you will experience a cleansing of your brain chemistry. An alcoholic needs to be sober for a number of days before the alcohol is completely out of his or her system. The same principle applies to those recovering from sexual addiction. Even fantasies produce chemicals in the brain that cause us to feel pleasure. These chemical reactions are a natural part of life. Sex addicts, however, have used this chemical reaction to medicate and escape their feelings. Ceasing all sexual activity can allow the brain chemistry to return to normal.[1]

The second benefit of abstinence deals with the addictive characteristic called tolerance. Tolerance means the addict requires more of the addictive agent to achieve the same ends. An alcoholic, for example, develops tolerance so he or she requires more alcohol to become intoxicated. You may have built up a tolerance for sexual activity. You may find that you need a greater amount of sexual stimuli than you once did. This may have led you into more frequent sexual activity or more dangerous sex. This may also have affected your ability to experience sexual pleasure with your spouse. The need for more and more may even have created impotence. Being abstinent for a period of time will help to reverse these problems. If you can complete the abstinence period, you will find that the joy of sex with your spouse may return. If it has not, you may have to seek more specialized counseling.

A third reason I recommend abstinence deals with changing your core beliefs. Addicts hold the core belief that: *Sex is my most important need.* A period of abstinence reverses this belief and gradually teaches that sex is not your most important need; you can get along just fine without it.

A period of abstinence will help you deal with another false core belief: *sex is equal to love.* When you abstain from sex and still receive love from your wife or husband, that continuing love challenges the core belief. If you are single, through abstinence you will learn that you can experience love from more intimate friendships than when you were sexually acting out.

The most obvious advantage of an abstinence contract for your marriage is that it takes the pressure of sex off your relationship and allows the two of you to begin building your relationship on a spiritual and emotional basis. For many couples, marital sex has been full of conflicts, arguments, and possibly even emotional pain. A period of abstinence allows you to begin to heal from some of this pain.

During a time of abstinence intense feelings may surface—feelings you have kept bottled up for years. The period of abstinence will allow you an opportunity to deal with and heal from these feelings.

A bonus reason for abstinence has to do with the reason Paul suggested abstinence in 1 Corinthians 7:5. Abstaining from sexual activity allows a couple to devote themselves to prayer and spiritual renewal. Time spent with God reminds us that our love relationship with God is our most important relationship and deserves first place in our lives.

**Do not deprive each other except by mutual consent and for a time, so that you may devote yourselves to prayer. Then come together again so that Satan will not tempt you because of your lack of self-control. –1 Corinthians 7:5**

✎ **Which of these reasons for abstinence could be an advantage to your marriage?**

_____

_____

_____

Abstinence must be a mutual agreement. Discuss the contract with your spouse. In my experience, spouses divide into two basic categories:

• Some spouses welcome a period of sexual abstinence. Sex has been emotionally painful for years. Perhaps too many demands have been placed on them, or the sexual activity has been unpleasant. Whatever the case, a period of no sex will be a welcome relief.

• Some spouses, however, fear abstinence. These spouses feel they need the assurance of a sexual relationship. They worry that their sexually-addicted spouses will continue to act out if sex is not present in their relationship. They may suffer from the belief that if they were more attractive or sexually willing, their spouses wouldn't have a problem. This belief is not true. I have known sex addicts married to beauty contest winners. Beauty and sexual willingness are not related to the spouse's sexual sin. The abstinence contract is important for such couples. It teaches them that the basis of their marital relationship should be spiritual and emotional, not sexual.

A married couple should not attempt a period of abstinence if they do not also have a plan for working on their relationship in other ways. This might include seeing a counselor or a variety of other strategies. Unit 4 contains ideas for developing healthy intimacy in a relationship without relying on sex. You will find a list of resources for marriage enrichment on page 222.

If you think that you can benefit from a period of abstinence, I would suggest the following guidelines:

1. Discuss the abstinence contract with your sponsor and your accountability group. Make sure the timing is right and that your intentions are good.

2. Discuss it with your spouse. He or she must agree to it. Make sure that you explain to your spouse the positive spiritual and emotional reasons for the period of abstinence. Present a positive plan for increasing your emotional and spiritual communication during the time of abstinence.

3. Establish the dates for your abstinence contract. Set a starting date and an ending date. This will allow you to measure your progress. You may want to agree together that when you achieve abstinence for the length of time you have determined, the contract can be re-negotiated. Some couples have extended their abstinence period. Others have chosen to build back up to genital sexuality with periods of hand holding, hugging, and kissing coming first. Go slow. Remember that you may have experienced significant emotional and spiritual damage in the past.

4. Get counsel. If either of you have experienced sexual trauma in your relationship, or if either of you are sexual trauma survivors, get some professional help. Your abstinence period may allow some of these feelings to surface.

5. Sign a contract describing your abstinence agreement in the presence of someone who will hold both of you accountable to it. This could be another couple.

✎ **What do you think would be the value of an abstinence commitment?**

_____

_____

The wife's body does not belong to her alone but also to her husband. In the same way, the husband's body does not belong to him alone but also to his wife. Do not deprive each other except by mutual consent and for a time, so that you may devote yourselves to prayer. Then come together again so that Satan will not tempt you because of your lack of self-control.
–1 Corinthians 7:4-5

✎ **If both you and your spouse are willing to accept a period of abstinence, fill out the contract below and sign it.**

*We agree that we will be sexually abstinent for _____ days, beginning on _____.*

*We also agree that during this time we will do the following activities to increase our emotional and spiritual intimacy: (use more paper if you need to)*

_____

_____

_____

_____

*Signed*_____ *(addict)*

_____ *(spouse)*

*Witnessed by:*

_____

Deb and I have found asking another person or couple to "sponsor" you in this endeavor to be helpful. You could ask your pastor, a counselor, or another couple you know that has experienced and successfully worked through similar problems. You may discover very supportive fellowship.

Abstinence is a tool that can be used more than once for your healing. If used carefully, abstinence can be emotionally and spiritually healing. In some ways, it is similar to a fast. Fasting is abstaining from food in order to concentrate on your spiritual life. A fast is always for the purpose of increasing our relationship with God and not for the purpose of punishing ourselves or others.

One couple who reluctantly went into a period of abstinence shared with Deb and me how wonderful things are happening in their relationship. They are discovering that God brought them together for reasons other than physical attraction. They are growing together spiritually and emotionally.

You will also find that as you maintain sobriety over time, trust will be restored. Read back over unit 4 to see how trust is built over time.

## Assignment for the Lesson

✎ **Write the date that you began your sexual sobriety. This is like a birthday and you will want to celebrate significant milestones (30 days, 3 months, 1 year, and so forth).**

My sobriety began on _____.

➤ Say the following affirmation five times.

I can be sexually sober.

➤ Pray for courage. Read 1 Corinthians 10:13.

*No temptation has seized you except what is common to man. And God is faithful; he will not let you be tempted beyond what you can bear. But when you are tempted, he will also provide a way out so that you can stand up under it.*

—1 Corinthians 10:13

➤ Ask that God will always show you a way of escape.

# Fire Drills

*You were once darkness, but now you are light in the Lord. Live as children of light (for the fruit of the light consists in all goodness, righteousness and truth) and find out what pleases the Lord. Have nothing to do with the fruitless deeds of darkness, but rather expose them. For it is shameful even to mention what the disobedient do in secret. But everything exposed by the light becomes visible, for it is light that makes everything visible. This is why it is said:*
*"Wake up, O sleeper,*
*rise from the dead,*
*and Christ will shine on you."*
*Be very careful, then, how you live—not as unwise but as wise, making the most of every opportunity, because the days are evil. Therefore do not be foolish, but understand what the Lord's will is. Do not get drunk on wine, which leads to debauchery. Instead, be filled with the Spirit.*

—Ephesians 5:8-18

Bill sought to walk in the light—to live out the commitments of his new life of sobriety. He confronted his sexual sins and talked about them with his pastor and others. He sought accountability meetings, chose a sponsor, and he and his wife completed a period of abstinence.

Bill's main challenge in sobriety was his busy travel schedule. He had acted out with prostitutes in cities all over the country. His ritual was usually to watch the in-room movies found in most motels, call a taxi, and go to the nearest massage parlor. To stop traveling would mean to change his career. This change would have been financially devastating to him and his family. Bill constructed the following plan.

1. Bill researched the meeting times and places of various recovery groups in the towns to which he was traveling. If he needed to go to a meeting, he knew where they were.
2. With the help of his pastor, Bill knew the churches in the cities he was to visit. In some cases he had the name of a pastor that he could call if he needed to.
3. Although he was not an alcoholic, Bill recognized that when he drank, he was more vulnerable to sexually act out. He decided to stop drinking, even if that was somewhat embarrassing with some of his business contacts.
4. Bill tried to find motels that didn't have in-room movies. When he couldn't, he asked the front desk to lock out the pornography channels. In one city, he even had the TV removed from his room.

5. At night, Bill checked his wallet into the motel safe. He could always get it, but he had to go to extra effort.
6. In every city, Bill tried to arrange visits to friends, meetings, or churches. He avoided being alone in his room.
7. Bill carried with him the phone numbers of men in his groups at home and of his sponsor.
8. Bill called his wife, especially when he was feeling lonely.

Bill pursued recovery with great energy. He wanted to establish sobriety. Occasionally he felt alone and angry because he couldn't act out, but he made sure he always had someone to talk to.

Bill is pursuing his recovery with wisdom. He recognizes that he is subject to temptation. Sometimes he is especially vulnerable. Sometimes he experiences what addicts call "automatic pilot." When he is on automatic pilot he may find himself going to the places he knows he must avoid. He knows he must plan ahead for these times.

Sometimes the desire for sex is like a fire burning deep inside. Contingency plans designed to avoid automatic pilot have been appropriately named "fire drills." They are designed to put out the fire.

Bill recognizes, also, that when he travels he must avoid certain dangerous situations. His fire drills consist of plans specific to each situation.

✎ **When you start thinking of fire drills for yourself, check the feelings that come to you.**

- ❑ They sound pretty restrictive. Can't I lead a "normal" life?
- ❑ It sounds like things my parents would make me do.
- ❑ Won't I expose my sexual sins if I have to explain to others why I can't do certain things?
- ❑ Others will not want to be with me if I can't participate in certain activities.
- ❑ Thinking about all of this makes me angry.
- ❑ Thinking about all of this makes me sad.
- ❑ This is about punishment.
- ❑ Will I have to do these the rest of my life?

Planning ahead and being ready requires preparation. Waging this war is restrictive. Some of the things you will have to do may even sound childish. This will be true particularly in the early days of recovery. You will have to treat yourself like a child in order to learn new disciplines. Such actions are not punishment however, they are for the purpose of living a sober and safe life. When I talk to my son about coming home at a certain time, I am not punishing him. I want to keep him safe.

You will be asking yourself to give up certain freedoms in order to have fire drills. One of the major enemies of an addict is free time. During free time your mind will play tricks on you and talk you into taking care of your boredom or any other feeling in a sinful way. You may feel a certain amount of rebellion in having to give up your free time. Make sure that you talk to someone about these feelings.

You will probably feel sad and angry about living with such restrictions. Recovery includes a process of grieving. You are stopping behaviors that have been life companions to you for years. These behaviors are like friends. You may not know how to cope without them.

**What do you think you will miss the most by living a life of discipline?**

_____

People in recovery find that they will have to say good-bye to certain activities or people in their life to stay sober. This could range from people with whom you had an affair to looking at pornographic magazines or watching certain movies.

 **In the margin make a list of the people or things to which you must say good-bye.**

 Review your list of ritual behaviors that you discovered in unit 8, beginning on page 140.

Your ritual behaviors are the key to understanding the kind of fire drills you will need to construct for yourself. A fire drill contains several key elements:

- Who you will be accountable to, your sponsor or group members.
- What you will do in preparation for an emergency.
- What you will immediately do in case of an emergency. (This can include meeting times and places that you know you can go to right away.)
- Who you will call at the first sign of danger. (This should include people that you know you can call any time day or night.)

You may also have more than one fire drill for different kinds of acting-out behaviors.

 **Create a fire drill for yourself, just like Bill did in our opening story. You will find a form on page 223 to copy. Use the form to create your own fire drills.**

 Show your fire drill worksheet to your sponsor or to your group and get their feedback.

Fire drills are designed to help you in an emergency. At times, especially in the early days of recovery, you may experience failures. You may fall into one of your old acting-out behaviors. If this happens to you, because of the deep sense of shame that you have felt for years, you may be so discouraged that you want to give up all of the good work you have been doing. Please rest assured you are not alone. Many people struggle just as you do and have fallen. No less a man of God than the apostle Paul wrote the words you read in the margin.

## Slips and Relapse

We generally refer to one-time failures or acting out experiences as "slips." If slips continue, the problem becomes relapse. In relapse a person has reverted back to an old pattern of behavior.

One way to look at slips is to view them as a _Short Lapse In Progress_. A slip doesn't have to cause you to revert back to old patterns. The key is whether or not you can learn from them. You can ask yourself the following questions and get feedback from your sponsor and group:
- What was I feeling just before the slip?
- Where was the breakdown in my program: what wasn't I doing to take care of myself?
- Why did my fire drills not work? What do I need to add to my fire drill strategy that will help in the future?
- Do I have rituals I wasn't aware of that I need to attend to and create prohibitions for?

I know that nothing good lives in me, that is, in my sinful nature. For I have the desire to do what is good, but I cannot carry it out. For what I do is not the good I want to do; no, the evil I do not want to do—this I keep on doing. Now if I do what I do not want to do, it is no longer I who do it, but it is sin living in me that does it.
–Romans 7:18-20

Slips can be just a short lapse in progress if you learn from them and modify your efforts so that they don't happen again. In the early days of recovery, you may have to experiment with fire drill strategies. A slip may also help you identify feelings you need to deal with. Getting help with those feelings will advance your recovery program. The key is not to beat yourself up about a slip. They may have serious consequences you may have to deal with, but don't get down on yourself. Learn and grow.

A relapse is more of an emergency situation. You will need to be very aggressive in the measures you take to deal with it. Some of the things you may have to try include:

- going to some form of treatment
- intensifying your effort to get counseling
- going to more meetings
- having stricter boundaries around your behaviors and increased accountability.

A relapse may mean that you haven't healed completely from the wounds of your childhood. Age-old feelings may still be plaguing you. Relapse may mean unhealed wounds from the past.

Maybe you came into recovery somewhat casually. You thought you could do it easily without the hard work of healing that many of us require. Reconsider. Humble yourself. Get the help you need.

### Assignment for the Lesson

➤ Recovery means eliminating obstacles that prevent you from experiencing healthy sexuality. Do something healthy and enjoyable for yourself today.

➤ Say the following affirmation five times.

   I have the energy and wisdom to stay sober.

➤ Pray, asking God for help and committing your sobriety to Him.

LESSON
5

# Family and Friends

*My command is this: Love each other as I have loved you. Greater love has no one than this, that he lay down his life for his friends.*

—John 15:12-13

*Here is a trustworthy saying: If anyone sets his heart on being an overseer, he desires a noble task. Now the overseer must be above reproach, the husband of but one wife, temperate, self-controlled, respectable, hospitable, able to teach, not given to drunkenness, not violent but gentle, not quarrelsome, not a lover of money. He must manage his own family well and see that his children obey him with proper respect.*

—1 Timothy 3:1-4

Tom had established several weeks of sobriety. His life went through many changes, some that were difficult to hide. His family and friends wondered what was going on. How would Tom tell them the reason for these changes?

Tom had not shared with his family his past sins or his need for sobriety. He was afraid his wife would become angry and leave him if he told her the truth. Tom also believed his children were too young to understand. He feared that his friends would think he was a terrible person if they knew. They, too, might abandon him. Even though he was sexually sober, Tom continued to live with a secret, always wondering who might find out.

Several months later Tom's wife learned about one of his affairs. Tom asked for her forgiveness and tried to assure her that his sexual acting out had stopped. She wondered, however, how honest he had been about his sobriety when he had not been honest about his acting out. Establishing honesty and intimacy in their relationship was much more difficult after Tom's wife learned his secret.

Several years later Tom discovered a stack of pornography in his son's room. Tom wanted to talk with his son about the danger of porn. Tom wished he had explained earlier about how much trouble he had experienced with pornography.

Tom read in the paper that his closest friend had been arrested for soliciting prostitution. The friend's life and family were in chaos. Tom was finally able to talk to his friend about his own sexual acting out and his recovery. Tom's friend was grateful for the support, but said, "If you had only told me sooner, I might have received the help I needed."

Tom was really no different than you are now. A desperate part of you wants to be completely free of all of the secrets. You have shared your story in the safety of a group or with your sponsor, but you may be afraid to talk to those who are closest to you. Some of you may be tempted to just blurt out the truth, to tell everyone everything immediately, and get it over with. You may think, for example, if you tell your spouse everything immediately, she will forgive you right away and you can move on with your life.

This lesson seeks to help you think through the decisions you need to make about telling the truth to family and friends. If you prayerfully enter into this as a process, you will find, as scary as the prospect of truth telling is, it can also be very rewarding.


## Your Spouse

In unit 4, we discuss building relationships, particularly with your spouse. Lesson 5 of unit 4 describes building trust after it has been profoundly damaged. Your sexual sins have done that kind of damage.

✎ **Here are some common fears that might keep you from telling your spouse about your past sexual sins. Check the ones that apply to you.**

    ❏ He/She will leave.
    ❏ The truth will hurt him/her too much.
    ❏ He/She will use this information to punish me.
    ❏ He/She will never be able to trust me again.
    ❏ I'll lose all of my freedom if I tell.

Obviously, telling the truth involves taking a risk. Do you want to spend the rest of your life wondering what others will do if they find out about your sexual sins?

Here's a list of do's and don'ts for truth telling.

  • Do tell the truth if you want to build intimacy back into your relationship.
  • Do tell the truth if you are truly sorry for what you've done.

- Do tell the truth if your spouse has the resources to get support and/or counseling for him or her self.
- Don't tell the truth in order to manipulate your spouse's forgiveness.
- Don't tell the truth to punish your spouse, that is if he or she had been different, more attractive, or more sexually available, you wouldn't have done these things.

So, how much do you tell? Rigid, clear-cut answers do not exist for the measure of detail to subject your spouse to at one time. Here is another checklist to consider.

- Start with a general outline of the truth. You do not necessarily need to report the dates, names, places, or details of sexual activity. You may want to be honest about how much money you have spent.
- Agree with your spouse that you will tell him or her any specific details whenever he or she wants to know. You both may need to meet with a counselor to help you decide how much specific details you should share.
- Be specific if it helps your spouse clear up old lies or misconceptions of what really happened in certain situations.
- Be specific if you were ever sexually involved with a friend of your spouse. He or she will need to make decisions about an ongoing friendship with that person.

Your spouse should also consider why he or she wants to know specifics. Following is a checklist for the spouse to observe.

- Don't ask for specifics if it is for the purpose of punishing your spouse.
- Don't ask for specifics if you think it will help you monitor his or her future behavior.
- Don't ask for specifics if you want to compare yourself with any affairs, pornographic images, or sexual practices. Sexual sin or addiction is not about your attractiveness or sexual performance.
- Do ask for specifics if you think it will help you understand and eventually get closer to your spouse.

Naturally, the two of you will need lots of support and counseling to get through this difficult time. The truth of the past has violated your marriage vows and damaged your relationship. It can be repaired, your love restored, and true intimacy can be built. As discouraged as you may be now, please understand that there are many couples who have not only survived, but whose relationship now is much closer than ever before.


## Your Children

✎ Check the following statements that apply to you.

- ❏ I haven't talked to my children about sex yet. How can I talk to them about my sexual sin?
- ❏ They are much too young to understand.
- ❏ They'll never respect me again if I tell.
- ❏ How will I have any credibility with them to discipline them?

Whatever the age of your children, honesty is the best approach. This does not mean you must reveal specific details. You may only tell them an outline of the facts. Something as important as honesty, however, should not be avoided. No doubt, your sexual sin has affected your behavior toward them. Maybe you haven't been the kind of parent you would like to be. Perhaps your children have seen times of anger, impatience, sadness, or fear. They deserve an explanation. Perhaps, also, you and your spouse have been distant or estranged and not the best example of a loving relationship.

I recommend that both you and your spouse sit down with your children and explain in general terms what has happened, and how you intend to change. The key is to assure them that this is not about them, and you and your spouse are not going to be divorced. In my experience, children want to know mom and dad are staying together. They are resilient. They have a breadth of understanding and forgiveness deeper than most of ours. Here is a possible format for both of you to follow.

- We both have something to talk to you about.
- This is serious, but it is not about us getting divorced.
- We both may be a little sad for a while, but we are OK and will always be here for you.
- You may have noticed mom and dad struggling with some things.
- If we've been angry with each other, it doesn't mean that we're leaving.
- If we've been angry with you, it may be more about our own problems than it was about you.
- Mom/Dad has been sexually unfaithful to our marriage vows. What that means is . . ..
- Mom/Dad is getting help and he/she intends to become faithful again.
- We are going to work on rebuilding our relationship.
- We may not always have been the best parents, but we intend to change and be better.
- There are some specific things that may change around here. Right now they are . . . . (for example, we're getting rid of cable channels for the TV, dad won't be traveling as much, mom and dad are going to sleep in separate bedrooms for a while). Again, with God's help, we're keeping the family together.
- If there's ever anything else you want to know, don't be afraid to ask.

**KEY POINT**
Don't ever expect to have the final or ultimate conversation. Expect to have a series of conversations throughout their lifetime.

We talked to our children when they were 5, 8, and 11. Each of them understood the information in different ways. As they have grown, they have asked more questions and we have told each of them different things at different times. As they have entered their adolescence, begun to date, and think about the opposite sex, we have been able to talk to them in ways that, when we were children, we never dreamed of talking to our parents.

Your children will also learn that to struggle with sexual feelings is OK. After all, we are sexual beings and have questions. So will they. Your children will at least know there are ways to deal with these questions. Painfully for some of you, your sexual or other behavior may have directly affected your children. This could include any of the forms of abuse that we talked about in unit 9. If this is possibly the case, you may need to find professional help for them. Be of good courage. You can change and your children can heal. Keep in mind that helping them to heal is more important than protecting yourself. They will ultimately respect you for being honest and willing to change.

**KEY POINT**
Model honesty, the expression of feelings, the ability to change, and humility. These are great gifts to give to any child.

### Extended Family

How much or little you tell parents, in-laws, brothers, sisters, uncles, aunts, or grandparents will depend on several key factors:

- How much do you look to them for emotional support? You will want to tell those individuals who support you. Again, I would recommend being general but honest.
- What kind of individuals are they? What is their level of maturity? How will they deal with the information?
- What are your family wounds? You may have issues of abuse or other concerns with some family members. Talking to them may be part of your ongoing healing. Serious confrontations are usually best done with a pastor or counselor present to help facilitate the conversation. Many of you may "shut down" or not be yourself around some of your family. You may have to experience a certain amount of healing before you can talk to some family members.

## Your Friends

In your early days of recovery, you may want to rush into the street and tell the whole world you are getting better. You may be overjoyed at the new things happening and want everyone to know. Or, you may be so humiliated that you just want to tell everyone and get it over with. You may just be so tired, you don't know what to do.

For most of us, friends divide into two categories: those we seek to have intimate relationships with, and those who are more casual acquaintances. With the second group, I would discourage truth-telling, at least at first. You don't know them as well, so you do not know how they will deal with the information. You need to evaluate your closer friendships individually to decide who to tell. You don't have to tell everyone at the same time. Truth-telling may be a process of one-on-one sharing. Always ask yourself the question, "Why do I want to tell? What is the reason? What good can come out of it?"

➤ Did you ever think you were the only one who had committed some of your sexual sins? How would you have reacted if someone had told you his story? Would you have felt less lonely?

I am always surprised when I tell my story. At least one person always relates to it and finds help. Your story may be a helpful witness to others. You cannot save the world from sexual immorality. Neither can you compensate for your own sins by converting others to a more moral life. Before telling your story, you need to be well on the road to sobriety. In telling your story, you may convince yourself that you are completely healed when you are not. You will always be vulnerable to sexual sin. You must rely on God's power to sustain you throughout the rest of your life. Thinking you have control can be Satan's trap to a slip. These thoughts stem from pride and shame. Be patient.

What if you tell your story and people reject you? What if the people nearest to you reject you? What if your worst fears come to pass? Although I know the results of appropriate honesty are generally positive, I cannot promise you that you will not encounter rejection. I can offer you some final words of encouragement to end this unit. The risk of hiding your sins is infinitely greater than the risks of confession. If you practice appropriate sharing, you will gain at least two benefits. You will gain self-respect, and you will diminish the fear of being found out. In addition I can assure you that Jesus will understand. He will never reject you.

## Assignment for the Lesson

➤ Ask God to give you the wisdom to talk to those who will be gracious in listening and be closer to you in the process. Ask Him to give you the wisdom to witness to those who need to hear your story.

➤ Say the following affirmation five times.

I have the courage to reveal myself to others. I am forgiven for my sins by Christ and can be by others.

➤ Read Proverbs 12:22, written in the margin.

The Lord detests lying lips, but he delights in men who are truthful.
—Proverbs 12:22

---

Notes
1. For more information see *Craving for Ecstacy: The Consciousness and Chemistry of Escape* by Harvey B. Milkman and Stanley G. Sunderwirth, (Lexington, MA: D.C. Heath and Company, 1987)

# The Process of Recovery

## FOCAL PASSAGE

*Since we are surrounded by such a great cloud of witnesses, let us throw off everything that hinders and the sin that so easily entangles, and let us run with perseverance the race marked out for us.*

—Hebrews 12:1

## MEMORY VERSE

Consider him who endured such opposition from sinful men, so that you will not grow weary and lose heart.
–Hebrews 12:3

### KEN'S STORY

Ken finally stopped his sexual sins after years of acting out. At first the excitement of his new freedom kept him involved in the recovery process. He went to meetings, maintained a relationship with his sponsor, and practiced honesty in his relationships. But six months into sobriety he began to tire of the recovery process. He had to travel to attend group meetings. He was tired of all the prohibitions. Ken hated the label "sex addict." He was tired of being different. His wife had been supportive and forgiving, but she never understood the problem or went to any groups for herself. She also seemed tired of recovery work. As far as she was concerned, if Ken stayed sober, everything would be fine.

Ken heard a TV evangelist preach on deliverance, and he felt delivered. *I have 6 months of sobriety, I must be cured,* he thought. Ken stopped going to meetings, lost touch with his friends in recovery—including his sponsor—and generally started taking his recovery for granted. Life continued to go well for Ken for several more weeks. Then one night Ken decided he no longer needed to worry about watching TV alone late at night. For the first time in months he turned on the set at 11 o'clock. Many of the same old pornographic temptations were there, but Ken kept flipping the channels and finally went to bed.

The following day, the images Ken viewed seemed to come into his head at the strangest times, but he brushed them off. That night, however, he watched TV for a longer period of time. This pattern went on for several weeks. Ken didn't think anything of it, he still hadn't "acted out," at least not in the old ways. Finally, one night when Ken's wife was angry with him for watching so much TV, he got in his car and drove to a familiar massage parlor.

## GROWTH GOAL

In this final unit you will explore ongoing recovery from sexual sin. You will consider several aspects of maintaining sobriety. Some of these may be life changing for you.

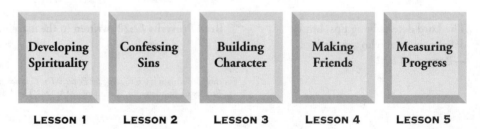

| Developing Spirituality | Confessing Sins | Building Character | Making Friends | Measuring Progress |
|:---:|:---:|:---:|:---:|:---:|
| **LESSON 1** | **LESSON 2** | **LESSON 3** | **LESSON 4** | **LESSON 5** |

# Developing Spirituality

*When pride comes, then comes disgrace, but with humility comes wisdom.*
—Proverbs 11:2

You met Ken in the unit story. He neglected his recovery process—with disastrous results. Perhaps you know Ken's pattern. You may have made a number of attempts to stop sexual sin and been successful for a while. Most addicts who achieve long periods of sobriety know they have to work continually on their recovery—even for the rest of their lives. At any point during sobriety you may drop your defenses. While this may sound discouraging, the positive changes of working a program can be quite exciting.

Ken discovered what many of us have experienced. The period of time between the 6th and the 12th month of sobriety is the most difficult. It is a time when we are tempted to think that we are well. We might also be tired of all the work of staying healthy. We are angry about being "different." We don't like the labels of "sex addict," "unhealthy," or "dysfunctional."

Bill Wilson had been a drunk for years. He tried to find a cure through psychiatry, but none of the efforts worked for any length of time. Finally, during one of his hospitalizations, he had a spiritual awakening which began to change his life. He found sobriety and for a time went around New York City looking for all the worst drunks he could find. He brought them into his house and tried to force-feed them the spirituality he had experienced. But his methods didn't seem to work.

While on a business trip to Ohio, Bill felt the old temptation and knew he needed to talk to another alcoholic. He started calling ministers, asking if they could "refer" him to a drunk. One of them sent him to see Dr. Bob Smith. Although he was a physician, Dr. Bob had been a drunk for years. Everyone considered him a hopeless case. Dr. Bob met Bill with considerable cynicism. He stopped Bill before he really got started, "If you've come here to preach to me, don't bother, I've been preached at for years." To which Bill replied, "You're mistaken. I didn't come here for you, I came here for me!"

These two hopeless drunks went on to found Alcoholics Anonymous, which has helped millions of men and women find sobriety over the last 60 years.

➤ **How does Bill Wilson's story relate to your recovery from sexual addiction?**

When Bill tried to force-feed others a remedy, no one got well. When he asked for help for himself from someone, the results were powerful in his life and in the lives of many others.

✎ **Can you name a Bible story in which a person finds God through his or her own accomplishment?**

_____

✎ **Can you describe a Bible story in which a person finds God through his or her own humility?**

_____

_____

**If you have played the fool and exalted yourself, or if you have planned evil, clap your hand over your mouth!**
**–Proverbs 30:32**

**KEY POINT**
The issue is not whether you have known moments of humility, but whether you can be humble over the process of time.

I do not believe you can name a Bible story in response to the first question. In answer to the second question, two of my favorite Bible stories are of the prodigal son (Luke 15:11-32) and the tax collector and the Pharisee (Luke 18:9-14). The verse in the margin describes the attitude of the tax collector.

➤ **In your sexual sins, or any of your sins, have you ever felt like the tax collector?**

In our opening story Ken was humble for a while. Then his pride regained control and he thought he was cured. Ken began to believe he could stay sober without help.

Have you ever considered whether asking God to remove your sexual sins might be a desperate attempt to control God—to get Him to do what you thought you needed and what you thought he ought to do? How many times have you told yourself that you could stop if you really wanted? How often did you try on your own to stop? We have discussed these questions before. Do you now see this kind of thinking as a matter of pride? You wanted God to work your way or you wanted to do it on your own. Maybe you thought you couldn't live without your sexual behaviors. Maybe you wanted God to remove all sexual thoughts from your life.

In our pride we want many things. In humility we have to surrender many things. In recovery we have to grieve over those areas of our lives we want to control but must accept that we cannot. In my own life, I will never again be a local church pastor. Every time I go to church this thought causes a twinge of sadness, sometimes even anger, when I remember what my life used to be like. Never mind that God has other ministry opportunities I never could have imagined, the chance of leading a local congregation is something I have to let go of. This is a humbling feeling, especially when I try to control my thinking that I could do a better job than the person currently behind the pulpit.

✎ **Sexual sins lead to many losses. A list of things you may have to grieve over appears below. As an act of humbly letting go, check those you acknowledge you have lost.**

❑ a marriage
❑ friends
❑ money
❑ a career
❑ a dream for your life.
❑ a person with whom you were sexually involved
❑ other _____

❑ a place from which you have had to move
❑ a church family
❑ the ability to regularly be with your children
❑ freedom through incarceration
❑ the pleasure of sexual acting out

➤ **Allow yourself to be sad for having lost these things. Can you give up your attempts to get them back?**

If you can, then you are on your way to humility and the act of letting go.

✎ **Choose the one person, place, or thing that represents your greatest loss. Write a letter of good-bye to this person, place, or thing. Express your sadness. Do not mail the letter. Check the box in the margin when you have done so.**

➤ **As you look to the future, can you let go of control of your own desires and prayerfully ask God to show you His will for your life?**

In the first year of your recovery relinquishing control may be especially difficult. You still have to deal with consequences of your sexual sin. Others may be angry with you, your spouse or other family members and friends may not understand, or you may be facing

❑ Letter completed.

legal, financial, social, or vocational difficulties. Some of these may not resolve themselves as soon as you like. You may be angry with God. You may feel that you've finally achieved sobriety, and yet your life doesn't seem to be improving.

✎ What consequences of relinquishing control do you most fear?

_____

_____

➤ Read the following passage:

*We have this treasure in jars of clay to show that this all-surpassing power is from God and not from us. We are hard pressed on every side, but not crushed; perplexed, but not in despair; persecuted, but not abandoned; struck down, but not destroyed. We always carry around in our body the death of Jesus, so that the life of Jesus may also be revealed in our body. For we who are alive are always being given over to death for Jesus' sake, so that his life may be revealed in our mortal body.*

—2 Corinthians 4:7-11

> Endure hardship as discipline; God is treating you as sons. For what son is not disciplined by his father? If you are not disciplined (and everyone undergoes discipline), then you are illegitimate children and not true sons. Moreover, we have all had human fathers who disciplined us and we respected them for it. How much more should we submit to the Father of our spirits and live! Our fathers disciplined us for a little while as they thought best; but God disciplines us for our good, that we may share in his holiness. No discipline seems pleasant at the time, but painful. Later on, however, it produces a harvest of righteousness and peace for those who have been trained by it.
> –Hebrews 12:7-11

We have God's promise that He will give us the ability to cope with life if we depend on Him. Nothing will ever happen to us so bad that it need destroy us.

We began this unit with Hebrews 12:1. The passage goes on to assure us that God only disciplines those He calls His children. See the verses in the margin. Many addicts I know count consequences as a blessing. They feel that God uses the consequences of their sins to keep them humble and in the process of recovery. Otherwise, their pride would have taken back control.

An ongoing part of spirituality is learning to trust. We learn that God brings consequences as a result of our actions. We learn that consequences are not necessarily punishment, but expressions of God's care. We learn to daily deny our pride, surrender our efforts to control God, and obey Him instead. We learn to obey Jesus' words from Luke 9:23: "If anyone would come after me, he must deny himself and take up his cross daily and follow me."

## KEY POINT
Turning your life over to God is a daily decision for the rest of your life.

## Assignment for the Lesson

➤ Read Romans 8:28. Make a commitment to seek and obey God's will.

➤ Say the following affirmation five times.

I can choose to surrender to God and obey Him.

✎ Below write a paraphrase of Hebrews 12:3, the unit Scripture memory verse. Begin memorizing this verse.

> Consider him who endured such opposition from sinful men, so that you will not grow weary and lose heart.
> –Hebrews 12:3

_____

_____

_____

➤ Consider recommitting your life to Christ, humbly asking Him to be Lord of all areas of your life, and to grant you His peace.

# Confessing Sins

*If we claim to be without sin, we deceive ourselves and the truth is not in us. If we confess our sins, he is faithful and just and will forgive us our sins and purify us from all unrighteousness.*

—1 John 1:8-9

In unit 11 you worked on honesty about your past behaviors. Confession is honesty in practical operation. Without confession you cannot build intimacy with the important people in your life. Confession also means more than simply admitting sexual sins. A life built on honesty and confession leads to positive relationships, openness, and freedom from fear. In this lesson you will explore confession as a key part of spiritual growth.

## Two Blocks to Confession

Many of us have two feelings that block our ability to confess our sins in a spiritually meaningful way: (1) anger and (2) shame. Have you considered the roots of these feelings in your life?

➤ **If you pictured the face of God, would you imagine Him smiling or frowning?**

❏ smiling ❏ frowning

If you often see God frowning, you probably picture God as angry and judgmental. Where does this picture come from for you?

✎ **From the following list, check the experiences that have influenced your life. Remember, you are not blaming others; you are seeking to understand yourself objectively.**

❏ You were put down as a child. Refer back to your work in units 7 and 8.
❏ You were exposed to preaching or teaching full of angry pictures of God's judgment.
❏ You were disciplined by those who told you God would be angry with your behavior.
❏ You have been judged or put down for your behaviors.
❏ God has never seemed to grant your requests for help.

You may be angry and fearful toward God for any of these reasons. If you find trusting God difficult, you may also have difficulty being honest with people.

➤ **Can you see that your anger toward God may be with others who have been judgmental or insecure and not with God?**

✎ **Can you think of a time in your life when someone was genuinely forgiving and loving with you? Describe the experience.**

_____

_____

Does this experience resemble what the Bible describes as God's character of forgiveness?

A second block to confession is shame. Feeling like a bad and worthless person is a core belief of sex addicts. This feeling drives us to find approval in a variety of ways including sexual behaviors. In previous units you have explored ways that your wounds from the past may have led you to shameful conclusions about yourself. Hopefully, you are beginning to heal from these wounds.

Confessing sins can lead to acceptance and the development of a healthy self-concept. We need to confess to others and to God. Confessing means we have given up our prideful attempts at earning forgiveness. A complete understanding of confession includes accepting God's forgiveness. Confession and accepting forgiveness brings powerful healing from shame.

✎ Have you ever thought your sexual sins were totally unique to you, no one else has ever committed such sins? Did they seem so bad, gross, or perverted that not even God would be able to forgive them? ❑ Yes ❑ No

✎ Where in the Bible do you find justification for the idea that your sin is impossible for God to forgive?

---

**Whoever blasphemes against the Holy Spirit will never be forgiven; he is guilty of an eternal sin.**
**–Mark 3:29**

The Bible does speak of one—and only one—unpardonable sin, the blasphemy of the Holy Spirit spoken of in Mark 3:29. Not all Christians agree about that sin. Some believe the passage refers to a person rejecting Jesus for so long that he or she loses all spiritual sensitivity. Thus the person is unaware of the activity of the Holy Spirit around him or her. Whatever the proper interpretation of the Bible teaching about the unpardonable sin, all legitimate Bible scholars will agree on one thing. The unpardonable sin has nothing whatsoever to do with a specific sin, such as sexual sin. Hopefully, you left the line blank. Many biblical passages describe God's grace through the gift of His Son. No sin is uncommon to man and nothing can separate us from the love of God in Christ Jesus.

*What, then, shall we say in response to this? If God is for us, who can be against us? He who did not spare his own Son, but gave him up for us all—how will he not also, along with him, graciously give us all things? Who will bring any charge against those whom God has chosen? It is God who justifies. Who is he that condemns? Christ Jesus, who died—more than that, who was raised to life—is at the right hand of God and is also interceding for us.*

*–Romans 8:31-34*

The true remedy for shame is two-fold. You need to break down the isolation that comes from feeling your sin is unique, and you need to be certain that your confession has been a complete accounting.

1. Hearing the stories of other sexual sinners and discovering that you are not the only one who has thought and done certain things combats shame. Since I have been involved in recovery, I can't think of any form of sexual sin, even the most perverted forms, that I haven't heard about many times.

➤ Where are you the most likely to hear these stories?

When recovering people tell their stories, they do not describe lurid details. Confession means honestly sharing the essence of sin. You're right, you will hear these honest confessions at meetings with other sexual sinners.

2. Making sure that your confession of sexual sin is a total and complete accounting of all your behaviors also combats shame. In the 12-steps, Bill Wilson called it a fearless and searching moral inventory.

✎ Such complete confession may take you some time—days, weeks, or even months—and it may require you to talk to others to get support while you are doing it. Do a life review beginning with your earliest memories. On separate paper make a list that includes the following items:

- every sinful behavior, sexual and otherwise, that you remember
- every attempt that you made to stop and failed
- every consequence you have experienced because of your sins.

Your list may be long. To feel completely forgiven we need to make a complete list. Leave nothing out. At various times in your life you may have tried to tell the truth about your sins to someone but you held something back. You told just enough for which you thought you could be forgiven. Maybe later you added to the list as you began to find acceptance. Eventually you must make a total list.

A moral inventory also includes remembering the good things that you have done.

✎ Make another list on your own paper. Account for your successes, your accomplishments, and your talents. What do you like about yourself? Maybe you will have to rely on what others have told you even if you didn't believe it.

✎ Who represents spiritual authority to you?

_____

This could be your pastor or someone else who represents positive spirituality to you.

➤ Make an appointment with this person to share both of your lists. Be sure to provide adequate time for this meeting. This could require an extended session. Do not waste the time, use the occasion specifically to share your lists.

This is confession to the highest spiritual authority in your life. The person's acceptance of you despite your worst sins will be a tremendous experience of grace for you.

❑ Meeting completed.

✎ Check here when you have completed this assignment:

You will not stop making mistakes and committing sins. As Paul says we all fall short. You will want to make acts of confession a regular and immediate part of your recovery. Alcoholics Anonymous puts it this way in Step 10, "Continued to take personal inventory and when we were wrong, promptly admitted it."

## Assignment for the Lesson

➤ Read James 5:16, which appears in the margin.

➤ Say the following affirmation five times.

Confess your sins to each other and pray for each other so that you may be healed. The prayer of a righteous man is powerful and effective.
–James 5:16

I can accept God's grace.

➤ Pray for courage to be fearless in your list making.

# Building Character

*Now when he saw the crowds, he went up on a mountainside and sat down. His disciples came to him, and he began to teach them, saying:*
*"Blessed are the poor in spirit, for theirs is the kingdom of heaven.*
*Blessed are those who mourn, for they will be comforted.*
*Blessed are the meek, for they will inherit the earth.*
*Blessed are those who hunger and thirst for righteousness, for they will be filled.*
*Blessed are the merciful, for they will be shown mercy.*
*Blessed are the pure in heart, for they will see God.*
*Blessed are the peacemakers, for they will be called sons of God.*
*Blessed are those who are persecuted because of righteousness, for theirs is the kingdom of heaven.*

*"Blessed are you when people insult you, persecute you and falsely say all kinds of evil against you because of me. Rejoice and be glad, because great is your reward in heaven, for in the same way they persecuted the prophets who were before you.*

*"You are the salt of the earth. But if the salt loses its saltiness, how can it be made salty again? It is no longer good for anything, except to be thrown out and trampled by men.*

*"You are the light of the world. A city on a hill cannot be hidden. Neither do people light a lamp and put it under a bowl. Instead they put it on its stand, and it gives light to everyone in the house. In the same way, let your light shine before men, that they may see your good deeds and praise your Father in heaven."*

—Matthew 5:1-16

Most of us are familiar with this famous passage called the beatitudes. These verses describe the character traits Jesus considers "blessed." In this lesson you will learn that, despite persecutions or consequences, growing in faith builds your character. We call the process of growing in grace sanctification.

## One Day At A Time

Alcoholics Anonymous is famous for many sayings, several of which have become part of our national language. One of the most well-known of these is the phrase "One day at a time." Thinking about staying sober for the rest of your life is overwhelming. Thinking about it for one day is less frightening and more manageable.

The one day at a time principle applies to building healthy sexuality. First look at actions that will achieve healthy sexuality and practice them for one day. Then repeat for a second day. Keep the process going until you have completed a week. As you work daily, keep in mind the progress that can result in a week, a month, a year. and eventually a lifetime of healthy practices. Work into each day definite actions that build healthy sexuality. Just as a person who is trying to develop the characteristic of kindness does one act of kindness a day until it becomes a habit, you will need to experience healthy habits daily.

One day at a time is a process of breaking the unmanageable, confusing, or overwhelming into more manageable, understandable, and less frightening parts.

We have already discussed one of the cornerstones of this character development—humility. In lesson 1 you examined humility as the ongoing daily process of surrendering our lives to God and of letting go. For the rest of your life you can seek God's will each day. In every situation ask yourself what God would want you to do, to be, or to decide.

Always strive to be as specific as you can. What are the specific acts that you can do to demonstrate the surrender of your will and control?

Another obvious character trait for those of us who struggle with sexual sin is freedom from lust. We need specific plans to avoid sexual temptation and to adhere to standards of moral purity.

➤ What is your plan for today to stay morally pure?

✎ The following is one sex addict's specific, one-day plan. Underline those activities you can use in your life.

- attend a meeting.
- talk to my sponsor and other members of my support and accountability group.
- stay out of video stores.
- make an amend from my amends list.
- leave the TV off.
- have a conversation with my wife.
- repair a broken relationship.
- make a counseling appointment.
- do my daily meditation.
- go for a 30-minute walk.

These are just a few examples from one individual. Your list for today will be totally specific to you and your needs. When you add up days like this, one day at a time, you will eventually find that you have a week, then a month, then a year, and then a lifetime of moral purity. But it all begins with one day.

✎ Here is a list of other character traits. Check the ones that you need to work on.

❑ kindness
❑ charity/generosity
❑ courage
❑ temperance
❑ compassion
❑ patience
❑ empathy
❑ trustworthiness

❑ peacefulness
❑ tolerance
❑ satisfaction
❑ endurance
❑ zeal
❑ honesty
❑ other _____

You may have other names for some of these. Others you may know by their opposites, like greed, impatience, prejudice, envy, or jealousy.

I believe in making very specific contracts with myself, my sponsor, my accountability group, and my support group to do specific things to work on these character traits.

✎ Choose one of the character traits that you checked. Write it in the margin.

Now, devise a daily plan for how you are going to work on it. Be specific.

_____

_____

_____

_____

Here are some examples in some of the categories:
- Patience and Empathy. Agree to wait until your spouse is through talking before you respond. Repeat back to her what she said.
- Charity and Generosity. Examine your budget to see how you might increase your giving to the church or to charitable causes.
- Temperance. Make an appointment with a counselor to discuss why you seem to be getting angry about insignificant things.
- Kindness. Perform a chore for someone that he or she normally does for you.
- Tolerance. Have a conversation with a member of a different ethnic or religious group.
- Satisfaction. Make a list of things you're thankful for.
- Courage. Do something you've always been afraid to try.
- Peacefulness. Apologize to someone.
- Zeal. Write your congressman or city councilman about upcoming legislation, or offer vocal support for a church ministry project.

Another helpful group slogan encourages you to: "Fake It Til You Make It." How good an actor are you? If you have lied to cover your sins, you probably have some acting skills. You can employ those skills in character development. The principle is easy—act like the character you're trying to develop. Act like you're kind, tolerant, charitable, or peaceful.

You may think that acting means being phony. "Why should I act cheerful when I don't feel cheerful?" In fact, acting means practicing. You can be pro-active. You can choose to be kind, or courageous, or cheerful and then act in the way you choose. Such choices are not being phony. They are choices to stop being a victim of your old habits. They are choices to take responsibility for yourself.

Practice what you'd like to be and eventually it will come more easily to you. Take any of the above strategies that you've decided to be accountable about and pretend you feel like doing them. So often we make the mistake of thinking we have to feel like doing something before we do it.

As you begin receiving positive feedback for your new actions, your nature will lean toward those actions. Before you know it, these new actions have become a part of you and you no longer have to "fake it." Congratulations—you've developed a new skill and made progress in recovery.

➤ In Acts 16 Paul and Silas were beaten and thrown into prison, yet they made the deliberate choice to sing and pray. Do you suppose they were singing because they felt like it, or did their positive behavior affect their attitudes?

**After they had been severely flogged, they were thrown into prison, and the jailer was commanded to guard them carefully. About midnight Paul and Silas were praying and singing hymns to God.**
**–Acts 16:23, 25**

Building character is a matter of practicing, experimenting with what works, and being accountable for giving the process a try. With small amounts of progress one day you might be someone else's role model.

## Assignment for the Lesson

➤ Practice kindness by telling a member of your *Faithful & True* group how much you appreciate him.

➤ Say the following affirmation five times.

I can make it and be who I want to be one day at a time.

➤ Thank God for the progress that you've made already.

# Making Amends

*Jesus entered Jericho and was passing through. A man was there by the name of Zacchaeus; he was a chief tax collector and was wealthy. He wanted to see who Jesus was, but being a short man he could not, because of the crowd. So he ran ahead and climbed a sycamore-fig tree to see him, since Jesus was coming that way.*

*When Jesus reached the spot, he looked up and said to him, "Zacchaeus, come down immediately. I must stay at your house today." So he came down at once and welcomed him gladly.*

*All the people saw this and began to mutter, "He has gone to be the guest of a 'sinner.'"*

*But Zacchaeus stood up and said to the Lord, "Look, Lord! Here and now I give half of my possessions to the poor, and if I have cheated anybody out of anything, I will pay back four times the amount."*

*Jesus said to him, "Today salvation has come to this house, because this man, too, is a son of Abraham.*

—Luke 19:1-9

Jesus' actions toward Zacchaeus must have mystified the people of His day. They couldn't understand why Jesus was spending time with someone of undesirable character. Yet Jesus' spirit of compassion and fellowship so changed this man that Zacchaeus sought to make restitution for his sins.

In this lesson you will learn how to develop a plan for making amends to those you have harmed by your sexual sins. This may be painful to consider. For many years you may have denied the harm your behavior caused. To face the effects of your behavior on others will take courage—one of those character traits that you examined in the previous lesson.

The word *amend* has three possible meanings. For many it suggests saying," I'm sorry." To amend may also mean, as in the story of Zacchaeus, to make restitution for the wrongs you have committed. Finally, to amend may mean to change the behavior that caused the damage in the first place.

I remember when my two boys were growing up. Deb and I would occasionally catch one of them misbehaving. Knowing we would be angry, he always would quickly and emphatically say, "I'm sorry." Translated, he really meant, "Don't be angry with me or punish me."

➤ Have you ever used an apology as a means to manipulate someone's reaction to you because you didn't want them to be angry?

This may still be the case for you. So often I see sex addicts say to their spouses, "I'm sorry. Don't be angry with me. I'm going to be better. You can trust me again." Sometimes, saying you're sorry is really an angry and controlling statement, "I said I was sorry, don't you dare be angry with me."

We need to move beyond control and manipulation. Being able to genuinely say we are sorry involves one of the character traits from our list in lesson 3, *Empathy*. Empathy means deeply understanding another persons feelings. As we genuinely understand how our behaviors have hurt others, we will be able to feel sorrow over the pain we have caused.

The Lord sent Nathan to David. When he came to him, he said, "There were two men in a certain town, one rich and the other poor. The rich man had a very large number of sheep and cattle, but the poor man had nothing except one little ewe lamb he had bought. He raised it, and it grew up with him and his children. It shared his food, drank from his cup and even slept in his arms. It was like a daughter to him.

"Now a traveler came to the rich man, but the rich man refrained from taking one of his own sheep or cattle to prepare a meal for the traveler who had come to him. Instead, he took the ewe lamb that belonged to the poor man and prepared it for the one who had come to him."

David burned with anger against the man and said to Nathan, "As surely as the LORD lives, the man who did this deserves to die! He must pay for that lamb four times over, because he did such a thing and had no pity."

Then Nathan said to David, "You are the man! This is what the Lord, the God of Israel, says: 'I anointed you king over Israel, and I delivered you from the hand of Saul. I gave your master's house to you, and your master's wives into your arms. I gave you the house of Israel and Judah. And if all this had been too little, I would have given you even more. Why did you despise the word of the Lord by doing what is evil in his eyes? You struck down Uriah the Hittite with the sword and took his wife to be your own.
–2 Samuel 12:1-9

David committed adultery with Bathsheba. Then he had her husband killed to cover it. Second Samuel chapter 12 gives us an example of how Nathan the prophet lead David to recognize what he had done and to experience repentance.

➤ Read the story of Nathan and King David, 2 Samuel 12:1-9 (in the margin).

Nathan used a story, as Jesus so frequently did, to get David to see himself. Boldly, Nathan says to David after he tells him the story, "You are the man!" We need to see ourselves and the damage that we've done. Painfully, I remember my wife asking me how I would feel if she had committed the sexual sins I had. Her question made a powerful impact on me. I experienced empathy. To empathize means to understand deeply the thoughts and feelings of another. I understood something of how Deb felt.

Throughout this study we have explored the emotional wounds your family inflicted on you. Hopefully, you have begun to allow yourself to feel honest feelings. Remember those feelings. Your own addictive actions have probably caused those close to you to hurt in much the same way.

➤ As you are doing the work of this exercise, you may feel shame. Take a gentleness break, remind yourself of God's forgiveness. My purpose is not to inflict more shame on you. I want you to empathize with those you have hurt so you can genuinely open up to them and share what's on your heart.

Your willingness to make restitution for the harm you've done is a good indicator of genuine sorrow. Zacchaeus was so transformed by the presence of Jesus in his life that he made a four-fold payback for his financial cheating. He also gave half of what he owned to the poor. Making restitution may not be as direct as making a financial payback. The damage you've done will not always be monetary. The damage is more often emotional and spiritual. Below is a short list of possible damages you may have caused.

✎ From the following list of possible results of addictive behavior, check each form of damage you have caused in someone's life:

❑ violated trust of your spouse, family, and friends
❑ wasted money on sexual activities
❑ destroyed marriages of those with whom you've had affairs
❑ lost valuable time with your children
❑ transmitted sexual diseases to your spouse
❑ created loneliness and fear in others
❑ exemplified hypocritical Christianity to those around you.

These are just a few examples of physical, emotional, and spiritual damage that many of us create.

How do you repair damaged trust, emotions, or spirits? You may not be able to directly repair the damage. What if the person you've offended is dead or gone? What if contacting someone would cause further harm? If you had an affair with someone whose spouse doesn't know about it, you can't really make direct amends to that person without creating further damage.

We must be creative with our amends. I know a pastor who had a number of affairs with women in his church. To repair the spiritual damage he set up a scholarship fund at a local counseling center that specialized in helping women who had been victims of their pastor's sexual addiction. This is indirect, but symbolically it was an act of restitution. Your amends may be symbolic of your humility and willingness to pay back. One of my acts of restitution is helping others find sexual sobriety. If I can help others get well, maybe I'll prevent further damage. I look at this as a way of indirect amends.

Direct amends can be the most rewarding experience. Making direct amends with those who might be angry with us can be a frightening proposition. The potential healing of the experience can be worth the risk. Amends consist of several components. Here are some ideas about the process.

## GUIDELINES TO MAKING AMENDS

1. Decide who you have harmed.
2. Determine the nature of the damage you've created.
3. Create a plan for restitution and change.
4. Get feedback from your sponsor or group about the appropriateness of your plan. Is the nature of the harm you've created really true? Is talking to the person(s) you've harmed reasonable at this time or will it cause further harm to him or her?
5. Arrange for time to talk to him or her.
6. When you meet:
   - State the reason you wanted to talk.
   - Explain the nature of the harm you believe you've created.
   - Apologize.
   - Explain your intention to make restitution and change.
   - Wait for his or her reaction.
   - Be patient and listen if the person needs to express anger. Don't be defensive.
   - Thank the person for his time and any expression of his feelings.

One word of caution. Because of the shame many of us feel, we may imagine we have caused more harm than we actually have. You may have been reared to believe you are responsible for other people's feelings when really you are not. This may be particularly true if you've experienced emotional incest. (Refer to the work that you did in unit 7 to review emotional incest.) People may have blamed you for their feelings when you were not at fault. Be careful about taking responsibility that doesn't belong to you. Feedback from others about your plan for making amends is important. Before you seek to make questionable amends, talk to a sponsor, pastor, or counselor to gain some objectivity.

✎ **Below is a form you can use to begin making a list of people you may have harmed and the plans you have for making amends.**

Person(s) harmed _____

Nature of the harm

❑ physical
❑ emotional
❑ spiritual
❑ monetary
❑ other _____

Plan for amends _____

_____

_____

**KEY POINT**
When you think of the type damage you've done to others, think of ways you might make amends to them and others, as well as prevent that kind of damage in the future.

Consider him who endured such opposition from sinful men, so that you will not grow weary and lose heart.
—Hebrews 12:3

You may encounter people who do not understand what you are doing. They may not be used to people offering apologies or trying to make restitution. They may not think they have been harmed or that they need any form of restitution. They may even discourage you from trying to make your amends. At these times keep in mind the Key Point in the margin.

Making amends is a way of reducing your shame. You will feel better if you can make restitution either directly or symbolically. It will be a part of your maturation process as you grow in character.

One more word of caution. The process of amends may take the rest of your life. Certainly the process of growing in grace and developing Christ-like behavior is a lifetime process. You may not always remember the persons you have harmed. You may not always have the resources or maturity to make restitution.

None of us are perfect, even in recovery. You will continue to cause harm occasionally by your actions. Growing in maturity simply says you realize when you have harmed another and you are humble enough to take responsibility and make amends.

## Assignment for the Lesson

➤ Practice with one of the members of your *Faithful & True* group a conversation in which you make an amend.

➤ Practice repeating Hebrews 12:3, your Scripture memory verse for this unit.

➤ Say the following affirmation five times.

Even though I have done many harmful things, God still loves and forgives me.

➤ Pray for those you have harmed by name and ask that they may find healing.

LESSON 5

# Measuring Progress

*Since we are surrounded by such a great cloud of witnesses, let us throw off everything that hinders and the sin that so easily entangles, and let us run with perseverance the race marked out for us. Let us fix our eyes on Jesus, the author and perfecter of our faith, who for the joy set before him endured the cross, scorning its shame, and sat down at the right hand of the throne of God.*

—Hebrews 12:1-2

The Bible occasionally uses the image of a race to illustrate the journey of faith. Addicts would like for the race to be a 100-yard dash. Those in recovery know it is more like a marathon. I once heard a gold-medal-winning runner give his testimony about his relationship to Christ. At the end of the Olympic race he was so tired he prayed to God, "Lord, if you'll pick up my legs, I'll put them down."

A runner can compare himself to other runners to know how he is doing. He can also use lap times as an indicator of his progress. How do we know how well we're doing over time?

## Tom's Story

Tom was angry at himself and determined that he would never sexually act out again. Tom knew he would do whatever he needed to do to stay sober. He stopped going to all the old places that had triggered him in the past. Actually, he stopped going very many places at all. Tom stopped initiating sex with his wife because of the sexual temptations that haunted Tom for days afterward. Their sexual relationship was almost non-existent. When his wife wanted to talk about it, he found excuses not to. Tom simply said, "I'm staying sober and that's all that matters."

Tom worshiped faithfully. At church, however, he was a picture of rigid control. He didn't seem to enjoy himself. He rarely smiled. His jaw was set and his teeth were clenched. Being at church seemed more like work than anything else. Tom attended meetings religiously. He always arrived on time and left as soon as the meeting was over. He didn't seem to enjoy any of the fellowship or friendships with the men around him. Whenever Tom was stressed out, which was often, he learned that eating helped him to calm down. In the time that Tom was sexually sober he gained 40 pounds.

On the first anniversary of Tom's sobriety, the men in his recovery group wanted to celebrate with him. He had a very difficult time accepting their congratulations. Tom felt more miserable and lonely than at any point in his life.

➤ **Are you discouraged by Tom's story?**

You might be thinking to yourself, *Here is a guy who has achieved what I've longed for and he isn't happy. What's the deal?* Tom's story illustrates that sobriety is only part of measuring progress. Tom has so tightly controlled his life, he can't enjoy anything. He isn't really working a recovery program. In an alcoholics group, people like Tom are known as "dry drunks." Don't misunderstand. Sobriety from sexual sin is the cornerstone of progress. Without it, nothing else would be possible. But, your recovery must include more.

Many of the same problems that caused Tom to sin sexually in the first place are still factors in his life. Tom has switched addictions. He has turned from sex to food. He may also turn to work or any other form of compulsive behavior. These may be less socially shameful than sexual sin, but they are cover-ups for the real problem. Tom is still lonely and angry. He has not improved his relationships or deepened his spirituality. He neglects his body. He is still a mess. A sexually sober mess, but still a mess.

✎ **Is your life still a mess? Below is a checklist of factors that may or may not be true for you. Check each of the factors that apply.**

- ❑ neglected or abused body (smoking, overeating, no exercise)
- ❑ neglected house or apartment (repairs are neglected, cleaning is not done, pets have no food)
- ❑ stressed at work (missed deadlines, desk is piled up, chronically late)
- ❑ no hobbies or interests
- ❑ financial stress
- ❑ neglected friendships
- ❑ neglected children and/or marriage
- ❑ developed other addictive or problem behaviors
- ❑ car is never washed or cleaned
- ❑ neglected spiritual discipline
- ❑ ongoing feelings of depression or anxiety.

How many of these did you check? When your recovery is going well, other areas of your life should improve also. A relationship exists between your recovery and the rest of your life. Healing from sexual sin is a matter of caring for yourself in all areas of your life. You will need to continue:
- healing your wounds from the past
- caring for your physical body and your surroundings
- healing old relationships and developing new ones, creating an ongoing community
- being aware of your feelings and the ability to express them to others
- deepening your spirituality, your relationship to Christ, and your worship of God.

Your recovery will involve all these areas. At times you may feel your life is out of control in some of these areas. Be aware; these are warning signs that your self-discipline is breaking down. You will be more vulnerable to temptations of all kinds, because you may be driven back into your anger, depression, or self-pity.

✎ **You may like to measure progress by numbers. One way to do that is to create a system for measuring yourself on a daily basis. Years ago Pat Carnes created such a way called the "Personal Craziness Index." Below is a way to create that for yourself.**

Go back to the checklist of ways to know your life is still a mess (at the bottom of page 218). Eleven items are mentioned. Pick the five most serious indicators for you. For each of those five, decide how you are doing today. Give yourself a 5 if you are really doing well in that area. Give yourself a 0 if you are doing poorly. Give yourself a 1,2,3,or 4 if you're somewhere in-between. For each of the five aspects you will have a number from 0 to 5. Add the total of all five of your indicators. The total should range between 0 and 25. Then create a chart for yourself that would look like this:

| Day of the Week: | Week Number: 1 | 2 | 3 | 4 | 5 | 6 | 7 | 8 | 9 | 10 | 11 | 12 |
|---|---|---|---|---|---|---|---|---|---|---|---|---|
| Sunday | | | | | | | | | | | | |
| Monday | | | | | | | | | | | | |
| Tuesday | | | | | | | | | | | | |
| Wednesday | | | | | | | | | | | | |
| Thursday | | | | | | | | | | | | |
| Friday | | | | | | | | | | | | |
| Saturday | | | | | | | | | | | | |
| Total for the Week | | | | | | | | | | | | |

For a 12-week period you will have a number for every day. If you forget to rate yourself on any given day, give yourself a zero for that day. Now measure your progress. Are your numbers increasing or decreasing over the weeks? If they are increasing, you are doing better. If they are decreasing, your personal craziness is getting out of hand. You are in danger of temptation. You need to increase the energy of the recovery tools you are using. Experiment with this method of self-monitoring and see if it works for you.

The first year of recovery is the most difficult. While you may be achieving sobriety from sexual sin, you may have neglected one or more of these other areas:
- Your spouse may still not be able to trust you. Your relationship may not have improved.
- You may experience ongoing financial, social, physical, vocational, or legal consequences.
- You may still feel spiritually empty.
- You may still feel lonely.
- You may still struggle with other destructive behaviors.
- Your wounds from the past may not have had enough time to heal.
- You may not have fully grieved the behaviors, relationships, or other things you have lost.

As a person accustomed to instant gratification, you may find the recovery process really disappointing and discouraging. Your disappointment over unrealistic expectations may contribute to your temptation to slip or relapse. Don't be fooled by Satan. Stopping sexual sin is like surgery. When you have surgery, your wounds may hurt as they are healing. The rewards of some of the new behaviors you are trying to build may take time before you experience a sense of deeper healing.

Part 1 of this workbook will help you work on and develop discipline in several different dimensions of your life. I call this a healthy sexuality model and it is about broadening health in all areas of your life as you seek sexual recovery.

## Where DO I Go from Here?

If you have studied Part 2 of *Faithful & True* first, I encourage you to go back and work through Part 1. If you have worked through both sections of the book, or if you have turned here at the conclusion to Part 1 because you do not want to do Part 2, allow me to make some suggestions for your continued spiritual and personal growth.

✎ Think about areas in your life in which you need to grow. On the following list number your top three priorities.

   \_\_\_ healing from the effects of sexual abuse
   \_\_\_ overcoming either anorexia, bulimia, or compulsive overeating
   \_\_\_ changing unhealthy relationships
   \_\_\_ conquering an addiction to alcohol or other drugs
   \_\_\_ understanding the Bible
   \_\_\_ developing your prayer life
   \_\_\_ knowing God's will
   \_\_\_ becoming a disciple maker
   \_\_\_ caring for your physical needs
   \_\_\_ other: _____

Remember that character development and spiritual growth are not instant. Worthwhile goals take time.

The following are some suggestions for further study and spiritual growth. All these resources are written in the interactive format you have used as you studied *Faithful & True*. All of these books are intended for group study along with daily, individual work. Determine a particular area in which you need to grow. Then use one or more of these resources to help you continue your spiritual growth. Your *Faithful & True* group may wish to continue to meet together, using one of these additional studies.

To build your self-worth on the forgiveness and love of Jesus Christ:
• *Search for Significance* Life® Support Group Series Edition by Robert S. McGee, Johnny Jones, and Sallie Jones (Houston: Rapha Publishing). This study will help you replace false beliefs about yourself with principles from God's Word. Member's Book, product number 0805499903; Leader's Guide, product number 090549989X.

To understand and deal with your family:
• *Breaking the Cycle of Hurtful Family Experiences* by Robert S. McGee, Pat Springle, Jim Craddock, and Dale W. McCleskey (Houston: Rapha Publishing). This study helps you understand how parents shape their children and how they pass family dysfunction from generation to generation. It teaches you how to break the cycle of generational family dysfunction. Member's Book, product number 0805499814; Leader's Guide, product number 0805499822.

To identify and replace codependent behaviors through a Christ-Centered 12-Step Process:
• *Conquering Codependency: A Christ-Centered 12-Step Process* by Pat Springle and Dale W. McCleskey (Houston: Rapha Publishing). The learned perceptions and behaviors called codependency—the compulsion to rescue, help, and fix others—often add to our addictive behaviors. *Conquering Codependency* applies the Christ-centered 12 Steps to these habits. Member's Book, product number 080549975X; Facilitator's Guide, product number 0805499768.

To conquer a dependency to chemicals or an eating disorder:
• *Conquering Chemical Dependency: A Christ-Centered 12-Step Process* by Robert S. McGee and Dale W. McCleskey (Houston: Rapha Publishing). Offers hope and healing for those who have developed a dependency on alcohol or other mood-altering drugs. *Conquering Chemical Dependency* applies the Christ-centered 12-Steps to help you overcome addiction. Member's Book, product number 0805499830; Facilitator's Guide, available for free download at www.lifeway.com/discipleplus/download.htm.

• *Conquering Eating Disorders: A Christ-Centered 12-Step Process* by Robert S. McGee, Wm. Drew Mountcastle, and Jim Florence. (Houston: Rapha Publishing). Applies the proved Christ-centered 12-Step discipleship process to help you overcome either anorexia, bulimia, or compulsive overeating. Member's Book, product number 0805499784; Facilitator's Guide, product number 0805499776.

To deal with the painful results of sexual abuse:
• *Shelter from the Storm: Hope for Survivors of Sexual Abuse* by Cynthia Kubetin, James Mallory, and Jacqualine C. Truitt (Houston: Rapha Publishing). Shelter guides the survivor of sexual abuse through the process of grief and healing. Member's Book, product number 0805499792; Facilitator's Guide, product number 0805499806.

To help you grow in developing a healthy lifestyle:
• *Fit 4: A LifeWay Christian Wellness Plan* addresses all four areas of life—heart, soul, mind, and strength. This wellness plan blends taking proper care of your body, being devoted to God, and maintaining healthy relationships with family, friends, and others. For more information contact LifeWay Church Resources Customer Service at 1-800-458-2772; FAX (615) 251-5933 or visit the Web site at **fit4.com**.

To understand God's will for your life:
• *Experiencing God: Knowing and Doing the Will of God* by Henry Blackaby and Claude V. King (Nashville: LifeWay Press). Find answers to the often-asked question "How can I know and do God's will?" This study helps Christians discover God's will and obediently follow it. Member's Book, product number 08054999547; Leader's Guide, product number 0805499512.

To learn more about the Bible:
• *Step by Step Through the Old Testament* by Waylon Bailey and Tom Hudson (Nashville: LifeWay Press). This self-instructional workbook surveys the Old Testament, provides a framework for understanding and interpreting it, and teaches Bible background. Member's Book, product number 0767326199; Leader's Guide, product number 0767326202.
• *Step by Step Through the New Testament* by Thomas D. Lea and Tom Hudson (Nashville: LifeWay Press). This 13-unit self-instructional workbook surveys the New Testament, provides a framework for understanding and interpreting the New Testament, and teaches Bible background. Member's Book, product number 0805499466; Leader's Guide, product number 0767326210.

To help you learn to think the thoughts of Christ:
• *The Mind of Christ* by T. W. Hunt and Claude V. King (Nashville: LifeWay Press). This course is a serious study of what it means to have the thoughts of Christ and to renew the mind, as Scripture commands. Member's Book, product number 0805498702; Leader's Guide, product number 0805498699.

To build a stronger marriage:
• *Making Love Last Forever, Adult Workbook* by Gary Smalley (Nashville: LifeWay Press). This 12-session interactive workbook reveals how to develop the best kind of love and balance your happiness with your mate's. Member book, product number 0805497919; Leader's Guide, product number 0805497900.

• *Building Relationships: A Discipleship Guide for Married Couples* by Gary Chapman (Nashville: Lifeway Press). This 12-unit course teaches couples sharing and communication skills, while guiding them into a deeper relationship with God. Member book, product number 0805498559; Leader's Guide, product number 0805498540.

• *The Five Love Languages, Video Pack* by Gary Chapman (Nashville: LifeWay Press). This video course helps improve a couple's relationship as they learn to more effectively express love in words and actions consistent with their partner's definition of love. Product number 0805498621.

To order any of the resources listed above or information on adult discipleship and family resources, training, and events, visit our Web site at www.lifeway.com/discipleplus or contact LifeWay Church Resources Customer Service, MSN 113; 127 Ninth Avenue North; Nashville, TN 37234-0113; FAX (615) 251-5933; email customer service@lifeway.com

Life can be an exciting adventure. The options you have reviewed present some possibilities for a lifestyle of continued growth, health, and service.

We heartily congratulate you for completing this workbook. Thank you for having the courage and tenacity to reach this point. This book ends, but the process of recovery continues—it is the process of victorious Christian living.

# MY FIRE DRILL

**ACCOUNTABILITY**

_____

_____

_____

_____

**PREPARATION (THE THINGS I WILL DO TO BE READY FOR AN EMERGENCY):**

_____

_____

_____

_____

**IN AN EMERGENCY I WILL:**

_____

_____

_____

_____

**MY PHONE LIST OF THOSE I WILL CALL**

**NAME**                                    **PHONE NUMBER**

_____        _____

_____        _____

_____        _____

_____        _____

_____        _____

_____        _____

_Your phone list should always include several names in the event that someone is unavailable._

Numbers for hospitals, treatment organizations, and support groups change. I have listed some numbers that should remain in service. Don't be discouraged if you can't get connected right away. Keep trying. Please feel free to write me or Eli Machen. We keep up with resources and will be glad to help you. Both Eli and Mark are available to do conferences and training seminars.

Mark Laaser, Ph.D.
P.O. Box 84
Chanhassen, MN 55317
(612) 949-3478

Eli Machen
206 Crestview Drive
Black Mountain, NC 28711
(704) 669-0309

## American Family Association
provides resources and workshops for sex addicts and couples as well as resources in the fight against pornography. Contact the Outreach Division at:

AFA
Outreach Division
P.O. Drawer 2440
Tupelo, MS 38803
1-800-FAMILIES (326-4543)

## Overcomer's Outreach
is a Christian organization that promotes 12-Step fellowships in churches for addicts of all kinds. For information about groups near you call:

Overcomer's Outreach
(714) 491-3000

## 12-Step fellowships for sexual addiction
Sexaholics Anonymous (SA) Of the national fellowships, this group's definition of sobriety is most consistent with Christian morality.
(615) 331-6230

Sex Addicts Anonymous (SAA)
(713) 869-4902

Sex and Love Addicts Anonymous
(617) 332-1845

# FAITHFUL &TRUE

## LEADER'S & FACILITATOR'S GUIDE

## ELI MACHEN

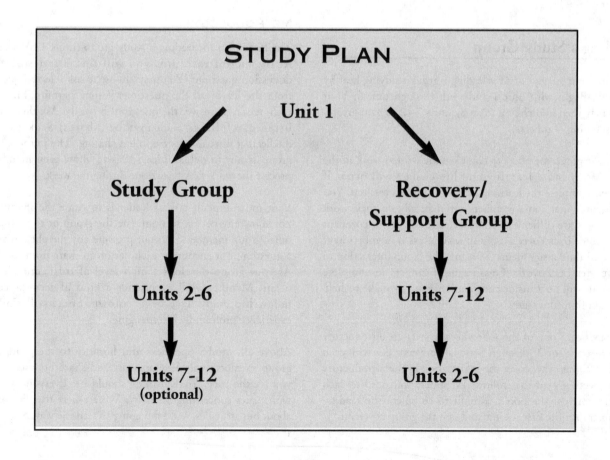

# Introduction to the Leader/Facilitator Guide

*Faithful & True* is a unique study designed for two different types of groups:
- For all adults, such as a men's group, it is a study of healthy, Christ-honoring sexuality.
- For persons who have developed an addictive or compulsive relationship with sex, it is a guide to recovery.

Note that *Faithful & True* may also be used in additional ways. Some persons will use it for personal study. They will benefit but will gain much more if they process their work with another person or group. Pastors and counselors may use it with persons doing intensive growth work.

The two groups will operate very differently. If your group fits the first description, leadership will be relatively simple. You need only read the portion of this leader guide entitled *Leading a Study Group*. If your group consists of persons recovering from addictive patterns, however, your task as a group facilitator will be much more demanding. You will need to read all of this guide carefully and prepare yourself for your task.

For purposes of clarity, I will refer to the *leader* of the first type group (a study group) and the *facilitator* of an addiction group (a recovery group).

## Leading a Study Group

Here are some suggestions for leading a group studying healthy sexuality. Begin with unit 1 and work through unit 6. Your group may then also choose to study units 7-12 to gain greater understanding of others.

Encourage group members to complete the written work in the book. Much more learning and life change will occur if members complete the learning activities between sessions. You will discover that some members automatically do their work while others are difficult to motivate. Use the group covenant on the inside back cover. At group sessions ask if members have completed their assignments. Structure the group interaction to involve members' work. Encouraging members to complete their work will be a major contribution you can make to help them gain from this study.

You may begin one of the following ways; 1) an introductory group meeting, or 2) through personal conversations with each member. Either way, cover the information in the introductory group meeting plan that follows. Members will need to each obtain copies of the book, commit to complete the reading assignment for the first session, and sign the group covenant.

If you choose to have an introductory group meeting:
- Review the introduction, pages 6-10. Encourage members to read the introduction carefully before the next session. It will help them understand how to benefit most from their study. Explain that they need to work through unit 1 before the next meeting.
- Give a brief overview of the book. Explain that Part 1 is for everyone while Part 2 is for persons recovering from patterns of sexual sin.
- Suggest that members may be surprised by what they learn in *Faithful & True*. Sexuality is not a physical act. We are sexual beings. In this study we will be learning how to develop a more effective life in all areas. Ask them to turn to the "Sexual Wholeness Model" on page 26. Explain that we will be dealing with all areas of our lives, not just the sexual area.
- Lead the group to discuss and commit to the covenant. Do not overlook or take lightly this step. Nothing you can do will save as many problems or enhance your group experience more than helping the members commit to the group covenant.
- Pray for each other and make plans to meet for the first week's study.

### METHODOLOGY

The basic plan for leading a study group (units 1-6) is simple. At the end of each unit you will find a series of group discussion questions. You may choose to ask selected questions from the list or all the questions if time permits. Encourage each person to answer the questions honestly. Ask the group to listen carefully as each member shares. Seek to avoid intellectual discussions or opinion sharing. The purpose of the group is not to debate ideas. It is to allow each member to process the work they have done during the week.

Your most difficult task as leader is to guide the sharing. Do not allow any person to dominate the group or to manipulate other group members. Do not pressure any member to answer a question, but encourage each person to share from the heart. As your group develops a high level of trust, miracles will occur. Members will experience a kind of acceptance and fellowship many have never known. Some will find this experience profoundly life changing.

Above all, model openness and honesty to the group. The group members will develop trust and share honestly only if you set the pace. Your attitude should be: Everyone struggles with issues concerning sexuality. We are here to talk honestly about our struggles, and I am going to lead the way.

Seek to create a safe, confidential, affirming atmosphere. Encourage members to share from their hearts. Be willing to confess your own struggles, weaknesses, and sins. Choose to be vulnerable, and your members will follow your lead.

## ISSUES TO CONSIDER

Even if you are leading a study group, be aware that some members may have experienced deep hurt in their past or have enormous amounts of shame in their lives. Someone in your group may begin to identify and deal with painful issues. If so, don't panic. Do not think that you or the group are supposed to "fix" the person. You can affirm and support him or her. Avoid advice and easy answers.

If you should have one or more members who need to deal with deeper issues, such as abuse in their past or addictive behavior in the present, you will need to make a referral. You can find more information about making referrals on pages 38-43 of *WiseCounsel:Skills for Lay Counseling* (0767326156). You may order this resource by contacting LifeWay Church Resources Customer Service 1-800-458-2772. Talk to your pastor or other church staff member for assistance in making referrals.

# Facilitating a Recovery/Support Group

Facilitating a recovery/support group is more demanding than leading a study group. Being a facilitator requires special skills. To facilitate, you need to be either a recovering person solidly in recovery—I suggest a minimum of two years sobriety—or a trained counselor.

A facilitator for *Faithful & True* should:
1. State clearly that a *Faithful & True* group is a support group, not a therapy group. The facilitator must not function as a therapist. The group covenant must clearly state that this is a support group, not a therapy group. The facilitator must commit to maintain a support group format.

In a support group each person is on the journey. The group operates as an affirming family. The facilitator serves as a guardian of the covenant rules for the group and keeps each member accountable to the covenant. In doing so, the facilitator *allows* group process to take place and work to the advantage of the individual members.

In therapy groups, the therapist *manipulates* the group experiences to the therapeutic advantage of the individual members. Such control and manipulation should be considered inappropriate for a facilitator and a support-group experience. Each group member must accept responsibility for his or her own recovery. The facilitator must not accept responsibility for the recovery of any other group member.

In the event you are a professional therapist leading this group, keep in mind your role is that of a facilitator, not a therapist. As a facilitator, self-disclosure and participation in the group process is important to maintain a support group format.

2. Establish a personal support system while facilitating the group. You need to have available someone to whom you can go for support. At times when facilitating a support group the issues of the group can be overwhelming. A facilitator needs to establish and maintain a solid clinical and spiritual support base for personal protection as well as for protection of the group.

3. Be willing to address unresolved sexual and personal issues in a support group format before attempting to facilitate a *Faithful & True* support group. A facilitator should have achieved a sense of healthy sexuality before attempting to facilitate a group in this area. Although a facilitator always experiences personal growth, do not attempt to facilitate a group as a means to resolve your own difficulties.

4. Be willing to invest considerable time and energy to learn about healthy sexuality, sexual addiction, and sexual gender issues. Take advantage of training opportunities.

5. If at all possible, co-facilitate a support group before facilitating a *Faithful & True* support group.

## ESSENTIAL FACILITATOR QUALIFICATIONS

The following basic qualities are essential for any group facilitator.
1. Be a growing Christian, a person of prayer, and a person who has faith in what God can do.
2. Be one who has sought to take care of his or her personal life and family first before helping others.
3. Have a general knowledge of the process of support groups.
4. Sense God's call to be in this particular ministry.
5. Be a good listener.
6. Be an active member of a local church.
7. Relate well with people in a spirit of humility.
8. Have a commitment to keep confidential information shared in private.
9. Be willing to give time and energy to help group members.
10. Have a teachable spirit.
11. Be in an accountable relationship with others.
12. Be spiritually and emotionally stable and mature.

Facilitators of *Faithful & True* support groups need to have demonstrated a commitment to their own spiritual and relational development. This can be done by participating in other LIFE and LIFE Support groups.

LIFE courses such as *Masterlife, Disciple's Prayer Life, The Mind of Christ,* and *Experiencing God* can help provide the spiritual foundation for leading a group. Facilitators will benefit greatly from an understanding of *WiseCounsel: Skills for Lay Counseling.*

Courses such as *Search for Significance* LIFE Support Group Series Edition, *Untangling Relationships, Conquering Codependency, Making Peace with Your Past,* and *Moving Beyond Your Past* can help provide the relational development needed to facilitate a *Faithful & True* group.

## HOW TO BEGIN

Refer to the facilitator guides that begin on page 229. The guides offer helps for each week's group meeting.

Your group will begin with unit 1. Then the group will go to units 7-12. Only after working through the recovery section will the group return to complete the "Healthy Sexuality Model" in units 2-6. You will notice that the group guides are arranged in the order you will use them (pp. 229-240).

Your group will probably not be able to complete units 7-12 in six weeks. The work in those units may take several months to complete. Your group can determine a plan for completing those units. Possible suggestions include:
- Study through the units on a one-unit-per-week plan, but with the awareness that the group will go through the units several times before moving on.
- Spend two to four weeks in each unit before moving on.
- Use an open-group concept. In an open group new members can enter the group at any time. Each member needs to get a sponsor and work through the material under the supervision of the sponsor. In this approach different members of the group may be at vastly different places in their recovery journey. The open and ongoing group has many advantages,

but note the method depends on the availability of good sponsors. As a result, the open-group approach is more difficult to establish.

With any of the plans, the important issue is that each person needs to complete the work in the book and share that work with the group, a sponsor, or an accountability partner.

## AFTER EACH SESSION

- Pray for each group member's specific needs.
- Call each group member. Encourage preparation for the next session. Assure each member that you are praying for him or her.
- Read "Before the Session" for the next Group Session, and carefully complete all the activities in the unit. If you are spending several weeks in one unit, review the materials you have covered and determine what the group needs to cover in the next. You will know the group has completed a unit when they have achieved the session goals.

## OPTIONAL METHOD FOR DEALING WITH GOALS

The most effective personal growth involves individuals setting or adopting and working toward their own goals. Group members have this facilitator material in their books. Consider leading the group members to accept the Session Goals as their own. Ask them to check off the goals as they are completed.

Some group members may need encouragement to check off any goals. Their perfectionism may keep them trying to complete each goal perfectly. You may want to make a time at the end of each session for group members to discuss and check off their goals. Thus they can affirm each other's progress.

# Group Session 1
# A Foundation for Sexuality

Note: these session guides are for a recovery/support group of persons seeking to deal with patterns of sexual sin. Study groups refer to page 226 for guidance in leading a study group.

## INTRODUCTORY GROUP SESSION

If you have not already done so, begin with an introductory group session as described on page 226. The following session guide assumes that group members have already signed the group covenant and done the work in the book for unit 1.

## SESSION GOALS

People caught in a cycle of sexual sin fear being vulnerable. They hide their thoughts and emotions from others. In this session group members need to commit to the idea of accountability and support. Your group members may be extremely isolated. They may have avoided relationships. They fear being found out and blamed. This unit begins the journey to build relationships. In this session group members will:

• Identify personal barriers that have inhibited sharing with others in the past;
• Agree to the rules of the group;
• Choose accountability partners;
• Begin setting personal growth goals.

In this early stage of the group process members may be experiencing anxieties and fears. Normalize these feelings by stating that every group member probably feels anxious and afraid. Assure them they will begin to feel more comfortable as the group progresses and members build trust.

## During the Session

### CHECK IN

• Give each member of the group a chance to express one feeling word that would best describe how he feels right now. Encourage each member to use only one or two words.
• Read with the group members the group rules from page 18 or from the group covenant.

### SHARE TIME

I have given you more activities than you will be able to cover in a single session. Choose the sharing questions that best fit your group's needs. Normally the bulk of the group time will be dedicated to sharing. In this session be sure to reserve enough time for the challenge at the end of the session.

• In the unit story on page 11, Fred was feeling angry over several issues related to sex. Like Fred, do you ever feel angry about sexual issues? Describe the situation.
• How could Fred benefit from a support group? What do you hope to gain from participation in this group?
• What does 1 Corinthians 10:13 say to you about even your worst thoughts and feelings?
• How has an unhealthy sense of shame impacted your life?
• How do you feel about developing a support system for yourself?
• Ask someone to read Hebrews 10:24-25. Point out to the group that God is their ultimate and complete source; however, by His design we need each other. Share what this passage has meant to you.
• Ask members to share examples of cultural messages which promote the idea that sex and love are the same (p. 21). Write the examples on a chalkboard or flipchart for the group to see. Ask how these messages make them feel.
• How would you respond to Jesus' question in John 5:6: *Do you want to get well?*
• Ask the group to share two items on which they need to work from the list on page 24.

### GROUP CHALLENGE

Explain that some group requirements are absolute. Before members can continue, they must furnish you with two things. Each must show you the completed personal crisis plan from page 23 and must have someone enlisted as personal support person. Explain that each member must have these two items by the next meeting.

Explain that the group will be working units 7-12 before coming back to Part 1. Instruct them to begin working on unit 7. Read 1 Corinthians 10:13 and say, *God has provided this group as one of the ways out. As He leads you to develop a plan of healthy sexuality, and to find a sponsor, pray for His wisdom and leadership. Each of you in this group are not here by accident, but by God's design, as a way out.*

### CLOSE IN PRAYER

Pray for your group and mention each person by name. Begin teaching your group the "Serenity Prayer." Refer to page 57. End the prayer time with the "Serenity Prayer."

# Sexual Sin and Sexual Addiction

## SESSION GOALS

You will know that the group, or an individual member, has successfully completed the work in this unit when they have done the following.

❑ Identify the difference between sexual sin and sexual addiction.

❑ Evaluate their sexual behaviors by the five elements of addictive behavior.

❑ Demonstrate a willingness to risk and trust others.

❑ Understand the cycle of addiction and examine their own behaviors for similar patterns.

❑ Learn the four core beliefs and their negative effect on sexual behaviors.

## During the Session

### CHECK IN

Lead members to "check in" by sharing a feeling. Read the group rules from page 18.

### SHARE TIME

• Review the stories of Ben and John. Ask, *What were the differences in the two stories.* Develop a list of positive behaviors for dealing with temptation.

• Discuss the five key elements of addictive behavior. Lead the group to compare these key words to the development of sexual addiction in John's life.

• Read Romans 7:23-24. Ask, *How is the struggle Paul describes an example of the addictive characteristic we call* unmanageability?

• Lead the group in a discussion of the difference between sexual sin and sexual addiction—the difference between addiction as a process and specific behaviors as sin.

• Display a list of the sexually addictive behaviors. Discuss the behaviors. Encourage each member to share with the group the behaviors he identified with from page 120.

• Lead the group in a discussion of offending sexual behaviors.

• Say, *Some of you may have felt deep shame as you discussed this lesson. What feelings have you experienced as you have studied?*

• Ask, *From the list on page 123 what behaviors have you used in an attempt to control your sexual behavior? Which behaviors were healthy and which ones were destructive?*

• Ask, *What have been your feelings when you were denied the opportunity to be sexual?*

• Ask, *Do you see yourself in any of the patterns of sexual overeaters, sexual anorexia, or sexual bulimia?* (See the examples of eating disorders from page 122.

• Ask, *What is the first thing you need to do to develop greater sexual health and faithfulness?*

• On a flipchart draw the cycle of addiction from page 125. Lead the group in a discussion of the cycle of addiction.

• Ask, *How often do you experience feelings of loneliness? What is usually happening or going on in your life at the time?*

• Encourage the group to share several things that trigger them sexually. Remind them that triggers can be sights, sounds, smells, touch, locations, or feelings.

• Encourage the group to briefly share which one of the three reasons from the list on page 126 would be most true of their fantasizing.

• Briefly review the key elements of Scott's ritual (p.126). Encourage members to discuss these elements of ritual and identify how they progress.

• Ask, *How have movies, TV shows, magazines, advertising, or life experiences taught you that sex is equal to love?*

• Ask, *Can you describe a time when you felt utterly worthless?*

• Ask, *Have you ever felt that you were not good enough for someone, or that someone didn't like you because of who you were? Who was it?*

• Ask members to share a time when they felt hurt or angry because they couldn't or wouldn't ask for help.

• Read and discuss Proverbs 11:1; 12:22; 28:13.

• Refer the group to the list at the bottom of page 131. Encourage the group to share from the list those elements they checked and to briefly explain their choice. Then lead the group in a discussion about how they think they will break through denial and delusion. Ask them each to set one goal for overcoming delusion and denial during the time you work together.

### CLOSE IN PRAYER

Seek to lead the group in brief but meaningful prayer activities each week to end the group sessions. Some of the time you may ask each member to pray, either silently or aloud, for the person on the left or right. Ask each group member to share a single personal prayer need and then have someone pray for each need. Demonstrate to the group that you value prayer. End your prayer time with the "Serenity" prayer.

# Powerlessness

## SESSION GOALS

You will know that the group, or an individual member, has successfully completed the work in this unit when they have completed the following.

❑ Honestly share with each other their lists of sexual behaviors, take inventory of their out-of-control behaviors and admit their unmanageability to one another.

❑ Examine their fantasies, recognize the feelings beneath the sexual thoughts, and determine how to deal with them.

❑ Identify their most common sexual sins and then be able to identify step-by-step their rituals leading to those behaviors.

❑ Establish self-imposed boundaries to achieve sexual faithfulness.

❑ Seek to replace old destructive rituals with healthy rituals.

❑ Gain an understanding of despair and two antidotes for it.

❑ Learn that healing from despair can begin if they are honest with others about their feelings of loss.

## During the Session

### CHECK IN

Lead members to "check in" by sharing a feeling. Read the group rules from page 18.

### SHARE TIME

• Repeat the unit Scripture memory verse together. Say, *Describe how you suppose it would feel to be "self-controlled, putting on faith and love as a breastplate and the hope of salvation as a helmet? (1 Thessalonians 5:7-8).*

• Ask, *Can you trust us enough to share the first time you knew you had done something sexually sinful?* Encourage members to be specific about the nature of the sin without being graphic. Ask them to share how the experience made them feel.

• Ask, *Did you try to talk with someone at the time? What was your experience? How did the person respond to you?*

• Read Proverbs 28:13 and James 5:16. Remind members that as they practice honesty and openness with the group they will begin to reduce the pain of secrecy. Ask them to share with the group the sexual sins they have committed. They may refer to their list on page 135, if they need a reminder.

• Ask the group to share which of the behaviors they did most often and three examples of how they tried to stop.

• Encourage members to refer to the list at the top of page 136 and share those characteristics they checked.

• Ask each individual member if he is ready to examine his feelings of unmanageability and give up these behaviors.

• Help the group members to recognize how much time they spend in fantasy and evaluate the nature of their fantasies. Encourage them to refer to the list of statements describing their fantasy life (p. 137) and share it with the group.

• Ask members to share their objective description of their most common fantasy and its nature (p. 138). Caution against being graphic. Remember to be gentle, this exercise can bring up a flood of feelings. Next encourage the group to share any feelings that they experience as a result of the sexual thoughts. Ask them to refer to the list they checked at the top of page 139.

• With this exercise the group can be extremely supportive of one another. Refer them to their work at the bottom of page 140 through page 141. Ask them to recall their most common form of sexual sin, then to think back to when they first became preoccupied with this sexual act. Encourage them to identify what triggered them. Then step- by-step have the group help each other identify how they move from the trigger to the acting-out behavior. Each person needs to understand how this process works. They will use this information as they establish effective boundaries.

• Have the group share what prohibitions they will enforce on themselves so they can stop their rituals. Encourage the group to help each other when necessary to establish effective prohibitions.

• Ask, *What healthy rituals would you like to establish in your life?* (p. 142).

• Ask, *Who has started or completed writing the assignment on page 145?* (the complete accounting of sexual sins). Strongly encourage them to share this accounting with another person if they have not already. They will not share this accounting in the group but with someone who will hear their confessions without trying to "fix" them.

• Lead the group in a discussion of the consequences they have experienced as a result of their sexual sins. Encourage them to refer to their lists on pages 147-148.

• Have the group specifically talk about their losses, every loss they can think of. Gently lead them to discuss their feelings about these losses.

### CLOSE IN PRAYER

Lead the group to spend some time in prayer for one another after hearing each other's losses. They will experience a lot of sadness and possibly anger as they deal with their grief. End with the "Serenity" prayer.

# Group Session 9
# Families (Part 1)

## SESSION GOALS:

You will know that the group, or an individual member, has successfully completed the work in this unit when they have completed the following.

❏ Gain a basic understanding of their family dynamics and how the family has influenced their lives.

❏ Describe the boundaries they learned growing up and how those boundaries affect their relationships today.

❏ Identify the rules they learned as children and determine how they continue to act out those rules today.

❏ Gain an awareness of the roles taught in families, and identify the roles assigned to them.

❏ Take an honest look at the way their families managed stress, and how they still use those strategies today.

# During the Session

## CHECK IN

Lead members to "check in" by sharing a feeling. Read the group rules from page 18.

## SHARE TIME

• Have each group member share his family map or genogram with the group (p. 152). Encourage members to provide as much information as they can. They may wish to include information about their grandparents.

• Review the examples of boundaries listed on page 154 and ask them to share examples of good and bad boundaries they learned growing up.

• Have each group member share how his parents either did or did not transfer control of boundaries to him or her. Ask, *Who is the captain of your ship?*

• Ask members to share one example of how boundaries in their families were violated by being too loose and one example of being too rigid.

• Ask, *Can you see how your sexual boundaries began to get confused? If so, explain.*

• Ask members to silently read Exodus 20:3-17. Ask, *Which of the Commandments are examples of good boundaries and why?* All of the Commandments are healthy boundaries. Lead members to discuss the Commandments as boundaries.

• Invite members to share their paraphrases of the Ten Commandments

• Remind the group of the five rules mentioned at the bottom of page 157. Ask each member to share how the rules were communicated, and give a brief example.

• Ask, *With which of these rules do you still have problems today?* Encourage members to share specifically how they have acted out these rules. If the group is small enough or you have time, you may want to discuss each of the rules separately.

• Ask, *What problems or issues were ignored or avoided in your family? Which remain as problems for you today?*

• Say, *Using your family diagram, describe what roles are played out in your current family situation.* If time permits, encourage members to share the roles of their extended family.

• Ask: *What do your sexual sins say about the roles you play in life? Describe one role you would like to change about yourself.*

• Ask the group to refer to page 165 and briefly share their list of emotions and the substances or behaviors their families used to deal with them.

• Encourage members to share how their families dealt with sexual feelings, information, or tension (p. 166).

• Gently, but firmly, encourage the group to honestly share what addictions or problems their current family is not confronting or dealing with. Ask what feelings are on the inside that they don't express.

## CLOSE IN PRAYER

As you have times of prayer, beware of certain pitfalls. Some people use prayer as a means to avoid personal application. When you ask what personal need the group can pray for, they emotionally distance themselves from painful issues by quickly mentioning the concerns of others. Do not allow the prayer time to degenerate into praying for concerns that distract from genuine issues.

Keep the prayer times brief, meaningful, and focused. Pray for the families of group members. Ask for the wisdom to see objectively, the grace to forgive others, and the courage to change our own behaviors. End with the "Serenity" prayer.

# Group Session 10
# Families (Part 2)

## SESSION GOALS

You will know that the group, or an individual member, has successfully completed the work in this unit when they have completed the following.

❏ Discuss the importance of understanding the abuse experienced in families or as children.
❏ Examine wounds in two categories, invasion and abandonment, and in the four areas: emotional, physical, sexual, and spiritual.
❏ Discuss with each other their honest feelings when they have experienced abuse.
❏ Learn that they can trust others to help them in their grieving and healing process.

## During the Session

### CHECK IN

Lead members to "check in" by sharing a feeling. Read the group rules from page 18.

### SPECIAL CONCERNS FOR THIS SESSION

A high percentage of persons who develop sexual addiction are themselves victims of abuse—often sexual abuse. You cannot determine for a person if he is a survivor of abuse, but you can create an atmosphere in which the survivor will feel safe and have permission to tell his story.

Members may feel and respond to powerful emotions during this group meeting. You can find additional information in *Shelter from the Storm: Hope for Survivors of Sexual Abuse,* and the facilitator's guide for *Shelter from the Storm* to help you prepare for this session. See page 221 for information on *Shelter from the Storm.*

### SHARE TIME

• Repeat together Psalm 27:10, the unit Scripture memory verse, and read Psalm 10:14. State, *This unit has been difficult for some of us. As we begin our work together, remember that God desires to provide for us any support, love, and acceptance our families were unable to supply.*
• Ask, *Why do you think some people have difficulty honestly examining their hurts?* Review the checklist on page 169.

• Review briefly the differences between abandonment and invasive abuse. You may find that to refer the group to the diagram on page 171 will be helpful.
• Ask each group member to share with the group his history of abuse. Encourage him to be as specific as possible in each area; emotional, physical, sexual, and spiritual. Be sure to cover both the invasive and abandonment elements of abuse. This group session can be a very difficult experience for some individuals. Be patient and sensitive to the Holy Spirit. If you need to stop and pray or just comfort someone, do so.
• Gently remind the group that they have just described a great deal of loss in their lives. Ask each one if she can accept the fact that she experienced loss and is ready to grieve so she can move on with her life.
• Ask if anyone checked any responses from the list on pages 178-179. If so, ask them to share these with the group.
• Ask the group to refer back to their chart of abuse (page 171) and share what they think was the effect of the abuse in each area of their lives.
• Ask the group to share their first sexual experience; how old they were and who was involved in the encounter.
• Have the group think for a minute of what the role models in their lives taught them about God. Then ask them they have struggled with God or with those who have abused them.
• Some members may have great difficulty with this session. They may experience a flood of emotions and feelings that will be a trigger for some to medicate. They may struggle with temptation and need additional support and encouragement from the group and their sponsors. Make sure everyone has a plan of action in place before leaving the group session.

### CLOSE IN PRAYER

Ask members to pray for each other. You may have each pray for the person on his right. Pray for courage and strength as members deal with loss and grief issues. End with the "Serenity prayer."

### BEFORE THE NEXT SESSION

In unit 11 members will create a set of fire drills—self-imposed restrictions to maintain sobriety. Make at least three copies of page 223 for each member. Distribute the copies at the end of the unit 10 meeting.

233

# Group Session 11
# Tools for Recovery

## SESSION GOALS

You will know that the group, or an individual member, has successfully completed the work in this unit when they have completed the following.

❑ Describe the difficulty of maintaining sobriety in isolation.
❑ Share the list of "fire drills" or contingency plans they have developed. Members will help each other fine tune their "fire drills" to provide well thought-out safety plans.
❑ Discuss together possible reasons for slips and relapses. Develop a strategy to respond to a slip or relapse.
❑ Help each other work through the difficult decisions of how and when to tell spouses, family, and friends their story.

## During the Session

### CHECK IN

Lead members to "check in" by sharing a feeling. Read the group rules from page 18.

### SHARE TIME

This session will focus on establishing plans and strategies for continued recovery. Members' recovery will only be as successful as their plans are thorough and honest. Constantly encourage the group to challenge each other in love when they see a weak point or loophole in another's strategy for recovery.

• Repeat Romans 12:2 together. State, *The tools for recovery are people and actions God uses to transform us by renewing our minds.*
• Read Ecclesiastes 4:9-13. Say, *The tendency to isolate is universal among those who have struggled with sexual sins.* Ask, *What are some of the reasons or practiced habits you have used to isolate?*
• Ask members to refer to their checklist on page 187 and share the approval-seeking strategies they have tried.
• From the list of characteristics of a sponsor on pages 190-191, ask members to identify those they checked. Ask them to describe their plans to enlist sponsors.
• Lead a discussion of sobriety. Make sure everyone has a clear understanding of what sexual sobriety means for Christians.
• The concept of an abstinence contract may be difficult for some of the group members. Lead the group to discuss the value of an abstinence commitment. Include the concepts of detoxification and reversing the core belief that sex is my most important need.

• Ask members to share what benefits might result in their marriages from an abstinence contract (p. 194).
• Ask the following questions related to abstinence contracts:
  –*What have you done on your abstinence contract?*
  –*How did you feel when you sat down with your spouse and worked on this contract?*
  –*If you came to a mutual decision, how long will you remain sexually abstinent, and what activities will you do to increase your emotional and spiritual intimacy?*
• Encourage members to share the date they began their sobriety. The group may wish to plan a way to celebrate as a group each member's sobriety date. (You may choose to give awards to celebrate "birthday's" such as 30 days, 3 months, and 1 year.)
• As members develop their fire drills, you will need to firmly encourage them to help each other be thorough.
• Ask the group to share how they felt when they started thinking about fire drills. Refer them to their check list on page 197.
• Ask members to share what they believe they will miss most by living a life of discipline and restriction.
• Ask members to share their lists of people or things they must say good-bye to (p. 198).
• Refer members to their fire drill form they were to fill out this past week. Ask each group member to share his fire drill strategy with the group. When each member has shared his strategy encourage the group member to ask the group for feedback.
• Briefly lead the group in a discussion about slips and relapse, the difference between the two, and what to do if they occur (p. 198).
• Lead the group in a discussion of common reasons they might want to tell their spouses about their past sexual sins. Refer them to the check list on page 200. Ask each member if he wants to spend the rest of his life wondering what his spouse would do if she found out.
• Encourage members to share their check lists from page 201. Ask them to share how they feel when they think about talking about their sexual sins with their children.
• Lead the group in sharing how they feel about telling their story to friends. Encourage them to talk about which friends they think they could tell and which ones they can't.

### CLOSE IN PRAYER

End the session with a time of prayer. Pray for wisdom, courage, and strength for the difficult work of recovery. Conclude with the "Serenity prayer."

# The Process of Recovery

## SESSION GOALS

You will know that the group, or an individual member, has successfully completed the work in this unit when they have completed the following.

☐ Discuss issues in their lives that limit their spiritual growth, and work together on ways to make the daily decision to dedicate their lives to God.

☐ Explore ways their anger or shame blocks their ability to confess sins to God. Work toward fully confessing their sins to another person.

☐ Help each other to develop daily individual character building plans.

☐ Work together to carefully and gently make an accounting of the damage they have done to others, and determine how they can best repair the damage to those individuals.

☐ Develop a plan to maintain ongoing accountability and evaluation of their recovery process.

## During the Session

### CHECK IN

Lead members to "check in" by sharing a feeling. Read the group rules from page 18.

### SHARE TIME

• Repeat Hebrews 12:3 together. Ask, *How does the verse encourage you to continue the process of change and discipleship?*

• Ask, *What do Proverbs 11:2 and 30:32 tell you about being a spiritual person?*

• Remind the group of Ken's story on page 204. Ask, *How many of you did similar things in your relationship with God? Do you now see your actions as pride?*

• Encourage members to describe times when they have struggled to control their sexual thoughts, acting out, or other areas of their lives. Ask, *Do you see your struggles to control as expressions of humility or pride?*

• Say, *Each of us have experienced losses because of our sexual sins. Can you share those things you believe you will have to grieve over as an act of humbly surrendering control? Refer to the check list on page 206.*

• Read 1 John 1:8-9. Ask, *Why is confession a key part of spiritual growth?*

• Lead a discussion of how each member views God, and from where his view of God comes.

○

• Ask members to share a time when someone was genuinely forgiving and loving with them. Ask them to describe who the person was and how the experience felt.

• Ask, *Have you begun working on your fearless and complete moral inventory? How are you doing with your inventory? Share any struggles or successes you are experiencing.*

• Ask, *Did you ever believe your sexual sins were so bad that not even God would be able to forgive you?*

• Ask members to share who they chose as their spiritual authority to hear their moral inventory. If any in the group have completed this experience, ask if they would briefly share how it went for them and how they felt afterwards.

• Ask members to share what character traits they need to develop (p. 212) and to describe their daily plan for working on those traits.

• Lead a discussion of appropriate and inappropriate amends. Caution against amends that would cause harm.

• Ask members to share several examples from their list and request feedback from the group on the appropriateness of the amends.

• Ask members to share how they felt as they worked through the list of people harmed and plans for amends (p. 216). Encourage them gently, and remind them of God's grace and forgiveness.

• Ask the group to share how, apart from sex, they know that their lives are still a mess (checklist p. 218).

• Ask members if any have filled out a "Personal Craziness Index" (p. 219) and if they would share it with the group. Encourage those who have not to do so and bring it to the next group meeting.

If the group continues through Part 1 then encourage them to bring their personal craziness index to group with them regularly until keeping it becomes an ingrained habit of their recovery process.

Strongly encourage your group to continue by working through units 2-6. However, if this is your final group session, encourage members to continue with other appropriate growth opportunities. Review the suggested options for further study on pages 220-222.

### CLOSE IN PRAYER

Congratulate group members for the work they have done. Challenge them to prepare for the next session by completing unit 2, dealing with the healthy sexuality model. Spend some time in prayer together. End with the "Serenity prayer."

# Group Session 2
# The Physical Dimension

Note that these facilitator guides are for the facilitator of a recovery group. If you are leading a study group, you will find guidance on page 226 and discussion questions at the end of each unit (units 1-6). If you read on, recognize that some of the questions and activities are much too personal and demanding for a study group format.

## SESSION GOALS

You will know that the group, or an individual member, has successfully completed the work in this unit when they have done the following.

❑ Identify experiences and feelings that left them with a sense of shame about their physical appearance.
❑ Begin to see themselves as God's handiwork, which He considers very good.
❑ Learn to give and receive healthy affirmation.
❑ Begin to establish healthy physical goals and accept accountability of the group in working towards them.

## During the Session

### CHECK IN

Lead members to "check in" by sharing a feeling. Read the group rules from page 18.

### SHARE TIME

• Read or ask someone to read Ted's story page 27. Ask, *In what ways do you identify with Ted's story? In what ways do you not identify with his story.*
• Ask, *How did you feel while listening to Ted's story?* Encourage members to share their feelings. Listen for feelings of sadness, frustration, loneliness or anger.
• Ask, *Would someone like to share with the group a similar story you may have experienced?* Encourage and support the group member who shares. This will model for the rest of the group the fact that no shame or judgment will result from sharing. Affirm and accept the person aside from the behavior. Remind the group that Christ came to forgive and set them free. Offer an opportunity for others in the group to share a similar story from personal experience.
• How do you react to the statement in the Scripture memory verses (Genesis 1:27, 31) that God considers you a "very good creation?

• Ask: *When you were an adolescent, how did you feel about your physical appearance? How do you feel about it now?*
• Lead members to describe a time when they felt put down or criticized about some aspect of their appearance.
• Ask, *When you were growing up, what attitudes did your family display toward sexuality and the human body?*
• Ask members to share their paraphrases of 1 Corinthians 6:19 (page 30). Ask, *What does it mean to be a "temple of the Holy Spirit"?*
• Ask, *If you are or have been married, how have you felt when your spouse says no to sexual intercourse?* Lead the group to identify and share their feelings, whether of anger, loneliness, rejection, or other emotions. State, *All the feelings you have described are normal. The important issue is what we do with them. We need to recognize and identify what we feel. Then we can make wise and Christlike judgments about how to deal with the emotions.*
• Invite members to describe their exercise plans.
• Ask, *How do you feel about Jesus' action of leaving the needy crowds to take care of Himself (pray, eat, and rest)? (Matthew 15:39)*
• Lead the group to discuss their answers to the assignment at the bottom of page 37.
• Encourage members to describe their feelings when they have considered or experienced sexual dysfunction.
• Ask, *Have you sometimes felt pressure to perform sexually or felt inadequate sexually?*

### CLOSE IN PRAYER

Ask each member to identify and share with the group two specific changes he needs in his life. Challenge members to listen and remember the two requests of the person on their left. Then each pray for the person on the left. Close with the Serenity prayer.

# The Behavioral Dimension

## SESSION GOALS

You will know that the group, or an individual member, has successfully completed the work in this unit when they have done the following.

❑ Identify messages about dealing with feelings they heard when they were growing up.
❑ Identify strategies they learned, and have used, to distance themselves or exit relationships.
❑ Begin to identify feelings they seek to numb.
❑ Disclose to the group any substances or behaviors they see as addictive or they need to confront.
❑ Identify fears and anxieties and share them.
❑ Develop and begin to practice a plan of healthy behavioral strategies.

## During the Session

### CHECK IN

Lead members to "check in" by sharing a feeling. Read the group rules from page 18.

### SHARE TIME

• Read to the group Bob's story from page 41. Ask members if they identify with Bob's situation. Ask the following questions, *Has anyone ever suggested to you that you may not be in touch with your feelings? Do you answer a question requesting how you feel with an answer of what you think rather than what you feel?* Ask them to explain an affirmative response.
• Ask, *Can you share a sad or painful family event? What was the family's reaction?*
• Lead the group to brainstorm and compile a list of sayings, put-downs, or remarks they heard growing up concerning emotions. Include such statements as "Big boys don't cry." Write the responses on a flip chart or chalkboard. Ask members to describe their feelings as they consider the list.
• Say: *After working on unit 3 this past week you may have seen new insights into your family. This is not about blame. Most of our parents do the best they can with the resources they have. We studied this unit to understand some negative beliefs behind our actions and what we can do to change those beliefs. What negative belief did you discover in yourself as you studied this unit?*
• Ask, *Were addictions present in your family? If so, what were they?*

• Read to the group Barry's story on page 46. Ask members to share any mood-altering substances they use or behaviors they have developed. Have them look at their diagram on page 46.
• Ask the group to look at their list on page 47. What moods do they seek to change? Ask: *Which of these mood-altering strategies are addictive and need to be confronted?*
• Say: *Describe a time when you were angry at your spouse about sex. Which of the core beliefs was the basis for your anger?* (See page 130—Note: members will only understand the core beliefs if they have studied unit 7. See page 228).
• Read the six ways we can deal inappropriately with anger from page 49. Ask the group which of these approaches they use. Encourage them to share an example.
• Remind the group that they may have feelings of anger toward God. State, *Several people in the Scripture were also angry at God and expressed that anger to Him.* Read Psalm 44:9-21, Psalm 88, and/or Jeremiah 20:7-18. Ask members to describe a time they were angry with God.
• Instruct the group to pair up and turn to their responses to the exercise at the bottom of page 50 and top of page 51. Ask the pairs to take turns reading their confessions of anger to their partner as if they were that person toward whom they felt anger. Then have the pairs pray for one another and for the person to whom the anger was directed. Time this exercise, keep it brief and bring them back together quickly. This exercise should only take 4 or 5 minutes.
• Lead the group in a brainstorming activity. Have them compile a list of ineffective ways and a list of better ways of dealing with anger (page 51).
• Ask members to share their list of fears from the activity on page 53.
• Ask, *What anxieties and fears must Jesus have faced (Matthew 26:36-45) as he prepared to go to the Cross?*
• Ask members to share two new healthy strategies they have chosen to manage stress in their lives. Lead them to ask the group for accountability and help with these strategies.

### CLOSE IN PRAYER

Suggest that members think of a time when they felt a strong emotion such as anger or fear. Ask, *Were you able to talk to God about your emotions?* Encourage them to talk to Him now about that occasion. Explain that they may pray aloud or silently. Invite them to share with God whatever changes they are experiencing in the group. Lead the group to spend a time in prayer. End the prayer time with the Serenity prayer.

# The Relationship Dimension

You will know that the group, or an individual member, has successfully completed the work in this unit when they have completed the following.

❑ Discuss the importance of intimate relationships.
❑ Describe the connection between sexual temptation and loneliness.
❑ Identify steps they can take to develop healthy intimacy with others.
❑ Evaluate how shame may be preventing them from being open and vulnerable with others.

## During The Session

### CHECK IN

Lead members to "check in" by sharing a feeling. Read the group rules from page 18.

### SHARE TIME

• Read Jonathan's story from page 58. Ask if anyone identifies with Jonathan.
• Read the characteristics of unhealthy shame appearing on page 59. Ask members to share a time when they thought no one liked them.
• Read Zephaniah 3:5. Brainstorm two lists. On one, list the results of a life filled with unhealthy shame. On the other, list the results of "Knowing no shame." Discuss the two lists.
• Read the Core Beliefs About Shame from page 59. Ask how the member's attitude toward these core beliefs have changed during the weeks you have been meeting together.
• Ask each member to state a feeling word that best describes how they feel when they consider sharing secret information about themselves. (This will normalize feelings of fear they are experiencing about sharing.)
• Ask the group to tell which of the four core beliefs they identify with most and why.
• Describe how feelings of shame lead to fears of rejection. Shame causes people to hide who they really are by holding back parts of themselves or their history. Ask for a volunteer to share from the list on page 60 any information he may have withheld that he feels shameful about. Have the group affirm each person who shares (teach the group to use statements like "That was courageous", or "I appreciate your honesty with us.")

• Encourage members to think back to childhood to recall times when they experienced a lack of love, care, or support from one or more important people in their lives. Remind them not to minimize their experiences by thinking like an adult. To a child the pain of rejection is intense. Ask members to share with the group the experiences they recalled.
• Ask for a volunteer to share how being honest felt. Did they have any fears of sharing? Ask them to reflect back to how the group reacted. Throughout the time the group has been meeting, have they been surprised to find acceptance when they feared rejection?
• Ask the group to turn to the continuum activities on pages 63-65 and describe how they evaluated themselves. What did this exercise show them about themselves? Remind the group that learning intimacy is a function of practice, taking risks just as they did in this group. Affirm members for the work they have done in the group.
• Ask members to turn to the checklist of symptoms for unhealthy dependency (page 67). Ask them to share how this list affects the way they feel about themselves. Remind the group to be gentle with themselves; fear of being alone is a natural reaction. Dependency is not a negative word. God designed us to practice a form of healthy dependency on Him and others. His word teaches us that we need both relationships with Him and with each other.
• Remind the group of lesson 4 where they looked at six contracts for change. Ask the group to share a particular contract that had some impact on them and in brief general terms describe their experience in trying to implement it in a significant relationship.(If they have not implemented a contract yet, then ask them to share how they feel about the prospect of doing so.)
• Ask members to turn to page 74 and review the Seven C's of Trust Building. Encourage them to briefly share one principle that had an impact on them or that they recognize the need for work on. Ask members to specifically consider the relationship with their spouse or another significant relationship they need to strengthen or rebuild.

### CLOSE IN PRAYER

Lead members in a time of prayer. Give thanks for the important relationships in your lives. Ask God to build in you the skills to have more meaningful relationships with Him and with others. End with the Serenity prayer.

# The Personal Dimension

You will know that the group, or an individual member, has successfully completed the work in this unit when they have completed the following.

☐ Discuss the importance of trust and emotions. Identify why as adults they struggle in relationships.
☐ Seek to identify their talents and possible reasons why they may or may not feel good about those talents.
☐ Explore the connection between talents and when they feel God's pleasure. Begin to develop their own mission in life.
☐ Examine their concept of sexual identity, its roots and healthy alternatives to possible incorrect assumptions.
☐ Consider reasons for feelings of loneliness and the connection to how they feel about themselves.

## During The Session

### CHECK IN

Lead members to "check in" by sharing a feeling. Read the group rules from page 18.

### SHARE TIME

• Have someone in the group read Matthew 19:13-14 aloud. Lead the group to discuss their thoughts about what Jesus meant by connecting His kingdom to children.
• Offer the opportunity for anyone in the group to share a time when his trust was betrayed, when someone they looked to for care disappointed him, let him down, or hurt him. Allow group members to volunteer to share what they feel comfortable in sharing. If someone wishes to pass, let him.
• Ask the group to review their list of emotions on page 81. Encourage members to share a time when they felt an emotion yet could not express it. Encourage those who are willing to share their scores with the group. (This exercise will allow members to get a sense of how others struggle with appropriately expressing their emotions.)
• Have someone read Matthew 25:23-30. Say, *Describe in one or two feeling words how this Scripture makes you feel.*
• Ask members to share any experiences or conversations they had with their parents that gave them a sense of approval or disapproval about their talents or abilities. Ask them what they felt at that time about those experiences.
• Ask members to share a number of their accomplishments or things at which they excel. Encourage them to share even if they have difficulty believing in their talents.

• Lead the group to brainstorm reasons they may not have been using their talents. List all the reasons; then ask members to choose the excuses they use most.
• Ask the group to share who's voice they most often hear when they think of what they are to do with their lives. Ask, *Why have you sometimes chosen someone else's direction rather than your own?*
• Ask, *What results have you experienced when you were working at cross purposes to God's will for your life?*
• Lead members to describe a time when they believe they were in touch with God's purpose for their lives. Ask: *How did it feel? What were the results?*
• Ask members who have written a mission statement if they would like to share their statements with the group. Affirm each person for any mission statement shared. Remind members that developing their mission statements is a process. They will continue to develop and change their mission statements as they go through life. They will add and delete as they mature and identify their talents and gifts.
• Refer to James' list on page 89 of lessons about life. Ask members to share any of the list they identified with. Open the discussion to any similar lessons they may have learned.
• Refer to the list of cultural categories on pages 89-90. Ask members to pick out a category that was particularly significant to them and share their examples with the group. (If time permits encourage them to share several).
• Ask the group to think of times when they feel alone and to identify the feelings they experience. Refer them to their lists on page 91. Then ask how they remedy these feelings of loneliness. Encourage them to refer to the second list on page 91. Refer to the list of healthy alone-time activities (page 92). Ask members to discuss several activities they would like to incorporate into their regular routine.
• Ask members to share one thing they are excited about changing in their lives over the coming week. Encourage the group by example to affirm each group member as they describe life-changing commitments.

### CLOSE IN PRAYER

End the group session with a time of prayer. Instruct members to thank God for the talents He has given. Ask Him to help them value the talents and gifts they have received. End with the Serenity prayer.

# Group Session 6
# The Spiritual Dimension

You will know that the group, or an individual member, has successfully completed the work in this unit when they have completed the following.

❑ Identify and discuss the foundational influences of their religious feelings and attitudes.

❑ Identify false beliefs about God's attitude toward them and contrast those false beliefs with Scripture.

❑ Evaluate how "magical thinking" or "thinking in the extremes" affects how they relate to God.

❑ Evaluate their spiritual disciplines and be challenged to make needed adjustments to become more Christ-centered.

## During The Session

- Ask members to share their spiritual history with the group beginning by giving a brief description of their parents' attitudes about faith and church.

- Ask the group to describe other people who have had a positive or negative influence on their spiritual journey. Ask: *What did this individual teach you about God?*

- Ask members to share their salvation experience and what motivated their decision, was it an attempt to control God's reactions or was it an act of surrender and love? Lead the group to help each other identify their motivations.

- Review the story in John 8:3-11. Ask members to describe what they think Jesus would say to Angie in the story on page 98.

- Ask the group if they have ever felt like a mistake. Have they ever felt like a mistake in the sight of God?

- Ask the group to think back over their lives and share what behaviors, thoughts, and actions caused them the most shame. Gently encourage them to share their lists with each other. If the group is uncomfortable sharing with each other, then encourage them to share this list with someone they trust and who represents spiritual authority to them.

- Lead the group in a discussion of the insights they gained from the Bible stores of the Prodigal son and the Samaritan woman at the well.

- Encourage members to share ways they have attempted to affect God's behavior—"If I do something, God will either do or not do something else."

- Lead the group in a discussion of ways they have learned to think in extremes . Encourage them to look at ways they may have searched for the correct formula, or have been more concerned with the rules rather than with the meaning or purpose of the rules. If the group is willing, encourage them

to share some of the formulas they have used to be more spiritual.

- Lead members to discuss times in their lives when they felt the real presence of God. Ask them to describe when, where, who were they with, and what were they doing.

- Encourage the group to share some of the things they listed on page 106 that they might do with the person they listed.

- Lead the group to share how they rated themselves on the three scales on page 107.

- Ask members to share a brief plan they could or already have put into place as a result of working through this unit. Ask them if they would like to commit to one another to work on these plans for the next 30 days.

- Review with the group the four dimensions of the healthy sexuality model.

- Encourage members to share possible roadblocks to their journey of sexual and spiritual wholeness. Refer them to their list on page 110.

- Encourage the group to share briefly what changes have impacted them most in this group. What legacies will they pass on to their families? How have group members encouraged them to grow and mature?

### FINDING GROUP CLOSURE

For some groups this may be the last group session. You may find it helpful to do some kind of closing ceremony or graduation of some kind. The group may wish to participate in planning a meaningful closing, suggest it and see. Every group will be different with its own preferences.